Tearmoon Empire

Volume 9

Author
Nozomu Mochitsuki

Illustrator
Gilse

Tearmoon Empire

Nina
Esmeralda's maid.

Elise
Anne's younger sister and the second daughter of the Littstein family. Mia's court author.

Matthias
Mia's father. Tearmoon's emperor. Dotes on his daughter.

Balthazar
A fellow disciple of Ludwig's cohort.

Liora
Tiona's maid. Hails from the Lulu tribe who live in the forest. An expert archer.

Adelaide
Mia's mother. Deceased.

Gilbert
A fellow disciple of Ludwig's cohort.

Galv
An old wiseman and master to Ludwig.

Musta
Head chef of the imperial court of the Tearmoon Empire.

Vanos
Dion's adjutant and former vice-captain of a hundred-man squad in Tearmoon's imperial army. A giant of a man.

Outcount Rudolvon
Father to Tiona and Cyril.

Equestrian Kingdom

Malong
Mia's senior. Club leader of Saint-Noel Academy's Horsemanship Club.

Kuolan
A Moonhare. Mia's favorite horse.

Kingdom of Sunkland

Monica
A member of the White Crows. Infiltrated the Kingdom of Remno as an attendant to Abel.

Graham
A member of the White Crows. He is Monica's superior.

Merchants

Marco
Chloe's father. Head of Forkroad & Co.

Shalloak
A powerful merchant who sells all sorts of goods to kingdoms throughout the continent.

Kingdom of Remno

Lynsha
The daughter of a fallen noble family in Remno.

Lambert
Lynsha's older brother.

Perujin Agricultural Country

Rania
The third princess of Perujin. Mia's schoolmate.

Arshia
The second princess of Perujin. Rania's older sister.

Story

Mia, the reviled selfish princess of the fallen Tearmoon Empire, is executed, only to wake up a twelve-year-old again after somehow leaping backward through time. With this second chance at life she resolves to fix the ills that plague the Empire... so she doesn't end up at the guillotine again. With the help of her previous life's memories and a healthy dose of overly-generous interpretation of her actions by those around her, she successfully averts a revolution, only to be told by her time-leaping granddaughter, Bel, that in the future Mia's entire lineage will end in ruin and she herself will be assassinated. In order to avert this grisly fate, it seems necessary for her to become Tearmoon's first empress...

Outcount Rudolvon's Family

Cyril
Tiona's younger brother. Super smart.

Tiona
The eldest daughter of Outcount Rudolvon. Looks up to Mia. In the previous timeline, she led the revolutionary army.

REVOLUTION

ARCHNEMESIS

ASSISTANCE

ARCHNEMESIS

Kingdom of Sunkland

Keithwood
Prince Sion's attendant. A cynic. But a competent one.

Sion
Crown Prince. All-round genius. In the previous timeline he was Mia's archnemesis, aided Tiona and eventually became known as the "Penal King." In the present he accepts that Mia is the Great Sage of the Empire.

[Wind Crows] Sunkland's intelligence service.

[White Crows] A team within the Wind Crows formed for a certain project.

SUPPORT

Holy Principality of Belluga

Kingdom of Remno

Abel
Second Prince. In the previous timeline, he was known to be an extraordinary playboy. Now, as a result of meeting Mia, he works to diligently improve his swordsmanship instead.

Rafina
The Duke's daughter. Saint-Noel Academy's student council president and the school's de facto decision maker. In the previous timeline, she supported Sion and Tiona from behind the scenes. Her smile can be lethal.

[Saint-Noel Academy]
A super elite school attended by all the highborn children of neighboring nations.

[Forkroad & Co.]
Chloe
The only heir of Marco Forkroad, whose company spans multiple kingdoms. She is Mia's classmate and book buddy.

Chaos Serpents
A group of chaosmongers trying to wreak havoc upon the world. They are deeply hostile toward the Holy Principality of Belluga and the Central Orthodox Church. Traces of their clandestine misdeeds can be found throughout history, but the details are shrouded in mystery.

Characters

Tearmoon Empire

Mia

Protagonist. The sole princess of the empire. Ex-selfish brat. Actually a coward. A revolution leads to her execution, but she somehow leaps back through time and wakes up a twelve-year-old again. She successfully avoids a repeat encounter with the guillotine, but then Bel shows up...

GRANDDAUGHTER AND GRANDMOTHER

Miabel

Mia's future granddaughter who leapt backward through time. Goes by "Bel."

The Four Dukes' Families

Ruby

The daughter of the Duke of Redmoon. A gallant lady with a wardrobe to match.

Citrina

The only daughter of the House of Yellowmoon. Bel's first friend.

Esmeralda

The eldest daughter of the House of Greenmoon. Self-proclaimed best friend of Mia.

Sapphias

The eldest son of the House of Bluemoon. Got into the student council thanks to Mia.

Ludwig

Young, motivated government official. Sharp tongue. Ardently believes in Mia and is trying to make her Empress.

Anne

Mia's maid. Born into a poor family of merchants. Mia's loyal subject.

Dion

The strongest knight in the Empire. In the previous timeline, he was Mia's executioner.

ARCHNEMESIS

※ ——— Future Timeline Relationship   ※ ·········· Previous Timeline Relationship

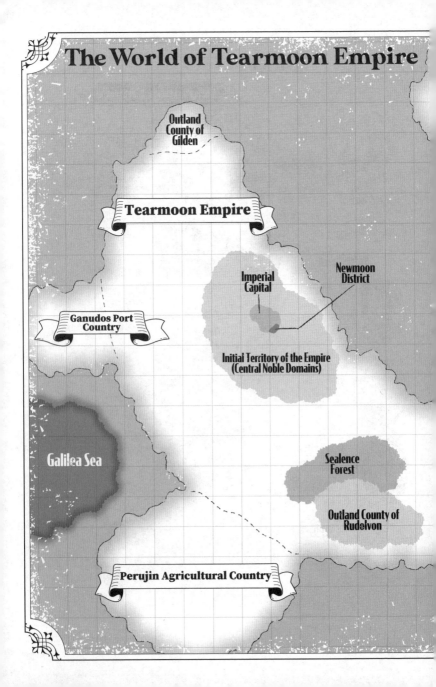

The World of Tearmoon Empire

Outland County of Gilden

Tearmoon Empire

Imperial Capital

Newmoon District

Ganudos Port Country

Initial Territory of the Empire
(Central Noble Domains)

Galilea Sea

Sealence Forest

Outland County of Rudolvon

Perujin Agricultural Country

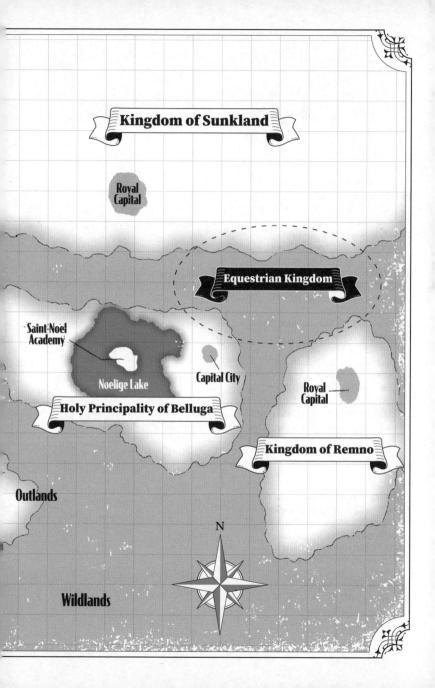

Tearmoon Empire: Volume 9
by Nozomu Mochitsuki

Translated by David Teng
Edited by Samantha J. Moore
English Cover & Image Lettering by Meiru

Copyright © 2022 Nozomu Mochitsuki
Illustrations by Gilse

First published in Japan in 2022
Publication rights for this English edition arranged through TO Books, Japan.
English translation © 2023 J-Novel Club LLC

Find more books like this one at https://j-novel.club!

Managing Director: Samuel Pinansky
Light Novel Line Manager: Kristine Johnson
Managing Translator: Kristi Iwashiro
Managing Editor: Regan Durand
QA Manager: Hannah N. Carter
Marketing Manager: Stephanie Hii

ISBN: 978-1-7183-7448-5
Printed in Korea
First Printing: September 2023
10 9 8 7 6 5 4 3 2 1

Part 4: To the Moon-Led Morrow III

Part 4
To the Moon-Led Morrow III

Prologue: The Doctrine of Empress Mia
–Ludwig's Important Duty–

Saint Mia Academy, located in the south of the Tearmoon Empire near the Sealence Forest, was an educational institution that served as a symbol of the Tearmoon Empire. Enrolling young and talented students from across the empire without regard to their status or heritage, it brought nobles and commoners alike together under its educational banner, training them to become future leaders of Tearmoon. In adopting this ideal advocated by Empress Mia, the academy produced a great number of capable graduates.

One of Mia's chief vassals, Ludwig Hewitt, had also received a direct order from her.

"As a professor of Mialogy, you are to teach the children about it."

The academy's most important subject, Mialogy, was the study of Empress Mia's feats and accomplishments, ensuring that future generations would remain informed about her historic exploits. It had come about a few years prior when Mia received a proposal for its establishment. She'd immediately gone to Ludwig, deeming him suitable for the task. Deeply honored by this show of trust, Ludwig had taken it upon himself to realize her vision, going so far as to deliver personal lectures to the academy's students a few times a year.

For the record, when Mia had first heard the word "Mialogy," she almost choked on her own spit. When she'd gone to Ludwig, she'd told him to "handle it accordingly," hoping he'd find some way to scrap the idea without upsetting anyone. She had not in any way asked him to take charge of the project, much less start teaching classes himself. But anyway, that was the reason for Ludwig's current visit to the academy.

After delivering a long lecture in which he passionately pontificated about Mia's greatest achievements, he left the classroom feeling the pleasant fatigue of a job well done. As he walked down the hallway, a voice called out to him.

"Mr. Ludwig!"

"Hm?"

He stopped and turned to find a young man with a strong frame. He was clearly from the forest tribe of Lulus and, more importantly, Ludwig *knew* him.

"Long time no see, Mr. Ludwig," said the young man.

"Ah, long time indeed. It is an honor to have my name remembered, Mr. Wagul."

He bowed toward the grandson of the Lulu chieftain, Wagul, who smiled bashfully at the deferential greeting.

"Please, Mr. Ludwig. The honor is mine. You helped me so much back then."

The words sent a flurry of scenes spinning through Ludwig's mind. Suddenly, he was back in the old Newmoon District. Ten years had passed since he'd walked into that forsaken district with Mia and witnessed its decrepitude. Since he'd smelled the death and rot. That day, Mia had saved a young boy. That young boy was now standing before him as a young man, sparkling with nothing but potential. Ludwig drew in a breath, moved by the profundity of it all.

"Is your grandfather, rather, the chieftain doing well?"

"Yes, grandfather's healthy as a horse. A little too healthy, if you ask me," answered Wagul, his speech now devoid of the inflections unique to the Lulus. His time in the academy had imbued him with not only fluency in the common tongue but an aura of scholarly intelligence different from the woodland wit of the Lulus.

"Correct me if I'm wrong," said Ludwig, "but I believe you're currently teaching here?"

"Yes. I help the children learn about the history and customs of the Lulu Tribe," Wagul replied with slightly reddening cheeks. "Oh, will you be staying here in Princess Town today?"

"I think I will, since I have another lecture tomorrow."

"That's great news. In that case, may I join you for dinner? I'd love to hear some of your stories," said Wagul, his eyes glowing with excitement and wonder.

"A compilation of Her Imperial Majesty's maxims?"

"That's right. I've asked Ms. Elise, her court author, to put together a compendium of Her Imperial Majesty's achievements, but in the meantime, I figured compiling a summary of her words would be equally meaningful."

Ludwig and Wagul sat in the dining hall of an inn, each with a glass of wine in his hand. There was another moment of profundity as Ludwig appreciated the fact that the young boy he'd once known was now old enough to enjoy a drink with him.

"That sounds like a great idea. There's a special power to Her Imperial Majesty's words. They give people courage," Ludwig said, nodding in heartfelt agreement.

"In that case, would you mind if I interviewed you for the compilation later? Surely, there are some gems among the words she has said to you. Some of her speeches to the academy must be worth writing down as well."

"No problem. I'd love to help with that."

And so, before Mia could have any say on—or even have any knowledge of—the matter, the two began excitedly discussing a draft of "Mia's Marvelous Maxims." It should be noted that when she would later be presented with the idea, she'd let out a sound that resembled the kind of grunt one might utter when taking a punch to the gut. Ludwig, of course, would not notice.

Now, back to the inn.

"By the way, Mr. Ludwig," Wagul added, "I happened to sit in on your lecture earlier."

"Oh, you did? I wasn't aware," said Ludwig, slightly mortified that he'd let himself get so carried away with the lecture that he lost track of his class. "My apologies. I always remind myself to keep a cool head during these lectures, but once I start talking about Her Imperial Majesty, I tend to lose myself…"

"Oh, no, I was actually hiding in the corner. I didn't want to disturb your class," said Wagul, shaking his hands. "The way you retraced Her Imperial Majesty's steps through the lecture was fascinating. I do have a question, though. Did Her Imperial Majesty really go to Sunkland just for her friend Esmeralda?"

"Ah. Good question." Ludwig nodded with the air of a teacher impressed by his pupil.

After befriending King Yuhal of Perujin Agricultural Country and the Merchant King, Shalloak Cornrogue, Mia had gone straight to the Kingdom of Sunkland without so much as a breather. Her official reason was to attend the engagement party of one of her closest friends, Esmeralda Etoile Greenmoon. As for the unofficial ones…

"I have a friend who said that if the House of Greenmoon were to form a union with the second prince of Sunkland, Echard, it could potentially lead to political chaos, and she probably went to deal with that. But this friend also said that there was probably more to it…"

"Hm…"

Ludwig found himself impressed. Clearly, Saint Mia Academy was producing some real talent. The people here were giving proper thought to the meaning of Mia's actions and trying to deduce her intentions. That boded very well for the future of the academy.

Also, they were right. There was definitely something more to Mia's trip to Sunkland.

I still don't know how she figured it out, but at the time, Her Imperial Majesty had correctly predicted an attempt on the life of her close ally, Prince Sion. The actions she took were all part of her monumental effort to prevent the impending tragedy while keeping any inevitable chaos in Sunkland to an absolute minimum.

It was an achievement of historic proportions. It was also one that had to remain untold.

Ludwig picked up his wine glass, then stopped and grimaced. What was he to tell this young scholar? Needless to say, he couldn't simply divulge all of Mia's feats. However, staying completely tight-lipped would be a discourtesy to Wagul's commendable spirit of inquiry.

Looks like I'd better remain relatively sober for this meal.

He put the glass back down and asked the owner for some water, which he used to rinse the wine from his mouth and throat.

"Let me think… There is *one* thing I can tell you… What Her Imperial Majesty did back then, she did indeed do for the sake of a friend."

Thus, in a quiet voice, Ludwig began to tell the tale of Mia's trip to Sunkland.

Chapter 1: The Secret behind That Dress...

Mia stood in Count Lampron's guest room—her temporary abode in the Kingdom of Sunkland—getting ready for the upcoming party. Anne was helping her into a dress that was meeting some resistance near the waist until she drew in a quick breath to focus her mind. The associated tightening of her tummy allowed the dress to slip right into place. With attire adorned, she closed her eyes to organize her thoughts.

I did a lot of thinking yesterday in bed, and I have to say, the situation is pretty complicated right now.

Bed-thinker Mia proceeded to lower herself into her preferred location of thought. Her eyes still closed, she began sifting through the vast amount of information she'd recently discovered. Piece by piece, she put them into their proper mental containers for further analysis.

As an aside, when people are asleep, their brain apparently uses the time to organize memories. Whether this bears any relevance to Mia's preferred position of thought, however, is debatable.

In any case, after going through everything she knew and giving them a good, long think, she reached a conclusion: *This time around, the easiest solution seems like just telling Sion about it and having him do something about the problem. He's got Keithwood too. They can't possibly still poison Sion if the pair of them are both looking out for it…*

Currently, Mia's knowledge of the situation was no longer limited to insight from the Chronicles. She also had access to the results of Citrina's investigation, which painted a fairly obvious picture of Echard having been in contact with the Serpents and potentially planning an assassination through poison. Given the same information, the Sunkland pair would surely arrive at the same conclusion and take steps to thwart the attempt.

For some reason though, Mia found herself reluctant to follow through with the idea. *How odd... I know that it's clearly the best solution, but somehow, I feel like I shouldn't do it... Like something will go wrong if I do... I wonder why?*

"Um, milady?"

Anne's voice pulled her out of her thoughts. She looked around to find that Anne had already stepped back, her work complete. She stood and walked up to a mirror.

"Hmm..." She spun in a circle, regarding herself, and nodded with satisfaction. "Perfect."

Mia was clothed in the same simple dress she'd worn to the dance party for welcoming new students to Saint-Noel. Having grown a little, she'd had the dress retailored for her new stature. That wasn't all, though. This time, she was in full gear. She wore a ribbon on her head. A pendant necklace hung from her neck, and tiny earrings twinkled on her ears. Finally, a translucent shawl gave it all an extra air of refinement.

"Thank you very much, Anne. Your work is impeccable."

"It's always an honor, milady." Anne lowered her head in a respectful bow.

Mia giggled. "Oh, look at you, all grown up and professional now. You look like a maid who knows what she's doing."

"I'm glad you think that. I do know how to bake bread now, and I can even ride horses."

"I'm not sure if riding horses is part of the usual job description for maids, though."

They shared a knowing look and laughed, after which Anne's expression gained a hint of concern.

"Um… Milady? Is something on your mind?"

"Oh? Why do you ask?"

"You've been looking downwards this whole time. I can tell, because I'm a maid who knows what I'm doing," said Anne with a jocular wink, "and the one thing maids know better than anyone is the person they serve."

"Oho ho, you've sure learned how to talk. But I suppose you're right. I can't seem to keep anything from you."

"That's right. You can't keep anything from me because I'm *your* maid, milady. That's why I also know that you'll be fine. I just want you to remember that if anything goes wrong, I'll always be here for you, so don't worry. Just go out there, give it your all, and do what you think is right." Anne held up her fists and let out a huff of encouragement. "No matter what happens, I'll always have your back!"

"Anne…" Mia smiled at her maid's stirring display of devotion.

"In that case…I guess I'll just have to go out there and give it my all then."

Whatever Anne saw in Mia's face, it reassured her, and her expression softened.

"All right, milady, I think it's time I went to help Miss Bel and Lady Citrina with their preparations."

"Certainly. Go ahead. I don't know about Rina, but Bel probably doesn't have much experience wearing dresses."

"Understood."

The door had barely closed behind Anne before it opened again, this time revealing Esmeralda.

"Hello, Miss Mia."

She wore a magnificent dress, and she wore it well, converting its extravagance into elegance with gentlewomanly poise. It was brilliantly emerald in color and lavishly frilly with Greenmoon family crests embroidered in various places using golden thread.

Mia looked her over. Rather, she looked her *abdomen* over, and found it slender and firm.

Hm, she's wearing a corset, isn't she…? That must *be a corset. The poor girl, she won't be able to eat much with such a tight corset on…* She nodded to herself as she eyed her friend with pity.

"My, Miss Mia, that dress…" said Esmeralda, noticing Mia's attire.

"You recognize it? It's one of my favorites."

Whenever she wore the dress, it would bring back a host of delightful memories.

I hope I'll have a chance to dance with Abel today… Oho ho, it'll be like reliving that time again, she thought, grinning to herself.

Her fantasies were interrupted by an unexpected reply from Esmeralda.

"Of course I do... It's the one made by your mother, Her Imperial Majesty Adelaide, isn't it?"

"Huh?" Mia stared agape in confusion. "Um, what do you mean by that?"

"My, you didn't know? I heard it from one of the tailors my family frequently deals with. I remember her saying how she was so nervous to re-tailor it because it was made by your mother. Apparently, her hands were shaking the whole time."

"N-No one ever told me that!"

"Really? I've also heard that in Her Imperial Majesty's hometown, they have a custom where mothers gift their daughters with handmade clothing..."

"Th-They do? Huh..." Mia murmured in a trancelike voice before looking down at the dress on her body. She ran her fingers across it, her expression suddenly sober and thoughtful. "This, from mother... No wonder... Now I know why father was so happy to hear I wore it..."

She recalled the time she told her father about how she'd worn the dress to the new students' dance party, and he'd all but exploded with glee.

"Truly? You wore that dress?" he'd exclaimed before demanding all the particulars, which she'd reluctantly told.

"Yes, it's a very nice dress. I've taken quite a liking to it— Oh, I was originally planning to wear the dress you got for me, of course, but that one got a little dirty because of...some circumstances, so I changed into this one."

She meant it as an excuse, but her father didn't seem to notice.

"I see... I see!"

Even more inexplicable was his ensuing delight.

"*So you wore* that *dress, did you...? My dear little Mia, wearing that dress...*" he murmured with the biggest and silliest of grins.

What in the moons? she wondered. *I was expecting him to get all sulky about me not wearing the dress he chose... This is all very confusing...*

Furthermore, when she mentioned that she'd grown out of the dress a little—vertically, in case anyone was wondering—he immediately had it re-tailored to her current height so she could wear it whenever she wanted. And on top of that...

"*Well, since we're renewing the dress, why not add a few matching accessories too? Cost is no concern. We'll have the continent's best—*"

"*No, no, father. Please don't. That would be a waste— I mean, uh... Oh! They'd clash with the dress. I'd rather have the dress stand out, so how about we go with some more modest accessories? Ones without any gems would be best!*"

"*Really? But—*"

"*Yes! Anyway, I'll pick the accessories, so you don't have to think about this anymore, okay?*"

"*I see... If you say so...*" The emperor had paused for a second before mumbling, "*By the way, Mia, there's something about that dress that you should, uh...*"

"*Hm?*"

Mia arched an eyebrow at her father, who then gave his head a slow shake.

"*...No. Never mind. I'm glad you like the dress. Do take good care of it, all right?*"

"*Huh? Well, of course I will. I like it, after all.*"

"Silly father... He could have just told me..." whispered a reminiscent Mia. "He must have been embarrassed. He can be such a child sometimes..."

She shook her head, the gesture more fond than frustrated, before slowly closing her eyes. She had precious few memories of her mother. Nevertheless, the gentle grain of the cloth, so wonderfully soft to the touch, evoked a deep nostalgia.

"Thank you, mother... Keep watching over me, all right?"

As she breathed the words, something flashed before her eyes. It felt like a faint vision of her mother's face wearing the kind of expression mothers did when they loved their children but found them a tad too reliant on motherly support. Mia felt her back straighten at the gentle admonishment. The look in her eyes grew more sober, more focused.

"All right then. It's time to go. Look alive now. Mother is watching."

Her voice was imbued with a newfound determination.

Chapter 2: Princess Mia Thinks...
and Thinks...

Decked out in full battle gear, Mia gave her cheeks a few invigorating slaps as she prepared to metaphorically ride out to war.

Fortunately, this time, she had a lot of pieces to play with. Esmeralda, Citrina, and Tiona were all hers to command, forming a powerful trifecta for her vanguard. This formation was further rounded out by Ludwig's impeccable smarts, and on top of that, she even had Rafina at her back. Anne, her walking, talking anxiolytic, was at her side, and Bel had come along too. The latter mostly because she was a rabid Sion fan, but anyway.

All right. I know what I have to do, so let's get down to business.

While giving herself the pre-combat pep talk, she sorted through her thoughts one last time.

There are two problems I have to deal with: The first is that if Esmeralda marries Prince Echard, it'll strengthen my political opposition. The second is that Sion is going to be assassinated... Actually, no. She shook her head. *The political opposition issue isn't something I should be thinking about. Ludwig said he had some ideas about it, so I should leave it to him. Right now, what I need to focus on is making sure Sion doesn't get assassinated* tonight. *Nothing else will matter if I can't keep him alive.*

Further consideration solidified her stance.

Besides, Esmeralda can help me on the political front. And once I tell Sion that I literally saved his life, I can have him back me up too.

Her sole mission right now was keeping the poison away from Sion.

According to the Chronicles, Sion dies by poison. And according to Rina's investigation, it's highly likely that Prince Echard received some sort of poison from the Chaos Serpents...

The Chronicles' passage alone had failed to explain how such a young prince had managed to get his hands on such potent poison. Citrina's report had bridged the gap.

She apparently has the antidote ready too...

Mia glanced at Citrina, who nodded back.

"Don't worry, Your Highness. We already have the item on hand."

"...Uh, what item?"

"The dried mushrooms. You picked them up on the way here to Sunkland."

"The dried mushrooms..."

"Yes. The people of the Equestrian Kingdom have a long tradition of using a yin-type poison to hunt. If I wanted to poison someone and make it look like the Equestrians did it, that's the poison I'd use. The mushrooms you picked up earlier have a yang-type poison which counters its effects, allowing them to work as an antidote..." Citrina paused for a second, one eyebrow arching. "But I thought you knew all this already?"

Mia gulped, forcing the reflexive "Of course I did!" back down her throat. She could certainly bluff her way through this question, and it'd surely deepen Citrina's trust in her, but...

"No. Unfortunately, I'm not as familiar with poisons as I'd like."

She chose honesty, for she knew that it never pays to play professor, especially when it came to poisons.

"I bought those mushrooms on a whim. It's actually a complete coincidence that we have them right now," she admitted. "Like I said before, I think it's very likely that poison is going to be used at some point, so I'm counting on you, Rina."

"Understood. I'll do everything I can, but there's one thing you should keep in mind, Your Highness. Countering poisons is very difficult, and no antidote is perfect. There's never any guarantee."

"I see. In other words, the best solution is to make sure the poison never gets into him in the first place. Hm…"

"By the way, are we not going to tell Prince Sion about this?"

Mia scrunched up her face at the question. "I've certainly considered the option, but…"

As a matter of fact, she'd already asked Dion to inform Keithwood about the suspicious activity surrounding Prince Echard. Considering the fact that Citrina's report was, at best, only circumstantial evidence, outright indicting the prince of plotting murder would be unwise, to say the least. However, she couldn't afford to say *nothing* either. Fortunately, Keithwood was a tactful fellow. If anyone could successfully navigate the diplomatic nightmare that was investigating a Sunkland prince on a foreign tip, it was him. Technically, Sion should be capable of doing so as well, but Mia felt a strong resistance to the idea of telling him, and she was beginning to understand why. The hint came from the dress she was wearing.

The one who's going to kill Sion…is his little brother…

That, she now realized, was the source of her reluctance. What would happen if Sion were to discover the plot and confront his brother? The criminal nature of the incident would likely require him to demand trial. And punishment.

Of course, Sion has changed. I doubt he'd do so willingly. But can he even refuse in the first place? Would Sunkland allow him to?

After everything they'd been through together, she felt like she knew Sion pretty well as a person. Being Mia, the details of her understanding might be questionable, but she nevertheless had an approximate grasp of how he saw the promised crown over his head and the standards to which he held himself. The Remno incident had, in her opinion, brought his near-neurotic fascination with justice and fairness down to a more reasonable level of dedication. He was no longer the Sion of old.

But that was during their adventures, where his homeland held little sway over his actions. Here, in the heart of Sunkland, where they prized just and righteous rulers above all else, an attempt to assassinate their crown prince would be met with a tidal wave of demand for fair trial, along with fair punishment. Fair, unbiased, and thoroughly unforgiving punishment.

He'd be forced to sentence his own brother to death... That'd surely scar him for life...

Mia's fingers tightened around the scarf on her neck. She had no siblings. The only family she knew was her father, the emperor. She wasn't even all that fond of him. If anything, she found him rather annoying. When he'd seen her wearing this dress, though... The dress that her mother—his wife—had made with her own hands... The beaming joy that had radiated from him was admittedly endearing. Not that it made him any less annoying, but... Back in the previous timeline, the news of him being sent to the guillotine before her had rattled her to no small degree. He was annoying, but not *that* annoying...

Besides... Though she had no memories of her mother, she certainly would have loved to know her. And, if possible, have her at her side. Such was one's family. They were precious beyond reason. She couldn't imagine Sion feeling any different.

I mean, yes, he's perfect and flawless and knows way too much for his own good, but it must still hurt him to be forced to sentence a family member to death.

Perhaps it was the fact that she was wearing her mother's handmade dress. For some reason, Mia couldn't stand the thought of the relationship between Sion and Echard turning so dreadfully sour. Offing an assassin or two was no problem, but if one of those assassins was Sion's own brother, she wasn't sure whether telling him about it would do him more good than harm.

Anyway, that's why it's absolutely imperative that no other nobles find out about this.

So long as the whole incident was kept under wraps, Sion wouldn't be forced into a position where he had to kill his brother for the sake of justice.

But assuming no one else finds out, and Sion chooses to forgive Echard, how would Echard feel about Sion?

She couldn't help but think that it would only make the younger prince more bitter, especially considering Keithwood's description of his character and the inferiority complex he suffered from. As the rift between the two brothers widened, it would leave them increasingly vulnerable to manipulation by the Serpents.

"Which would be even nastier. Honestly, I'd rather deal with assassins."

What made the Serpents so problematic was their ability to turn well-behaving citizens into their pawns. Vital pieces of the intricate system that was society would become corrupted, but their function would be no less vital. A regular assassin could be eliminated with minimal harm to Sion's conscience, but doing so to a brother who'd become an assassin would cause a lot more collateral damage.

Dealing with the incident at hand would require utmost finesse.

"I think...saving Sion's life is going to be the least of my problems this time."

There was no guarantee the Princess Chronicles would warn her of every impending crisis. If she identified a potential problem down the road, it was best to nip it in the bud.

"Let's say I have Rina follow Sion around. Esmeralda can stick with Prince Echard. As for Tiona...maybe I should assign her to Sion too..."

As she contemplated how to deploy her forces during the party, one issue slipped her mind.

When it rains, it pours.

Misfortunes never come singly.

Bad things come in threes.

She failed to consider the implication of these well-known proverbs. With the princes' estrangement and the Serpents' involvement, the stage was set for a third bout of trouble to come hopping along like that two-legged guillotine of her dreams.

Chapter 3: Mia...Isn't Living a Lie!

The ball took place in the main hall of Solecsudo Castle. The lavishly decorated space was currently teeming with guests.

"Your Highness, in addition to Sunkland nobility, there are, as we expected, a great number of foreign dignitaries," Ludwig said in a swift whisper after scanning the hall.

"Are you certain?" asked Mia.

"Yes. I've identified a number of people who match the descriptions from Balthazar."

"Hm... Well, knowing that Miss Rafina and Abel were invited, I already figured it wasn't just a normal party..."

The fact that the event was being hosted by Sunkland's royal family and a main guest was Esmeralda, who belonged to one of Tearmoon's Four Houses, made it all but impossible for the party to be small in scale.

The thing is, I still don't know what this party is supposed to be about. What are we even celebrating? she thought as she looked around.

"Hello, Mia."

Her idle rubbernecking was cut short by an approaching figure. Rafina Orca Belluga, clothed in formal ball attire, walked up. Her hair floated gently behind her, silklike over skin as pure and immaculate as fresh snow. Her dress was a pale blue with a twinkling translucence that evoked the flowing beauty of mountain streams.

34

"My, Miss Rafina. It's a pleasure to see you again." Mia curtsied with the utmost respect. "Thank you for having lunch with me the other day. It was wonderful."

"I'm so glad to hear that. You're such an epicure that I was worried the food might not be up to your standards..."

Their conversation triggered a wave of chatter among the surrounding nobles.

"Hey, that person talking to Lady Rafina..."

"Yes, I know what you're thinking, and you're probably right. It's Tearmoon's princess..."

Unbothered by the sudden attention she was garnering, Mia continued to look around until she found Abel on the other side of the room.

"Hey, Abel! Over here!" She promptly stretched a hand up as far as it would go and waved.

Abel noticed immediately and walked over. "Well, someone's looking lovely today, isn't she?"

"Oh, Abel, you're such a flatterer! Feel free to flatter me more, by the way!"

Within seconds, she'd forgotten the reason she'd come here and begun flirting with Abel, so it was perhaps fortunate that an announcement forced them to stop.

"Welcome, everyone, to this ball hosted by our great kingdom of Sunkland. I thank you all for attending." It was Count Lampron, formally greeting the guests.

That reminds me... He's supposed to be the master of ceremonies today.

Mia idly watched him give his speech, the contents of which she found entirely uninteresting until...there was a sudden turn of events!

"As a matter of fact, I have the honor of delivering some magnificent news to our esteemed guests here. A public statement will be made soon, but it is my pleasure to announce that the second prince of our kingdom, His Highness Echard Sol Sunkland, is officially engaged to Lady Esmeralda Etoile Greenmoon of the Tearmoon Empire."

Count Lampron's booming announcement was met with a round of applause.

"What?!"

Esmeralda, faced with this unexpected development, could do little but let out cries of bewilderment. The news took Mia by surprise as well, but the shock was soon replaced by a wave of relief. Why relief, you ask?

I see! So that's the point of this party. Now I know why they invited Miss Rafina and Abel and all these other nobles but left me out... It's because they didn't want me meddling with their plans, and definitely not because I'm unpopular, or they all hate me, or all my friendships are a lie and I'm actually terribly, terribly alone... Phew! What a relief!

At last, Mia figured out what Count Lampron was trying to do. It was the good old fait accompli technique—by preemptively claiming that the engagement was official, he made it awkward for the involved parties to refute.

Basically, he's forcing Esmeralda into a position where she can't say no anymore. Hm, hm. This is a pretty smart move on his part. Esmeralda might act like a tyrant at home, but she can be such a wimp when she's outside.

Not that Mia was a paragon of mental fortitude or anything, but anyway...

He's probably talked this out with the Greenmoons already. Esmeralda's probably the only one who doesn't know. The poor girl... They set her up, thought Mia, feeling a pang of pity for her friend. *But wait. Do I actually* need *to do anything about this?*

It wasn't like Esmeralda hated Echard's guts. In fact, she seemed...kind of fond of him.

I'll probably miss her a little, but having Esmeralda marry into Sunkland's royal family should make it easier to manage the relationship between Sion and Echard.

After all, averting tonight's assassination wouldn't mend the pair's bond. Whatever grievances Echard felt toward his brother would likely remain. In that case, it was better to leave someone she could trust, like Esmeralda, by their side...

Her thoughts were interrupted by the figure beside her speaking up.

"Congratulations. I offer my best wishes to the bride and groom, and hope that this union will strengthen the bond between the two nations," said Rafina, placing her hands on her chest. "My good friend, Mia Luna Tearmoon, is surely overjoyed to witness this moment as well. Isn't that right, Mia?"

Faced with that chillingly courteous smile of Rafina's, Mia uttered a whimpering, "Uh..."

At that moment, it dawned on Mia that Rafina was complying with Ludwig's request. *This* was the countermeasure he'd prepared. It was playing out as they spoke. The problem...was that it revolved around *her.*

Chapter 4: Nod, Nod...Nod?

After a brief mental blank, Mia's brain started working again. Rafina's sonorous voice had shifted the whole room's attention from Lampron to Mia.

Wh-What is happening right now?!

She had no idea what Rafina was expecting her to say, but she knew she had to say *something*. A moment's hesitation was followed by resolve.

I'll have to ride this out! I don't know where this wave is headed, but as long as I make like a jellyfish and go with the flow, I probably won't drown!

She let out a short breath. The next instant, a brilliant smile adorned her face.

"Yes, this marriage between the House of Greenmoon and the royal family of Sunkland is indeed terrific news. Prince Echard is a marvelous individual. I'm so glad that my dear friend Esmeralda has found herself such a wonderful bridegroom."

The sentiments she voiced were genuine. People tend to grow through marriage. If Echard could become a more mature individual through this arrangement, it might rid him of the desire to plot further assassinations. Theoretically, Mia stood to benefit from this marriage, allowing her to speak from the heart. For this part of the proceedings, at least.

"As am I," concluded Rafina. "May the Lord bless their coming days together with much love and happiness."

After Rafina spoke her blessing, the hall came alive with chatter. Count Lampron smiled at the hastily conversing nobles, his expression vaguely smug. This very situation was the reason he'd arranged for Rafina to be present. Acknowledgment by the Saint of Belluga lent the proposed marriage a legitimacy that made it difficult, if not impossible, to annul. This was further reinforced by the presence of numerous foreign dignitaries, all of whom could bear witness to her endorsement. The purpose of this party was to make this marriage a done deal.

"To have the Kingdom of Sunkland and the Tearmoon Empire, two pillars of our continent, brought closer through marriage is truly a wonderful development," said Rafina as she turned to Mia. "And I'm sure it will greatly assist you in what you're trying to do as well. Isn't that right, Mia?"

It took Mia a moment to figure out what Rafina meant. Fortunately, the answer dawned on her before she let out any telltale gestures of confusion. What Mia was trying to do...referred to the sustained provision of food during a widespread famine. She had, after all, made an appeal during the entrance ceremony for mutual and open food support between nations. To that end, establishing friendlier relations with Sunkland was certainly beneficial.

Given Sion's personality, he probably won't say no to food-assistance measures. Still, it can't hurt to have more insurance, and Esmeralda becoming his in-law will be pretty good for that. In that sense, this marriage is actually a pretty good deal. I mean, once the famine hits, nobody will have the time for political power struggles anyway.

But was it really that good of a deal? Considering the fact that it was a trio of Mia fanatics—Ludwig, Rafina, and Anne—behind this plan, was that *truly* the extent of their vision? Of course not. Theirs was a far grander scheme.

"You've been keeping yourself quite busy lately, haven't you?" Rafina continued. "I heard about your tour de force in Perujin."

Before Mia could respond, a nearby Sunkland noble interjected. "Oh? Might that be related to the news of Tearmoon expanding their food reserves?" he asked loudly, clearly intending for the question to be heard by others.

"What a coincidence. We were wondering about the same thing too."

More nobles waded into the conversation.

"There have been…concerns in our kingdom that Tearmoon is stockpiling food in preparation for an invasion."

"Well, I've actually spoken to His Majesty—" Mia stopped, realizing that someone far more qualified to answer their concerns was quietly approaching—her loyal subject Ludwig. That's right. This time, Mia had come prepared, equipped with not only her right hand but her brains too! It did beg the question of "if her right hand and brains were all other people, then how much of Mia was actually *Mia*?" Alas, there was no time for such philosophical pondering.

Hm… Yes, I should definitely leave this to him. He'll do a much better job.

A carefully worded response was necessary to avoid rousing more suspicion. Carefully wording responses was brainwork. Therefore, it only made sense to use her brains, aka Ludwig.

"About that matter… I understand that there are many misunderstandings afoot. Fortunately, I have one of my most trusted vassals here with me. Allow me to introduce you to Ludwig.

He will explain to you the true nature of the matter," said Mia, expecting him to deliver a perfect explanation that left no room for doubt.

Which, he did. He sure did. His explanation left absolutely no room for any doubt.

After receiving the metaphorical baton from Mia, Ludwig nodded.

"I assume you all wish to know why Her Highness went to Perujin…" He gave his glasses a tap. "The reason for her journey… was to establish a continent-wide system of mutual food aid that would not be hindered by sovereignties and borders."

Mia folded her arms and nodded with satisfaction at this answer.

"And in order to realize her vision," Ludwig continued, "she needed the cooperation of a number of merchant companies to build the organization that would manage this effort."

Mia continued her arm-folding and head-nodding, but her eyebrows began to take on a curious slant.

"The ones who will aid in this effort are Forkroad & Co. and the renowned merchant, Shalloak Cornrogue."

The latter's name sent a wave of commotion through the nobles.

"Cornrogue? Isn't he supposed to be greed on legs? She brought *him* on?"

Had it been Cornrogue alone, the announcement might have garnered more censure than praise. Shalloak Cornrogue frequently employed aggressive business tactics that garnered him no small number of enemies. However…

"Well, if Forkroad is part of the operation too…"

Forkroad, though smaller than Cornrogue in scale, was known to be a trusty and upright merchant. Even neighboring nations were aware of his reputation of doing fair and honest business.

"Also, weren't those two supposed to have been at each other's throats lately?"

Many nobles frowned in bafflement, having heard of Cornrogue's hostile actions toward Forkroad. Regardless, if Mia had managed to secure support from both of them, that could mean only one thing—she'd not only made peace between the two, but won both of them over. Those who knew of the Great Sage of the Empire only by name found themselves dumbfounded. No longer were she and her feats the stuff of rumor and hearsay. Now, they were personally witnessing one of her incredible achievements. In real time, to boot. The experience was far more visceral.

But Ludwig wasn't done. He wasn't going to stop until he'd left them completely breathless.

"Her Highness wishes to completely and permanently eradicate all famine from the continent. That is why she is building this organization. And that is why she went to Perujin."

"What does Perujin have to do with this?" asked a voice from the crowd. "And aren't they a vassal state?"

Ludwig nodded at the questioner. "A valid question. It is an undeniable fact that there is considerable criticism regarding the relative positions of the empire and Perujin Agricultural Country, and that criticism is certainly fair. However, undoing our current arrangement is by no means simple, because Perujin is completely nonmilitarized. If they were to be invaded by a hostile nation, they would not last long. To that end, they require the empire's military power for their protection. Given this difficult relationship, and all the complications and baggage it brings, I trust you can all see how the criticism of Perujin's vassal status to the empire is, while valid, a problem with no easy solution," said Ludwig, growing ever more loquacious as he spoke. "However, despite having full knowledge of this difficult context, Her Highness took a look at the arrangement... and rejected it!"

Passion flowed through his every word. He gesticulated. His speech quickened without any loss of eloquence. Every fiber in his body seemed to buzz with energy, and waves of exhilaration coursed through his veins.

Basically, he was experiencing what happens when geeks get to talk about their favorite thing.

"That is why Her Highness went to Perujin!" he declared, chest filling with pride for the historic achievement of the princess he served. "To demonstrate the path forward that she believes in! A path not cut by blades. Not scorched by war. But paved with respect. She went not to do battle, but to *teach* battle! By placing the headquarters of the merchant's organization in Perujin, she showed them how to fight for themselves—to protect themselves without weapons and arms!"

Food shortages could occur anywhere. Befall any nation. And when it did, who would make an enemy of the nation that offered aid? Should that nation then suffer an invasion by malevolent forces, who would refuse to offer aid in return?

"The true enemy of Her Highness, the one with which she intends to go to war...is a foe no one has even considered before. She wishes to fight famine itself! And to do so, she is building an organization that spans nations, borders, and cultures, and it is in Perujin where this grand vision will first take shape!"

The conclusion of Ludwig's speech was met with pin-drop silence.

A beat later, Rafina spoke. "Incredible... Absolutely incredible. I've never been more proud to call Princess Mia my friend." Rafina turned to Mia. "It is an honor, and with every passing day, I grow more uncertain if I deserve it."

With that, the Saint of Belluga gave her seal of approval to Mia's grand vision, thereby setting the greatness of her feats in stone. That was what Ludwig had been after. It was, in a way, an attack on Sunkland's "justice." What Mia did in Perujin, and what she was planning to do thereafter... What *was* the organization she was building? What did it represent?

It was an organization of peace. An organization of true justice that would fight against a common foe of all mankind—famine.

Ludwig's speech could be summarized as "Her Highness is trying to uphold a justice that is not limited by borders. One that is universal across all nations." Its righteousness did not in any way pale in comparison to what Sunkland expected of its rulers. In fact, it was *better*. He was challenging the justice championed by Count Lampron and his kind by presenting an alternative one and, after demonstrating its superiority, dared them to oppose it. Would they stand opposite her in this struggle? Take the side of famine?

Absolutely not. And so long as they couldn't, the marriage between Esmeralda and Echard would work in Mia's favor. Sunkland was a kingdom of justice. If Mia's justice was more true, they would have no choice but to join her.

Thus concluded Ludwig's master stroke, in which he used Sunkland's values against them...to *further* their values. He fought justice with justice, and in doing so, made them one and better.

"...Huh?"

Needless to say, all of that went straight over Mia's head.

Chapter 5: Fond Visions of Four-Eyes Past

"I'm moved beyond words. Your dedication to the people… Not just Tearmoon's, but *all* the people of this continent… It's nothing short of awe-inspiring. It is my earnest hope that this new bond you've formed with Sunkland will be an invaluable boon to your efforts," Rafina said on the heels of Ludwig's speech with an enthusiasm that rivaled if not surpassed his.

And who could blame her? After all, she'd effectively been sidelined during this whole incident. Despite being her friend—no, *because* she was her friend—Mia had refrained from asking her for help. The inability to help Mia had left her sorely disappointed, and this was her chance to make up for it. She was raring to go!

"I am so proud of you," Rafina continued, taking Mia's hands in the process. "And you should be too. This accomplishment is one for the history books. If there is anything Belluga can do to help you, you need only ask."

Faced with her unbridled praise, panic began to set in for Sunkland's nobles. The Holy Lady despised being made an instrument of nobles to flaunt their influence. She was also famously averse to favoritism. This was not someone they could sweet-talk, much less bribe—or so they thought, but in actuality, she was not only willing but *eager* to offer highly biased help to her friends.

Now, Rafina, who was largely immune to persuasion, was applauding the greatness of Mia's feats. The significance of that could not be understated. The Holy Lady was, for all intents and purposes, acknowledging the righteousness of Mia's justice.

Huh... I'm not quite sure what's going on...

Mia found herself at a loss. Judging by the fluid interplay between Ludwig and Rafina, this was likely part of their plan. The problem was that Mia had already entered hands-off mode, figuring she could take a step (or three) back and let Esmeralda do the remainder of the heavy lifting. Instead, she found herself at the forefront of the matter again. Her initial panic, however, was soon replaced by puzzlement as she gave the situation more thought. Why, she wondered, was this organization thing even being mentioned? She understood the necessity to explain to Sunkland's nobles why she'd gone to Perujin, but how was that relevant to this marriage proposal and its effects on her political opposition?

What is the point of all this? What is Ludwig up to? That was when it hit her. *Oooooh, I get it now... This is plan B, isn't it?*

It occurred to her that even Ludwig couldn't think of a way to call off this engagement. Instead, he'd decided to make the most of the situation and excavate some new talent for their budding organization.

I bet he's planning to make Sunkland provide some useful personnel for the organization!

She could hardly be further off the mark.

That's why he teamed up with Rafina. He asked her to help him pressure Sunkland.

They were currently in the presence of not just Sunkland nobles but many other foreign dignitaries. Having Rafina pledge her support in front of so many people was a decisive move that would force Sunkland to offer help as well.

I have to say, though, I'm impressed. I had no idea Ludwig was building an organization like that behind the scenes. She pursed her lips thoughtfully. *A mutual food aid network that spans borders, huh? That never even crossed my mind. But now that I think about it, an organization like that would indeed be pretty useful when the empire is dealing with the famine. As long as people have food to eat, they probably won't haul me off to the guillotine. Hm… At first, I was panicking because I had no idea what he was talking about, but wow, this whole thing is actually thought out pretty well.*

As she looked at Ludwig with renewed appreciation, he declared in the proudest of voices, "For the sake of convenience, we have decided to name this organization in honor of its original proponent. I hereby formally announce the establishment of the Mianet."

I…also had no idea Ludwig was coming up with such terrible names behind the scenes.

"Mianet"? Seriously? She could feel the beginnings of a headache.

Okay, so assuming I make him change the name later… This is still pretty good. He definitely deserves some credit for making the most out of a losing battle.

They might not win the battle, but they wouldn't lose the war. Though their enemies would have their way this time, Mia still had Esmeralda, whose future actions could turn the tide in her favor.

That's why I originally wanted to leave it to Esmeralda, but Ludwig managed to take advantage of the situation and score some points for us. Oho ho, good for you, you not-so-stupid four-eyes. No wonder you managed to keep a failing empire standing for so long back then.

She recalled—almost fondly by now—the final days of a despairing empire. Under Ludwig's instructions, she'd spent most of her time on the road, going desperately from place to place trying to keep the empire from toppling. He'd been with her every step of the way. Him and his stupid glasses. All the way to the guillotine.

Very well. I'll be his puppet again. A pawn in his plan. In terms of fighting losing battles, this is nothing. Especially compared to back then.

Enjoying the brief wave of nostalgia, Mia stepped forward with renewed vigor. "Thank you very much, Ludwig. That was a wonderfully articulate explanation. I'm sure it made the situation much clearer for everyone."

Then, she smiled at Rafina. It was part performance— reinforcing the image of their intimacy—and part gratitude. Whatever the circumstances, Rafina's gesture of support deserved thanks.

"I've always meant to speak to you about the effort at some point and ask for your help, Miss Rafina," she said, emphasizing the name for good measure. "But…I didn't think you'd agree so readily. I'm very glad you did, though. Thank you."

Finally, she addressed the guests in the hall.

"As you've heard from my retainer, I believe it is in the continent's interest to establish a system for fighting famine, and I intend to ask every nation for their cooperation. That, of course, includes your great kingdom of Sunkland…"

Now that she understood the gist of Ludwig's plan, Mia did her best to help him with his staffing concerns. Granted, though they were soliciting useful personnel for the definitely-yet-to-be-formally-named Mianet, indiscriminate acceptance of help from all sources ran the risk of causing chaos within the organization. Fortunately, she didn't have to worry about that for this particular source…

and it was all thanks to Rafina. Her influence was prevalent throughout the continent, but it was arguably strongest here in Sunkland, whose sovereignty based its guiding principles on the Holy Book of the Central Orthodox Church. Should the personnel provided by a Sunkland noble prove problematic, what would happen?

Well, Mia would tell on them! She'd go straight to Rafina and have her give them a good scolding. That would likely ruin the noble's reputation. The threat of having the Holy Lady on their behinds should keep them from getting questionable ideas.

No wonder he asked Rafina for help! Good call, Ludwig!

And so, princess and subject worked in tandem, the vectors of their efforts aligned on every axis except the ones that mattered. Their divergently united performance was interrupted, however, by someone who found it hard to stomach.

"With all due respect, Princess Mia, I *must* protest!"

Chapter 6: Princess Mia…Speaks with a Bit of an Accent

"Are you, in your position as the leader of this Mianet organization, telling all us Sunkland nobles to subordinate ourselves to you?"

A stern voice cut through the hall's chatter. It belonged to the man acting as the event's master of ceremonies, Count Lampron. He sneaked a quick glance at King Abram, but the Sunkland sovereign showed no signs of speaking. That didn't surprise Lampron. The vision presented by Princess Mia was in the interest of the common people. Its justice was valid—indisputably so. Nevertheless, he couldn't afford it any legitimacy.

If Princess Mia seriously believes what that vassal of hers is claiming…then we have absolutely no way of refuting her. To oppose her position is to oppose justice. It would undermine everything we stand for.

Peace protected by the rule of a just and righteous king… That was the most central pillar of Sunkland's existence as a kingdom, and it was the principal justification for their expansionism. So long as they hoisted peace for the people as their banner, they had no way of opposing Mia's stance.

But that's not all… There's more to it…

A chill ran down his spine as he realized the graver danger that Mia represented—a justice that rivaled or even trumped that of the King of Sunkland. A chief argument of the Sunkland conservatives was that all people were best ruled by the King of Sunkland, because he was most capable of ruling in a virtuous fashion. There was an inherently requisite condition to this argument, though. The King of Sunkland couldn't be less virtuous than any foreign nobility; his superiority had to be plainly evident. If people were to see Princess Mia as a ruler of similar competence and virtue as King Abram...

Lampron gritted his teeth. That couldn't be allowed to happen. He needed a plan, and he needed it fast.

Bah... I thought all the talk about the Great Sage of the Empire was just exaggerated hearsay. Who knew it actually had some substance?

She had the initiative to invite herself as a friend of the Greenmoon bride, the wits to turn the tide of the party in her favor, and the extraordinary gumption to take something from the realm of empty ideals and lip service, and turn it into reality. She defied just about every expectation he had of her. Princess Mia, he now realized, was no distant mirage. She was a Goliath. Towering, powerful, and completely real. Even so, he couldn't back down. He had to fight, no matter the odds. He looked upon her, feeling as if he were in her shadow, and furiously racked his brain looking for a way to find fault with her claims.

"...I'm sorry? Subordinate yourselves to me? As the leader of the organization? Please, that's just about the last thing I'd want you to do. It'd be so ann—rrogant of me." She covered her slip of the tongue with the politest "*oho ho*" she could muster. "The one who should lead the organization is neither me nor the King of Perujin. And it's not the King of Sunkland either. Not even Miss Rafina. No, it should be led by an expert in that field."

"By which you mean..."

"I believe the task should be given to someone nominated by either Forkroad or Cornrogue."

Her answer was both simple and reasonable. Merchants, being experts of distribution, would know best how to set up supply routes. They'd also have a good grasp of how much food was available in each nation. Those were the very problems the organization needed to solve, so the one to take the reins should not be herself but someone with extensive knowledge in the relevant matters.

"You would yield the prestige and glory to someone else? Even a commoner from another nation?"

"It is my opinion, Count Lampron, that being able to eat filling and delicious meals at all times is a great blessing. What greater glory is there than to provide that for all people? To have everyone rest easy at night knowing there will always be bread in the morning?"

And there it was. The perfect response. Well, *almost* perfect. Her pronunciation of "arrogant" had a bit of a strange accent to it, but that was a minor detail.

Bah, I have to concede this point. Arguing would only make a fool of myself.

With teeth clenched, he shot her a glare, only to be met with the most benign of smiles. The young princess, standing there in a gorgeous dress that seemed to exude the purity and benevolence of her soul, looked positively radiant.

"Hunger kills nations. It kills their people, their nobility, and their kings and emperors alike. It is our common foe. Should we not then join together and fight this threat as one?"

As she delivered that final blow, Lampron felt the last vestiges of his fight leave him. His legs suddenly felt weak, and he had to make an effort to remain standing. What Mia was trying to accomplish was a feat of historic proportions that would be told and retold for generations, and faced with opposition, she not only did not brush him aside as an enemy but instead continued to offer her hand in good faith.

The fight was over. No matter how hard he looked within, he could not dredge up any more ways to remain her enemy. He was done. Not beaten, no. He had not despaired at the disparity of power. He'd simply lost his reason to fight. At the same time, he also realized why Sion, who'd always advocated the same ideal of prosperity through the rule of the righteous Sunkland king, had changed. It was because he'd met *her*—the Great Sage of the Empire.

"Enough, Count Lampron. I believe you've addressed all the questions our guests might have had. We have now reached concordance."

At last, King Abram spoke. He turned to Mia, eyes narrowing as if looking at something all too bright.

"Princess Mia, I am deeply impressed by your profound ingenuity. It would be our honor to help craft this grand vision of yours," he said with a regal smile. "And allow me to formally thank you for affording my son, Sion, your friendship. May he continue to be blessed by it all his life."

"Of course he will, Your Majesty. Not just friendship, though. Esmeralda is my kin. Once she marries Prince Echard, we will be family. Blood will be shared by Tearmoon and Sunkland." Mia turned toward the crowd. "Forgive me, everyone. I have taken too much of your time. The guest of honor for this occasion is not me, but Prince Echard and my very good friend Esmeralda. They have been brought together through a proposal of marriage, and I wish them all the best. May this wonderful arrangement proceed with the smoothness and gaiety it deserves."

Those present would not soon forget the resplendent smile that adorned her face.

Chapter 7: Spark

Mia never fails to impress... Sion let out a deeply affected sigh. *Forget Count Lampron. She's holding her own against father.* The gulf between their abilities only ever seemed to widen. *The Great Sage of the Empire, huh?*

"Hey, Sion. Long time no see."

He pulled himself out of his thoughts to find an old friend looking at him. "Ah, Abel. Long time, yes. I was hoping to say hi at school but, well, not everything goes my way."

The semester had already begun at Saint-Noel. Normally, Sion would be in Belluga by now, but he'd postponed his departure to attend this party. The school was used to such situations, though. Saint-Noel enrolled a great deal of nobility, and important events back home frequently required students to miss class. In such cases, extended absence was permitted.

"It's okay. These kinds of things happen," Abel said with a shrug. "Besides, isn't it a pretty novel experience for the student council to be meeting here in Sunkland? You didn't even need to come. We pretty much brought the council to you."

Sion smiled and shook his head. "Novel, yes, but also sort of embarrassing, considering I'll have to introduce all of you to my family."

"Sion?" asked Echard, who walked over. "Who might this be?"

"Hm? You don't remember? I'm pretty sure you've seen him once, but I guess you were too young. This is Abel Remno.

Second prince of the Kingdom of Remno, fellow member of the student council at Saint-Noel…and my friend."

Abel scratched his head, mildly embarrassed by the candid remark.

"Wow, 'friend'? To whom do I owe the honor?" he said, hiding his discomfort behind the joking tone. Then, he addressed Echard. "Abel Remno. It is a pleasure to meet you, Prince Echard. I come on behalf of my kingdom to extend our best wishes to this engagement."

"Thank you very much, Prince Abel," answered Echard. "I'm still a little shaken because it was very sudden, but I'll try my best for the sake of Sunkland."

That got an amazed stare from Abel. "For the sake of Sunkland? Ha ha, you're a far better prince than me. When I was your age, I sure didn't have the smarts to be thinking about my kingdom." He let out a hearty laugh. The prideless playboy of the past was nowhere to be seen.

You sure have changed, haven't you? Sion remembered when he'd first gone to Saint-Noel. Back then, Abel had at times exuded an uncaring aura, almost as if he'd given up on himself. Not anymore. *You've conquered your inferiority complex toward your brother. Freed from its burden, you've become a prouder man.*

Sion regarded his confident friend, appreciating his courage, integrity, and his steadily improving swordsmanship. He then looked at his own brother. Would Echard, he wondered, one day become like Abel? Could this meeting of the two change something for the better? He then looked around. It wasn't just Abel. Everyone around Mia, from her subjects to her friends, were upstanding people. He hoped they'd rub off on Echard. Their influence could only be good for him.

If only they could do for Echard…what they'd done for *him*. Free him from the old, ossified values that imprisoned his mind.

"I have to say, though, Mia really is something else."

Abel's comment woke him from his musing. "She sure is… Not once has she failed to amaze me."

Nodding in agreement, he regarded the girl who was no older than himself but could hold her political own against his father.

"That vision of hers…is the stuff of history books. It's going to shape the future of this whole continent," Sion murmured.

It wasn't just a countermeasure against famine. Its true significance was in its ability to reshape thought. It would change how people looked at the world.

The continent, by and large, conformed to the values of the Central Orthodox Church. Particulars varied from kingdom to kingdom, but there broadly existed a shared understanding of what was right and what was wrong. For example, ideas like "those in need should be offered help" and "the power given to nobles also confers upon them a duty to ensure the peace and safety of their people" were agreed upon by most as part of a basic system of morality.

That agreement, however, was largely superficial. Are the inhabitants of strange and distant lands truly the same as us? What if they only look similar but are actually terrible demons on the inside?

Such concerns, though vague, always occupied the dark recesses of people's minds. Because they'd never met. Because they'd never conversed. There was always a seed of doubt. A sense that they couldn't be trusted. As a result, it was easy for the people of foreign nations to look more and more like enemies. Sure, they worshipped the same god and championed the same justice. But *they* were the ones saying it. No matter how much they looked the same, true trust was never easy to come by.

But if Mia's vision became a reality... It would very literally change the world. The flow of people and goods would grow in both volume and consistency. New routes of trade between nations would develop, leading to new channels of communication between people. New bonds would form. Many would see for themselves that those inhabitants of strange and distant lands were indeed the same.

"Speaking of which... Mia really could afford to be a little more arrogant," said Sion.

"What do you mean?"

"She's the Great Sage of the Empire, for crying out loud. Who could be more fit than her to lead an organization like that?"

Abel nodded. "That is a very good point. But..." he said before letting out a short laugh.

"Hm? What's so funny?"

"Oh, I was just thinking about her speech. Maybe she was nervous, but you remember how she said 'ann-rrogant'? I just find it amusing that even the Great Sage of the Empire can get tongue-tied every once in a while."

Sion pursed his lips. It was certainly an endearing moment, offering a glimpse at the girl behind the sage. However...

"Was it nerves...or tact?"

This time, the one to respond was not Abel, but Echard.

"Tact?" He frowned. "Do you mean she did that to make her seem more approachable? Because of that saying? The charismatic are followed by many, the perfect by none?"

"That's right. It occurred to me that for someone of Mia's caliber, maybe it's possible to intentionally trip up for effect."

Echard frowned even more.

"Can you really plan that kind of thing?"

"For her, I think the answer is yes. It seems simple, in fact, compared to some of the other things she's done," Sion said before looking Echard in the eyes. "If Mia has a vision like that in mind, then the marriage between you and Lady Esmeralda will doubtlessly have a great deal of significance. You'll have a part to play as a prince of Sunkland, so make sure you make everyone proud."

He infused his voice with expectation, for he knew Echard's struggles. He knew his sweat, toil, and pain. Echard tried hard to fill his princely role, but being constantly compared to Sion had left a scar deep in his heart.

He's trying to become me, but he doesn't need to. He can have his own goals. His own way of living.

Talents and gifts varied from person to person. Just as Sion had his strengths and weaknesses, so did Echard. There were some things that only Echard could do. He prayed that Mia's vision would be a spark for him. Push him to see things in a new light. Then, one day, perhaps they could work together on this grand project. How wonderful it would be if they could, as siblings, play a part in bringing her vision to fruition.

That was his sincere hope. And it was what he'd hoped to convey.

"As a fellow prince of Sunkland, I'll do my best to help Princess Mia too," said Sion. "Let's both give it our all."

"Yes… Of course."

Echard's response was quieter, spoken with his face downcast. His expression was hidden from view.

Chapter 8: A World of F.A.T.

Count Lampron's sudden interjection left Mia flummoxed.

"...I'm sorry? Subordinate yourselves to me? As the leader of the organization? Please, that's just about the last thing I'd want you to do. It'd be so ann—rrogant of me."

She *oho ho*'d reflexively as a drop of cold sweat rolled down her back.

Sweet moons, I almost said "annoying"... Okay, I need to get my act together.

Realizing that a new current had developed in the conversation, she refocused her mind, trying to follow its flow.

All right, my "arrogant" save has got me covered on the humility front, but it leaves me wide open in terms of responsibility...

For endeavors like this, the natural assumption was that whoever came up with the idea would assume responsibility for it. Since the organization was Mia's brainchild, the obligation of leading and managing it might very well fall to her. But that'd be so much work! What she needed was a line of reasoning that would exempt her from the onus of work.

And then it hit her. "I believe the task should be given to someone nominated by either Forkroad or Cornrogue," she said, holding back a smug grin.

A brilliant idea, if I do say so myself! If I nominated someone from my own empire, it might ruffle some feathers, but if it comes from a third party...and not just any third party but a merchant—an expert in the field—no one can complain about me playing favorites that way. On top of that, if the person messes up somehow, it won't be my responsibility.

"You would yield the prestige and glory to someone else?" asked a shocked Count Lampron.

Her brows twitched at this question.

"Prestige and glory..." she whispered musingly. If words had taste, these would come bitter.

Mia was no stranger to glory. As the princess of the Tearmoon Empire, she was well aware of the prestige it afforded her. However, she was also well aware of something else—the guillotine. Glory... Prestige... Social eminence... None of those would stop a blade from slicing through her neck. A fast horse was way more useful. In fact, she'd be more than happy to trade all her glory for a carrot cake. The carrot cake, at least, she could feed to Kuolan and keep him running.

With that said, running away implied that her head was already in danger of rolling. She'd much rather keep the guillotine from coming after her in the first place. And what was the best way to do that?

She regarded Count Lampron and spoke in the slow, slightly patronizing tone one took when explaining something to a particularly dense child. "It is my opinion, Count Lampron, that being able to eat filling and delicious meals at all times is a great blessing."

That's right. A full tummy a day keeps the guillotine away. To eat a cake today and know that there will be mushroom stew tomorrow is a blessing greater than any glory. The full enjoyment of eating said cake, however, rested on a certain condition—

the full stomachs of everyone nearby. Nothing robbed a cake of its sweetness as quickly as the sight of starving people below the castle walls.

"What greater glory is there than to provide that for all people? To have everyone rest easy at night knowing there will always be bread in the morning?"

'Twas not glory that averted the guillotine, but gorged guts. People needed to feel assured that they could eat to their hearts' content today and still have plenty of food tomorrow. *That* was what truly kept heads on shoulders, because what happened to people after they ate that much? Food comas. After pigging out, people start to feel like there's a pig weighing them down. They get sleepy. Their body slows; their mind dulls. They stop caring so much about things—like questionably competent princesses— so long as they could enjoy a good night's sleep and another good meal tomorrow. Well, *she* stopped caring so much, at least, and surely she wasn't all that different from everyone else.

That was Mia's ideal world. A world where everyone was happy. And carefree. And at a severely elevated risk of developing F.A.T.

With that thought in mind, she favored the hall's guests with a smile, turning the cordiality of the expression up as much as it would go to mask any breakthrough smugness, and said, "Hunger kills nations. It kills their people, their nobility, and their kings and emperors alike. It is our common foe. Should we not then join together and fight this threat as one?"

The enemy was hunger. So it was for the masses, so it was for the nobility. Kings and emperors, Sunkland and Tearmoon—it was the same for all. And the enemy of an enemy...had to be a friend! That was the implicit meaning of her statement and her true aim—to wring some capable personnel out of Sunkland for the organization. Soon after delivering her statement, she knew that she'd prevailed...

"Princess Mia, I am deeply impressed by your profound ingenuity. It would be our honor to help craft this grand vision of yours."

...For the King of Sunkland Abram himself voiced his support for her cause. The cordiality in her smile did not last through this development. With mildly discernible smugness, she addressed the hall.

"Forgive me, everyone. I have taken too much of your time. The guest of honor for this occasion is not me, but Prince Echard and my very good friend Esmeralda. They have been brought together through a proposal of marriage, and I wish them all the best."

By promptly shifting the focus toward Esmeralda, she sought to send a message to her opponents. Yes, she couldn't stop the marriage from happening. In that sense, she'd lost this battle. But they'd better enjoy their victory while it lasted, because they hadn't won the war. How things played out from here was entirely dependent on Esmeralda, and she was, as Mia pointedly mentioned, her *very good friend*.

"May this wonderful arrangement proceed with the smoothness and gaiety it deserves."

She added that final line for good measure, meaning it as a sort of "Go ahead, have your marriage. I don't even care." Then, she spun on her heels and strutted away with what she assumed was an air of elegance instead of, well, sour grapes.

The grapes she walked *toward*, however, were definitely not sour. Nor was anything else around it. She made a beeline for the sweets section of the buffet table.

Ugh, that was way too much brainwork. I'm starting to feel dizzy. I need sugar.

CHAPTER 8: A WORLD OF F.A.T.

The proceedings had thoroughly expended her energy stores, leaving her body in dire want of sweets.

And so, Mia marched forward, each step bringing her ever closer to her ideal world. Literally. A world of F.A.T. awaited her on that table.

Chapter 9: Mia Channels Her Inner Seductress

Food... I need food... Cakes, preferably. Where can I find some cakes...?

Mia scanned her surroundings. The shock of her speech had yet to wear off. At Lampron's direction, the event had moved on to its dance and dine segment, but there remained an anxious energy throughout the hall. Guests whispered furiously to each other, and few—even those partaking in it—seemed to pay much attention to the dancing.

The hall was largely divided into two areas. A large open space was reserved for dancing, and another was lined with tables full of food and drink. The dining space was positioned next to the balcony, presumably to allow guests to marvel at the stars with a glass of wine in hand.

Mia wasn't interested in any of that. She'd rather know where her friends were. She didn't need to look, though; one of them was already approaching.

"Bravo, Mia."

Abel walked up to her with a wine glass in each hand.

"My, Abel. Is that for me? Thank you very much."

She took one of the glasses and sipped at the drink inside. It turned out to be juice. The mild sweetness with a refreshing hint of tart suggested it was based on apples. She swallowed, enjoying the coolness of the liquid as it flowed down her throat.

Soon, she felt the sugar making its way into her brain, and she let out a satisfied breath.

Suddenly, a thought occurred to her, and she stared at the glass.

I wonder if this is how they poisoned Sion. By slipping it into a drink like this.

In case anyone forgot, her main mission here in Sunkland was still ongoing. She'd done a good job of going along with Ludwig's plan, but that had done nothing to avert Sion's assassination.

What am I going to do...?

She grabbed a nearby macaron and popped it into her mouth to keep a steady supply of sugar going. As she chewed, she examined her surroundings once more. The dining area was filled with countless foods. If the poison had been hidden in any of them, avoiding it was going to be extremely difficult. It'd be best if Sion could just, you know, neither eat nor drink the whole night, but...

"Something on your mind?"

She looked up to find a worried Abel. As she studied his face...

You know, now that I take a good look, Abel has really long eyelashes. They're so straight too. And his eyes are so pure and dreamy. Just like him...

...She had absolutely no constructive thoughts whatsoever. If anything, her ability to produce any was actively hindered, as her brain had immediately switched to relationship mode.

"Uh... Mia, would you mind looking in, uh, some other direction every once in a while?" Abel said as he awkwardly averted his eyes. "It's sort of embarrassing when you stare like that."

"H-Huh? Oh, my. I'm sorry. I was, um, thinking...and I lost myself for a second."

Uh-oh. This is not good. If he asks me to dance, I'm not sure I can stay focused. I need to somehow— Wait, that's it! A dance!

Inspiration struck her like lightning.

What if I asked Sion to dance with me? And just kept him dancing the whole time so he has no chance to drink anything?

Even the superhuman Sion couldn't *possibly* drink while he was dancing. Eating would be out of the question too.

Okay, let's think about this. If I ask him to dance, he probably won't turn me down. And considering it's him, *once I get him on the dance floor, there'll be throngs of people lining up to be his next partner. He can still grab drinks between dances, but as long as I can make sure that's the only time he gets to go…*

Mia turned to face Abel and lowered her head. "I'm sorry, Abel, but as a gesture of respect, I'd like to first ask Sion for a dance this time. Would that be all right?" She then gave him the pleading puppy dog eyes.

"Hm? Of course. Go ahead. Dances are a part of diplomacy, after all. Showing everyone that you're on good terms with Sion should help keep your opponents in check."

Abel smiled gently at her. There was no hint of concern in his expression. No discomfort. No…anything. He wasn't even the slightest bit upset, almost as if it was perfectly reasonable for her to be dancing with Sion and *she* was the weird one for even bothering to ask. And that made *her* a little upset.

Seriously, Abel? she thought, feeling a pang of jealousy. *I just told you I'm going to dance with Sion, and you're just…okay with it?*

Relationship-mode Mia roared to life, and along with it came all the pesky nuances and sentiments that young lovers tended to inflict upon one another. When she was talking to other boys, she expected *some* pushback. Not too much, of course, but just enough for her to relish the hint of adoration that could be glimpsed from the jealousy. Oh yes, she'd become *that* kind of girl.

"Are you sure, Abel? Just so we're clear, I'm going to *dance with another boy...*" she said, going so far as to emphasize the latter part of her sentence.

Abel answered her with the straightest of faces. "Am I sure? Hm... Well, I'd be lying if I said it didn't bother me at all... But I've already made up my mind. Your affection isn't something I'm going to demand. It's something I'll earn—by becoming someone who's worth it."

Pierced by his unwaveringly earnest gaze, Mia's heart skipped a beat.

"Abel..."

"That's why... If you ever find yourself drawn to someone else, it's okay. Because I'll fight them, no matter who they are. Even if it's a friend like Sion. I'll fight him for your affection, and I'll win. I will earn my right to be by your side."

This bold declaration of love knocked the air out of her lungs. She could feel her face growing hot, and her thoughts melted into a jumbled haze. There was the sensation of a hand being placed on her back, followed by a gentle push.

"Go ahead. It's fine. Sion probably can't start dancing with other girls until you ask him, and it'd be a shame to keep all of them waiting."

Etiquette stated that one did not begin dancing before someone of higher rank. In terms of status, Mia and Rafina were definitely the highest of the women present. Rafina could certainly get the ball rolling, but she seemed to be holding back. That was probably why Sion just kept smiling at all the girls flocking to him. It definitely felt like everyone was waiting for Mia to make her approach.

"I-I suppose so. All right then..."

Mia took a deep breath, let it out, and composed herself.

Okay, focus. Focus! Right now, the first priority is stopping Sion's assassination!

Abel watched Mia go. After she disappeared into the crowd, he let out a quiet sigh.

"...Looks like I still have a long way to go." He shook his head.

As far as he could tell, the bluff had worked—but that didn't change the fact that he'd been bluffing. Deep down, his emotions were far more turbulent than they appeared.

"It's just a dance. I'm just letting someone else be her first partner. And *this* is how much it flustered me?" he muttered, holding up his clenched fist. "If I had more confidence in myself, maybe... But, hah, easier said than done."

Without even knowing it, Mia had channeled her inner seductress and toyed with an innocent boy's feelings!

Chapter 10: The Dance of Her Dreams, and Then...

After leaving Abel, Mia went straight to Sion. As expected, he was besieged by an army of young women. She grimaced at the sight of him, a lone isle in a sea of damsels.

Moons, I have to swim through that *to get to him? Ugh…*

Just thinking about it made her tired. As she approached, however, the sea parted before her as if she were some ancient prophet. The girls all stepped aside, and she walked through their ranks down the newly revealed path. Sion turned toward her and smiled.

"Greetings, Princess Mia."

"Greetings, Prince Sion. Might I have the honor of your first dance tonight?" she asked with graceful cordiality.

"Oh? You certainly may, and the honor is very much mine. Truth be told, I wasn't expecting you to ask."

"My, but if I didn't ask, how would we begin? After all, you've never been one to offer your attention sans demand, right?"

"Huh?" Sion quirked his eyebrow at the remark, eliciting an amused giggle from Mia, who then calmly extended her hand.

Mia, you see, knew an important fact of life. To wait is to waste—one has to *act* to acquire. Don't keep glancing at someone and hope they notice your gaze. If you want someone's attention, you have to go get it! So, she extended her hand. There would be no ambushes here tonight. She was going on the offensive.

Sion took it with the utmost care and led her gracefully toward the dance area.

"All right, Princess Mia. Shall we begin?" He straightened his back, placed a hand over his chest, and bowed.

In response, Mia bent at the knees and gave her skirt a polite tug. "Yes, Prince Sion. Let us enjoy this dance."

The hall's orchestra noticed their presence. The current piece quickly faded away. After a short pause, a new melody began at the perfect tempo for dancing.

"My, this is…"

Mia knew this number. It was frequently used to practice fundamentals. In other words, it was an easy piece meant for beginners.

Wow, they sure are playing it safe, aren't they? I guess I can't blame them. This is the princess of Tearmoon and their crown prince dancing. The last thing they'd want is for someone to embarrass themselves.

She glanced up at Sion. He smiled wryly, clearly aware of the unsolicited courtesy as well.

Considering Mia's recent flings with various other activities such as swimming, horse riding, and cooking (with questionable results for the last one), one could hardly be faulted for forgetting that she did, in fact, have a proper consort. Let it be reminded, however, that her real gift was dancing! It was her forte of fortes. She could dance to any music, no matter its style or rhythm, and effortlessly to boot!

"I appreciate their consideration, but it's really not necessary. I feel there is a need to make that point clear. What do you say, Sion?"

"Ha ha ha, the crime of underestimating the Tearmoon princess is a grave one indeed. Very well then. You have my full cooperation."

They looked at each other, took a quick breath in unison, and broke into a sequence of perfectly matched steps. A dance between Sunkland's crown prince and Tearmoon's princess naturally commanded the hall's attention. At first, the audience's gazes were mostly curious ones. Before long, they'd turned into admiration and astonishment.

Sunkland nobles were well aware of Sion's dancing prowess, but Mia's proficiency took them completely by surprise. Some of them, still bitter from the night's developments, had been hoping to vent a little by scoffing at her when Sion showed her up. The mouths of these would-be malefactors were forced shut.

Mia's motions were flawless. They accurately read every one of Sion's moves and matched them. Each swing of her arm, every flick of her wrist, was precise and deliberate. It was as if her control extended to every nerve and muscle, all of which had been recruited to optimize the beauty of her performance. The sight of her drew from the crowd long exhalations of awe, leaving them breathless.

"So that's Princess Mia... Magnificent... Simply magnificent."

As the music drew to a close, Sion shot the orchestra a meaningful glance. The conductor nodded and quickened the baton's rhythm.

"My, this is..."

"Well, you have a point to make, right? I figured one piece wouldn't be enough to establish your reputation. Now that we're warmed up, why don't we show them something with a bit more...*oomph*?"

Mia chuckled. "Go ahead then. Allegro or andante, I'll dance whatever you prefer."

Oho ho, how convenient of him to keep dancing. At this rate, I'll just need a few more girls to keep him busy afterward. If they preoccupy him for the rest of the night, it'll be mission complete!

After a few more numbers, fatigue finally caught up with Mia and she stepped back from Sion for a break. She'd expected the other girls to fill the void immediately, but instead…

"Are you thirsty, Sion? Here's a drink, if you'd like…"

It was Echard who walked up. In his hand was a glass of juice made from twilight grapes.

Whoa! If that's not suspicious, I don't know what is!

She hastily turned to him again and said, "U-Uh, actually, Sion, how about one more? I'm not quite ready to stop dancing yet."

"Really?" Sion frowned at her. "I mean, I don't mind, but what about Abel…?"

He began looking around for Abel, only to stop and bite his lip. He exhaled, seemingly reaching some internal conclusion.

"…You know what? I'm not quite ready to hand you over either," he said, staring pensively into the crowd. "No one wins by conceding all the time, after all."

Then, he turned to Echard.

"Sorry, Echard, but could you hold that for me? I'll drink it after I finish dancing."

"Huh? But it's nice and cold right now. If you wait, it'll—"

Before he could finish, the glass was snatched away from him.

"Now, now, Echard. One should never place themselves between a young man and a young woman who have business with each other." King Abram, glass in hand, grinned at his son. "You can have another glass made for him once he's done. This one, I'll enjoy for myself."

"Ah—"

Before Mia could react, King Abram downed the glass of juice. A few seconds later…

"Ugh…"

A grunt escaped his lips. His regal form began to sway. He took a few unsteady steps toward the balcony. Reaching for the handrails, he grabbed…and missed. His body folded over the banister, moments away from falling.

"Your Majesty!"

A girl's scream split the air. Mia, frozen in shock, could naught but watch as a feminine form dashed toward the ailing king.

Chapter 11: A Turn for the Worse

"Your Majesty!"

The first to reach Abram's side was Tiona. Her timely response was not the result of any anticipatory awareness, but simple coincidence. At Mia's instructions, she'd been staying as close to Sion as she could, but once he'd started dancing with Mia, she'd been left with nothing to do.

What should I do now...? I wonder where the other student council members are.

Just as she began looking around, she heard a voice from behind.

"Oh? You must be..."

Caught slightly off guard, she hastily spun around.

"Y-Your Majesty?!"

Standing before her was Sion's father, King Abram. He regarded her for a moment, then shook his head.

"Oh, for him to be leaving his friend alone by herself like this... My son clearly still has a long way to go." He addressed his entourage. "I would like to speak with my son's friend. Please, give us some space so the young lady can relax."

The men surrounding him, presumably all important Sunkland officials, lowered their heads respectfully and stepped away. Once they were gone, King Abram turned back toward her and smiled.

In that moment, the aura of regality about him that always made him seem so unapproachable diminished ever so slightly.

"Now then… Miss Rudolvon, I believe? Your father is an outcount of the Tearmoon Empire?"

"Yes, Your Majesty. It's an honor to make your acquaintance."

Tiona curtsied. The motion was a little stiffer than she'd liked. During dinner, she'd been in the company of both Mia and Esmeralda. Now she was speaking with him one on one. Some degree of nervousness was unavoidable.

"Were I a decade or two younger, I'd have requested your hand in a dance, but alas…I am a married man, and you are the same age as my son. Being seen on the floor with you would doubtlessly lead to a storm of censure about His Majesty's uncontrollable salaciousness. For the sake of not upsetting my wife, I must ask that we limit our interaction to conversation."

Tiona felt some of the tension in her shoulders ease at the jocular tone of his voice. "Thank you very much for your thoughtful words, Your Majesty, but I am only a noble in name. Having grown up in the countryside, I have very limited familiarity with dance."

"The Rudolvons are in the southern part of Tearmoon, I believe?"

"Yes, that is correct. My home is very far from the capital."

"I see… I heard that newly instated nobles from remote regions are met with considerable disdain in your empire… Is that true?"

"Unfortunately, it is. There is certainly a tendency to look down on us… But Her Highness is different. She is not bound by convention. She reached out to me. Spoke to me as a friend. And when I was faced with adversity, she came to my aid without the slightest hesitation."

Tiona recounted her experiences during her earliest days at Saint-Noel. She described how she'd been harassed by daughters of high-ranking nobles and how Mia had helped her. Then, she told the story of the welcome ceremony and its dance party.

"I used to hate the central nobility. That hate controlled me. Defined me. And it's thanks to Her Highness that I can now live free of that burden. She has a deep passion for justice and no tolerance for injustice. In a way, you could say she's similar to Prince Sion."

Yes, similar like pyrite and gold, but too bad no one was there to deliver this witty quip.

"They're similar, you say? I see…" said Abram, his eyes narrowing as he regarded the dancing pair. "That boy harbors an unrequitable love then. A pity, truly."

"Huh? Um… I'm not sure I understand what you mean," said Tiona, baffled by the remark.

Abram considered his response for a moment before speaking.

"Princess Mia is undoubtedly an exceptional individual. The question is… Would Sion be content with playing second fiddle to her? To be at her side, but propping her up instead of pulling her along? The makings of a leader… What it takes to be king… From talent to temperament, he has it all. His is a gift that, though perhaps lesser to Princess Mia's, is nonetheless too great to let wither. That is why he could never resign himself to living in her shadow." Abram spoke with the quiet profundity of a sage who'd seen some higher truth. "Sion is a natural king, but he can be nothing but. No matter how hard he tries, even if he were to surpass her through sheer grit and effort, his talent would only clash with hers."

It was then that Abram's expression gained a hint of surprise. "You seem…saddened. Why?"

"I…" Tiona's lips tightened. "I think that's just awful. I feel sorry for Prince Sion."

Tiona Rudolvon had lived a life of grit and effort. Fueled by her desire to get back at the central nobility, she'd strived and strived to better herself, hoping for…at least an acknowledgment that her hard work was worthwhile. That it meant something. And Mia had given her that.

What of Sion then? From her place on the isle of reward looking back across the waters of endeavor, seeing him swim and struggle in futility… Knowing that his hard work would never bear the fruit he desired… It was too much.

Seeing the pain in her expression, Abram gently smiled.

"I see that you have a kind soul… Do not burden it so. The hearts of boys are meant to be broken. It is by putting the pieces back together that they grow and mature."

It was then that Abram's eyes narrowed, and his gaze grew grim.

"That must be…"

His words faded into a deep sigh.

Abram walked away, leaving a conflicted Tiona. As she grappled with her feelings, she turned her attention back to Sion and Mia and watched them finish their dance. She saw Echard approach them and offer a drink, only for Sion to turn it down, saying he'd dance one more number. Abram took the glass and drank it instead. Then, she watched as the king slowly walked toward the balcony, his steps strangely floaty.

It was because she'd been studying him that she noticed the oddness of his gait. As he reached for the railing, time seemed to slow. She saw his center of weight shift and his body start to tilt outward, into open air.

"Your Majesty!"

A desperate dash brought her to his side just in time for her to throw her arms around his waist. She tried to hold him, only to be pulled forward by his taller form. They both began to fall.

"Liora!" she screamed. Not at the hall. Not to any petrified guest. She screamed the name of her most trusted subject.

"Miss Tiona!" Her attendant and friend, Liora Lulu, answered her call. In the blink of an eye, she was opposite Abram, feet planted and fingers clenched firmly around his clothes.

"Nnngaaaah!"

She could almost hear the powerful muscles in Liora's back tighten as she hauled the king back over the railing with one mighty heave. But things only took a turn for the worse. As they laid the king back onto solid floor, they found his face lifelessly ashen!

"Don't move him!"

A sharp voice cut through the hall. Tiona looked up to find a girl walking toward her through the crowd. She recognized her floral aura.

It was Citrina.

Chapter 12: An Ancient Poison
—Coincidental Encounter—

While the entire hall's attention was focused on the toppling king, Citrina got to work. Under Mia's orders, she'd been shadowing Echard the whole time to prevent this kind of situation, but King Abram had taken her completely by surprise.

Who'd have thought he'd do something like that...?

It was definitely the unexpectedness of his behavior, and not her mind being occupied by Bel's concerningly long trip to the bathroom that had delayed her reaction. Honest. Even if she'd been fully alert, the king's action was far too sudden for her to respond in time. Sudden, but not unreasonable. He was simply taking a drink that his younger son had offered to his older son, because the latter couldn't drink it right now. How could he have known that one son was trying to poison the other? That the poison was in the very glass he held?

His actions were entirely understandable, and therefore predictable. She should have been ready.

"It's okay. He can still be saved..." Citrina whispered.

She'd blundered, but not fatally. She could still turn this around. In fact, she had to. This was the very situation Mia had been preparing for. It was why she'd brought Citrina along.

If I can't be useful here, I might as well never be. It's time to pull my weight. Her lips tightened. *Okay, think. What should I be doing...?*

Off to the side of the hall away from everyone's attention stood a young boy in shocked silence. She quietly approached him.

"Prince Echard, there's no time, so we need to get straight to the point. Tell me, how much did you put into the drink?"

"Huh?" Echard's shoulders twitched. What little color remained in his face drained away.

"If you don't want patricide added to your list of accomplishments," Citrina said, her voice low but forceful, "then *tell me*. How much?"

The boy cracked under her quiet pressure. In a trembling voice, he answered, "O-One pinch."

Citrina mused on his confession as she walked toward the king. She waded through the clamoring onlookers, most of whom had now noticed the incident, and squatted down over the supine king with Tiona at her side.

"Don't move him!" she said in a commanding voice to dissuade any exacerbating actions.

Then, she regarded the king's face. Half of it had turned morbidly black as if death itself was encroaching through the skin.

Well, that confirms it. This is definitely the sign of shadowbane. And it's progressing fast. Ecliptic toxicosis is already setting in.

When consumed, shadowbane caused a condition known as ecliptic toxicosis, which got its name from how the way the skin on the victim's face would darken from one side to the other resembled a lunar eclipse. Its toxic effects were, in a nutshell, decrease in stamina, weakening of the heart, and reduced circulation leading to a body-wide breakdown of vital functions. Shadowbane was remarkably effective and had once been feared for blackening the faces of many rulers throughout history. However, it was an ancient poison and had now faded from the collective consciousness.

The reason was simple—it was relatively easy to treat by administering an appropriate dose of lightbane, its opposite poison.

Lightbane caused prominence toxicosis, named for its stimulative toxic properties. When consumed, it would greatly excite the heart, causing it to double or triple its rate. This would be accompanied by an infusion of energy that caused hyperactivity. Blood vessels would soon rupture from the intense pressure, and the victim would die flailing as blood spilled forth from every pore and orifice. The violent end resembled the solar prominences witnessed during solar eclipses, hence the name.

Treatment, however, was also simple. One simply had to administer an appropriate amount of its counter, shadowbane. Due to their mutually neutralizing qualities, they were useless against the prepared, making them unsuitable for assassinations. Over time, they faded from history. Then, over more time, so did knowledge of their antagonistic properties. The true nature of the two banes were now known only to a select few.

I heard that even the Equestris, with their long history of using shadowbane for hunting, don't touch it anymore.

Citrina, for her part, had never seen any shadowbane. There was none in the Yellowmoon stock. Lightbane, likewise, she only knew by name. Had they not discovered those mushrooms during their journey to Sunkland, she'd have nothing to cure the poison.

Two poisons whose only antidote is each other... Good thing we ran into that merchant on the way here. Otherwise... she thought as she took out a small bottle containing lightbane.

According to Echard, he'd put in one pinch. That tracked with the extent of the blackened skin.

Which means the dose for the antidote would have to be...

"Wh-What in the name of the sun?!"

Just as she was about to administer the lightbane, the Sunkland nobles who'd begun crowding around her saw the darkened patch on the king's face and recoiled in horror.

"Wait… Is that…shadowbane?"

A few nervous whispers entered Citrina's ears. Apparently, some of the nobles knew about the poison. It made sense; those whose positions placed them at risk of assassination would likely have studied up on such things.

"The physician! Someone go get the physician!"

Citrina ignored the frantic yelling that broke out and regarded Tiona.

"Miss Tiona, please keep your hands on His Majesty and hold him steady," she said as she began pouring the lightbane into a wine glass, trying to accurately procure the amount needed to neutralize one pinch of shadowbane.

"You! What do you think you're doing?!"

"Insolent girl! Remove your hands immediately! That is an affront to His Majesty!"

She paid them no mind. Their ignorance was apparent in the frivolous nature of their outrage. What concerned her were the less ignorant ones, the ones who understood that their king had just been poisoned. After all, she was just a little girl, and a foreigner at that. They definitely wouldn't want someone like her near their ailing regent right now.

The problem was that she *had* to be here, because she was certain that nobody else could save Abram's life. So, she swept her gaze across the hall looking for someone who could keep the nobles at bay. Someone whose grasp of the situation trumped that of everyone else's…

CHAPTER 12: AN ANCIENT POISON
—COINCIDENTAL ENCOUNTER—

Mia was sensitive to high-powered gazes, being able to employ such things herself. Perhaps that was why she felt it immediately and, against her better judgment, turned to meet it.

At first, she'd been as flustered by the sudden incident as everyone else, but she calmed a little after seeing Tiona and Liora haul the king back over the railing. Then, when she saw the resident poison expert Citrina rush over, she breathed out a sigh of relief, figuring everything was under control.

Which made the meeting of their gazes all the more upsetting.

No way. Seriously? You're throwing this to me? Now?

The receding panic reversed its course.

Oh, moons. Okay, think, think... How do I get out of this one? I need to pick my words carefully...

Just as she reluctantly forced her brain back into work mode, she felt another gaze on her. This one was much closer. In fact, it came from right beside her.

"Mia..."

She glanced over...only to be left speechless. Sion Sol Sunkland, the princely paragon of perfection, was looking at her with such doubt, such apprehension in his eyes that he was all but pleading for help. The instant she felt his insecurity, she instinctually nodded.

"Don't worry, Sion. It's okay," she heard herself say before turning toward the crowd and declaring with a confidence that baffled even her, "This girl is my vassal. She is one of the empire's foremost specialists, and I implore you to leave this matter in her capable hands."

Even Sion did a double take at her address, but her words had their intended effect, prompting him to breathe out and gather himself. Then, he addressed the crowd as well.

"All right, everyone. You heard the princess. Let the girl work. Also, someone go get a physician already," he said, directing the onlookers with an authority that masked his unease from everyone except Mia.

She alone saw the tiny tremors in his tightly clenched fists.

Chapter 13: Two Noble Girls Who Dared Rage...and One Princess Who Definitely Didn't Dare and Must Watch with Horror!

After taking out enough powdered lightbane from the bottle and dissolving it in water, Citrina poured the solution into the king's mouth without the slightest hesitation.

Tiona, having rested the king's head on her lap, watched the process with bated breath. Some of the liquid spilled from his mouth, staining her skirt. She wasn't bothered; in fact, she didn't even seem to notice. Her gaze never left the king's face.

Mia watched the treatment from afar as she assessed the situation. A thought suddenly occurred to her. *Wait a minute... Now that I think about it, if this doesn't go well...wouldn't it become my fault? I mean, I know that Rina's trying to treat him right now, but if King Abram doesn't make it, they might claim that we're the ones who poisoned him...*

This was a worrisome realization. She quickly conducted a tactical analysis of the room and tallied up her forces in case things suddenly went south. On her side, there was Liora the master archer and Tiona, who knew her way around a sword. She could certainly count on Abel to protect her, and likely Sion as well.

A-Actually, I'll be fine. I have Dion with me, after all. As long as he's here, most things shouldn't be a problem...

She mentally recited "Dion Alaia is my friend" three times. Only then did she feel a measure of calm return to her. With her composure restored, she looked toward Abram again.

"How is he, Rina?" she asked.

Citrina stood up. The wine glass in her hand was now empty. "He'll be fine…" She nodded, then added, "Probably."

Mia felt that last word in her soul. The desire to append grammatical disclaimers to statements was one she greatly sympathized with. Unfortunately, she was on the receiving end this time, and no amount of sympathy could change the worrying nature of the word.

"But I did everything I could, so…" said Citrina.

Her words rang true, and the darkened area began to recede from the king's face. His countenance improved as they spoke. It was then that a group of physicians belatedly arrived. The sight of the unconscious king left them as shocked and disoriented as everyone else. Citrina walked over to one of them and explained the situation, describing in detail how the king had been poisoned with shadowbane and given a dose of lightbane as an antidote. After confirming that the physicians were sufficiently informed to take over, she returned to Mia.

"Thank you very much, Rina," Mia said with a smile. "That was some great work."

"Your Highness is very welcome. I'm glad I managed to live up to your expectations." Citrina returned a smile, but of relief rather than her usual flowerlike front. It felt more *real*—more genuine. "With that said, I already knew the poison was shadowbane for sure, so the only thing I had to pay attention to was how much antidote to give. It really wasn't all that impressive."

"Oh? Is that so?"

"Yes. You definitely don't want to give too much lightbane— it's much worse. It makes you hyperactive, and you die with blood pouring out of every pore."

"My, how *dreadful*. Blood pouring out of every pore— Hm?"

Mia frowned. The description sounded strangely familiar.

Is it just me, or have I read about a death like that in the Chronicles? Hm...

Before she could ponder the issue further...

"Poison? Did you say poison?"

One of the younger nobles, having badgered a physician into explaining the king's condition, raised his voice in alarm.

"So you're telling me...that His Majesty was the victim of a targeted assassination attempt by poisoning?"

The hall immediately exploded with commotion.

"Assassination?!"

"Someone tried to poison the king!"

The frenzied murmurs entered Mia's ears, making her grimace. She knew what was next, and she didn't like it.

Well then. Here comes the finger pointing...

Suddenly, all the guests in the hall were seized by the upsetting realization that any one of them could have consumed a poisoned article of food. Tension in the air grew and grew, reaching a palpable thickness. Eventually, the young noble who first raised his voice spoke again.

"Well, it doesn't look like anyone else has been poisoned," he declared, looking around. "In that case, the most suspicious one is..."

Mia *tsk*ed. Echard, being the one to have handed the wine glass to the king, was the most likely suspect, but his implication would severely complicate matters. To her surprise, however, the young noble turned in her direction.

"You! You claimed you were treating His Majesty, but what if you'd secretly poisoned him in the process?" He pointed his finger at Citrina.

Mia looked from Citrina, who stood beside her, to the accusing noble, and *hmph*ed. His aim was immediately apparent. *Pfft. I know what he's doing. He doesn't even want to find the actual culprit. He's just using this as fodder to attack us.*

This gathering had, after all, been designed to strike at the alliance between her and Sion. King Abram's sudden collapse had certainly muddled the situation, but it did not seem to dissuade the Sunkland conservatives from pursuing their original goal.

"No. That is a false accusation. This young lady undoubtedly treated the king." A calmly voiced retort was heard, and it came from the most surprising of sources. "Younger nobles like you might not know," said Count Lampron, "but the poison used on His Majesty is known as shadowbane. Consuming it causes a distinctive black shadow to spread across the face. The shadow was already visible before she approached His Majesty. That, I can confirm."

Despite the count's testimony, dissent continued, this time from a different angle. "But the timing was too perfect. It feels *staged*. Could this not be a charade devised by the so-called Great Sage of the Empire?"

"That's…"

Count Lampron's ensuing silence was understandable. Shadowbane was an ancient poison, which raised the inevitable question of why a guest from Tearmoon happened to be carrying the antidote on hand. Even those unfamiliar with poisons could tell the coincidence was too convenient to be entirely natural.

"The very fact that she had the antidote is proof of her guilt! What better evidence can there be? Even if this girl *does* have the knowledge to diagnose this ancient bane, why in the name of the sun would she be carrying the antidote on her? And here of all places!"

"He's right!" Another noble joined in. "It's too unnatural! It can't be a coincidence!"

Oh my, the tides have turned in a rather worrying direction...

Mia started to panic. It wasn't because she feared for her own safety. No, it was far, far worse. She feared...Rafina. A glance in her direction revealed...

"Eep!"

Mia's hands shot up to her mouth to blunt a squeal of terror. At first, Rafina had been as startled by the king's collapse as anyone else, but she gradually recovered as she watched the developments. Now...she was *mad*. Her teeth bit into her lips, and her milky cheeks had turned an angry red. Rage flared in her eyes like flames.

Uh-oh. This is bad. This is very, very bad. Miss Rafina is about to blow her top!

She hadn't seen Rafina this mad since the student council election. Mia grimaced. She'd only recently come to realize that apparently, Rafina considered her a friend—a *close* friend, at that! This was of course great news, but right now, it might as well have been a hornet's nest.

Basically, by blaming me, that stupid noble there just bad-mouthed someone the Holy Lady considers a very good friend!

He was very rude about it too. Even Mia had felt a rush of indignation at his allegation, but she'd refrained from defending herself. Doing so would require her to point out the true culprit, and she didn't want to publicly accuse Sion's brother of attempted patricide. Not only would that complicate matters, she also didn't have proof. What Mia wanted was the universal wish of the chickenhearted—to minimize the size of problems until they went away. This problem had already gotten big enough with the king being poisoned. The last thing she wanted to do was to further embiggen it with accusations.

Fortunately, the Chaos Serpents are involved in this, so I should be able to shift all the blame to them and their assassins. So long as I have the Serpent card to play, all I need is for everyone to keep calm and stop pointing fingers at us.

To her dismay, the situation was heading in a decidedly uncalm direction. If Rafina blew her top, it might lead to a dispute between her and Sion. That could in turn create a fissure between Belluga and Sunkland. Serpents *loved* fissures like those.

Moons, how do I keep this from spiraling out of control? She racked her brain to no avail. Just as her panic quickly reached its peak, a cry of profound indignance echoed through the hall.

"Silence, you *barbarian*! I will not stand for such insolence!"

The voice rang like the crack of a whip, demanding attention. All heads turned toward the speaker. There, at the center of attention, stood Esmeralda, her chin upturned with pride and outrage. She swept her gaze angrily across the hall.

"Don't you dare say another bad word about my dear friend and princess, Mia Luna Tearmoon, or you'll have to answer to me!"

Esmeralda Etoile Greenmoon, proud Etoiline of the empire and bride-to-be of the second prince of Sunkland, made her displeasure known. Loudly and furiously. Having grown up a tyrant in her household, she was used to getting her way. She was hardly the type to swallow her rage, so she let it out on the nobles, cowing them with her lionlike manner. One, however, did not draw back. Echard was watching her with wide eyes, too mesmerized by her performance to react.

Esmeralda's speech created an opening for a second figure to ascend the stage. In the ensuing silence, another Etoiline, whose reputation had borne the brunt of their attacks, stepped forward.

Chapter 14: Citrina...Finally Sees the True Nature of the Great Sage of the Empire...or Does She?

"As a matter of fact," said Citrina, "there's nothing unnatural about it at all." Her voice was even, neither daunted nor indignant. She spoke in her usual, sweet tone.

The man who'd started the whole blame game retorted again. "Nonsense! Are you claiming it's pure coincidence that you just so happened to have the exact antidote with you? That hardly seems reasonable, unless you wish to further claim that the Great Sage of the Empire somehow has insight into the future."

"Of course not. For a human to see into the future is, to my knowledge, an impossible feat."

It also wasn't the way of the Great Sage. That, Citrina knew. Mia was no god. She had neither control over the workings of reality nor knowledge of that which had yet to occur. Not everything would always go as planned for her. Otherwise, she'd surely have prevented this poisoning from happening in the first place.

The truth, however, was that even Mia with her sublime wisdom wasn't able to foresee this sequence of events. So why was it, then, that she could still respond in such a precise and timely manner? Why was she capable of countering the Serpents so effectively? Because she was prepared. It was nothing more than that.

Exhaustive preparation was the secret to Mia's success. It wasn't that she knew exactly what it was she had to deal with; it was that she could deal with anything that came her way. The truth of this observation had fully impressed itself on Citrina during this trip. The very fact that she'd been brought along was simply one element of that preparation.

"I'd rather not do this, if I'm being completely honest," Citrina continued, "but I suppose my dignity is a small price to pay…"

Contrary to her words, she carried herself without a hint of shame, pinching the hem of her skirt and lifting it gracefully above her waist. It would have been a fine curtsy had it not revealed too much to be proper. Bared for all to see was the pale skin of her dainty legs, the shapely bulges of her tiny knees, and the incongruous set of leather belts wrapped around her slender thighs. Each belt was fitted with numerous slots that held a dizzying array of small finger-sized vials, the contents of which caught the light in the hall with iridescent gleams.

She drew out one vial and placed it on the table in front of her with a sharp clink. "This is an antidote for paralysis poison." She drew out another, placing it beside the first. "And this is an emetic to induce vomiting." A third followed. "And this is…"

Vial by vial, she emptied the slots on her belts. As the row of antidotes and the like grew in length, the commotion waned in proportion. By the time she placed down the final vial, the hall had gone dead silent. The nobles stared at the staggering exhibit, words failing them so utterly that time itself seemed to stop until she spoke again.

"Her Highness Princess Mia is irreplaceably important to us. No matter the time or place, no harm can be allowed to befall her. That we would prepare exhaustively for all eventualities is not only compulsory but blatantly obvious. I did not *just happen* to have the exact antidote on me—I have *many* exact antidotes. So I can deal with *any* poison."

The arsenal she carried was the distillation of Yellowmoon's extensive expertise in the art of poison. Having employed thousands of banes and studied thousands more, they'd prepared through their knowledge a careful selection of the most relevant substances, targeting the most likely poisons to be acquired around Sunkland. But even with Citrina's know-how, she hadn't anticipated the involvement of lightbane and shadowbane.

And that's what makes Her Highness so amazing. She came across some mushrooms en route, learned that they could be used as antidotes, and immediately purchased some.

Mia's genius wasn't only preemptive; it was also reactive. The way she could play things by ear, trusting her judgment to make decisions on the fly, had left Citrina in awe.

But none of that matters right now.

With her full complement of vials laid out on the table, Citrina favored her audience with a sweet smile...

"Given Her Highness's importance, this kind of preparation is, honestly, common sense. I assumed you afford your dignitaries the same protection here in Sunkland, but judging by your reactions... Perhaps I was wrong?"

...Before taunting them like a *boss*. Which then made her realize something.

Huh... Am I...angry?

She mused for a second, trying to deduce the source of the anger. She'd been feeling pretty good about saving the king's life. It was the first time she'd used her skills to do a good deed. Before she could even appreciate the feeling, though, they'd *spoiled it* with their petty accusations. That must have gotten to her. Should she be taunting people in her current emotionally charged state? What if she went too far? For a moment, she considered showing some restraint.

"So, now that you've all had your fun, who's going to take responsibility for making a young lady like Rina embarrass myself, hm?" She smiled. Restraint, she decided, can go suck on a lemon. She was going to make them feel as guilty as possible. They *had* made her angry, after all. It was their fault for starting it.

"That's right! Shame on you! All of you! Miss Citrina did what anyone would naturally do in her position. She helped a person in need. But instead of thanking her, you *humiliated* her! You forced her to suffer a terrible indignity."

To Citrina's surprise, the first one to respond to her provocation was, of all people, Esmeralda.

"Be proud of yourself, Citrina," she continued, "because your actions were nothing if not commendable. As the principal Etoiline, I offer you my finest compliments. We fair maidens all have our secrets, and I know how mortifying it must be to have them exposed.

97

To be so thoroughly *humiliated*... Oh, the humanity! Be strong, Miss Citrina!"

Citrina wordlessly watched the outpouring of commiseration, resisting the urge to make such remarks as "Since when were *you* the principal Etoiline?" and "What secret? I just wear belts on my leg to carry my antidotes." There was, however, one aspect of the impassioned speech she couldn't ignore.

"Um... Miss Esmeralda, it really wasn't *that* embarrassing for Rina. You don't have to make it sound so indecent..."

Well-intentioned or not, she'd rather not have the entire hall being told over and over how she'd been "thoroughly humiliated," as if she'd been forced to strip naked in public or something. Besides, when it came to indecency, going for dips in the sea with a throng of handsome young bodyguards every summer seemed far more damning.

"It's okay, Rina," said Esmeralda, clearly missing the point. "It's okay. I know it's a hard topic for you. Such indignity... Such humiliation... Oh, you poor girl!"

She proceeded to pull Citrina into a tight embrace.

"I-I just said, it's not that—"

"Say no more! You did well out there! Good for you!"

Oh, jeez. I provoked the wrong person...

Esmeralda's overbearing manner and sudden invasion of personal space were, frankly, quite unwelcome, but her words...

"You lived up to Miss Mia's expectations, and I'm proud of you!"

Her words made their way into Citrina's heart. Expecting exasperation, she found fondness instead. For Citrina, the other three dukes and their families had been nothing more than potential targets of assassination. Someday, she might have to kill them.

So, she kept her distance accordingly, knowing not her Etoiler peers—only *of* them.

So this is the young Greenmoon, Esmeralda... A simple girl, driven by emotions. Easily provoked and probably just as easy to manipulate. She seems like a pushover, honestly, thought Citrina, finding that the prior information she'd had of Esmeralda's character matched her behavior completely. *A simple girl...but not a bad one.*

There was a warmth to the girl's simplicity, a sincere depth to her compassion that Citrina didn't entirely dislike.

If I had a mo— I mean, a sister, would it feel like this?

Citrina, for her part, wasn't half bad of a girl either, being considerate enough to correct herself in her thoughts. Unlike her friend, who to this day still couldn't stop calling a certain someone grandma!

Hmm... I think I'll start showing up at the Clair de Lune parties more!

When it came to pushovers, Esmeralda was in good company.

The sight of Esmeralda protectively embracing the younger Citrina was like a bucket of ice water over the heads of the Sunkland nobles. The coolheaded among them quickly realized that the people they were denouncing were, in fact, young girls who not only deserved their protection as guests but likely just saved the life of their king. Silence gripped the hall, only to be broken by a cry of alarm.

"Your Majesty!"

King Abram, supported by his closest aides, stood up. His face was twisted in pain, and there was a worrying amount of sway to his gait, but he clenched his teeth, straightened his back, and slowly walked toward Citrina.

"Young lady, you have my deepest gratitude for saving my life. I can offer only an apology for the discourtesy of my fellow statesmen, and I beg your forgiveness."

"It is no matter, Your Majesty," replied Citrina. "Please, be at ease. You should seek rest."

The smile she showed Abram was less saccharine—more tender. A measure of relief entered his gaze, abating the tension in his expression.

"Count Lampron, I leave the rest to you. Ensure that our guests are afforded the utmost courtesy."

With that, he left the hall, accompanied by Sion and Echard.

"Phew… Looks like everyone's going to make it out in one piece."

The sudden comment from behind gave Mia a start. She spun around to find Abel, who stood within touching distance. She had no idea when he'd approached, and his right hand was closed tightly over the neck of a wine bottle.

"My, Abel… What's with the bottle?"

"Hm? Oh, uh, nothing much. I just thought…that you might be thirsty. How about it? Would you like a drink?"

"Oh, Abel, you scoundrel. Are you trying to ply me with wine?"

"Huh? That's not— Uh…"

His flustered response amused her.

He must have mistaken it for a bottle of juice… It's so nice of him to think of bringing me a drink, but he can be such an adorable klutz sometimes.

She smiled. For the big sister in Mia, having some lighthearted fun at the expense of younger boys never got old.

"You certainly have a way with words, Your Highness," said Ludwig, walking up as well. "But humor aside, it is indeed very good that the situation was resolved in a peaceful fashion."

Mia regarded him to find that he was also sporting the wine-bottle-in-hand look. She arched an eyebrow.

"My, that's not something I expected to see."

She hadn't pegged Ludwig for someone who'd drink at occasions like these.

"Your Highness..." he said, as if taken aback—almost hurt—by her comment. "When push comes to shove, I am a man as well. At the very least, I think I can secure an escape route..."

Sadly, only the first half of his mumbled protest entered her ears.

*My, is that so? "When push comes to shove," huh? I suppose this
wine provided by the Sunkland royal family is pretty rare. I don't
blame him for sneaking in a sip or three.*

It was, she figured, probably the same feeling as when she
was presented with rare sweets or exotic mushrooms. She pursed
her lips, feeling like she'd discovered a new side to Ludwig that she
empathized with.

"By the way, where's Anne?" she asked.

"I asked Miss Anne to stay with the guards for her safety. Just in
case," answered Ludwig.

"Just in case... I see. Smart choice. I knew I could count on you."

"I have to say though," said Abel, "I'm surprised Sion stayed
mum the whole time. I thought for sure he'd give those nobles a
good tongue-lashing. The shock of his father collapsing must have
really gotten to him."

"That...is probably not the reason," Ludwig said with a shake of
his head.

"Indeed..." Mia agreed with Ludwig.

*Sion probably realized that his brother's the one who slipped
the poison in the drink. That can't be something he wants to publicly
announce to his court. Granted, he's probably still reeling from the
double whammy of his brother trying to kill him and his father being
poisoned instead.* She grunted in thought. *What are we going to do
about Prince Echard, though?*

There were ways to fudge the fact that Echard had poisoned the
drink. Frankly, they could just blame everything on the Serpents.
It wouldn't be hard; blame-shifting was second nature to her.
Technically, the Serpents *were* responsible anyway. They were the
ones who'd given Echard the poison. So long as she could get Abram
and Sion on board, Operation Serpent Blame would be a go.

Being in Sunkland gave her a further advantage. The pride and joy of the kingdom's intelligence network, the Wind Crows, had previously succumbed to snaky influence. Bringing that up would force them to consider whether it was possible that a Wind Crow could have carried out this kind of poisoning. Having witnessed the capabilities of an ex-Wind Crow, who currently worked as a Yellowmoon butler...

It certainly feels possible, especially for someone like him...

The argument seemed sound, and if it was possible for a Wind Crow, it was surely also possible for the Serpents, who'd proved themselves capable of manipulating the organization. The scenario could be that the assassin slipped the poison in the drink, then slipped away under the guise of a guest and left the hall. Given Sunkland's prior experience with the Serpents, it couldn't be that hard to force this explanation through.

The problem, though...is what King Abram and Sion will think. Also, what Prince Echard himself will think. Hm... Hmmm...

Her contemplation was interrupted by a soldier.

"Pardon me, Princess Mia. His Majesty would like a word with you."

"...Huh?"

Little did Mia know, her true battle had only just begun.

Chapter 15: Miabel...Goes on an Adven- Tour of the Castle!

Going back a bit in time…

"Man, what a trip… Sure glad it's almost over. Once the day ends, things should settle down."

Connery, the guard captain under Count Lampron, let out a weary breath as he patrolled the outside of the hall. Ever since heading to Tearmoon to pick up the guest of honor from the Greenmoons, he'd been wound tighter than a spring. You couldn't blame him either; an Etoiline was technically higher in rank than his own boss. That alone was enough to give him a stress ulcer or two, but then her "friend" had to show up and turn a bad situation into a complete and utter nightmare. He was now tasked with guarding not just one very important girl, but many, one of which was arguably the most important in all of Tearmoon. Talk about unexpected difficulties…

"Once the ball ends, the Greenmoon girl should be going home to Tearmoon. The rest of her friends will probably follow suit."

With that thought came a great deal of relief, but also a hint of regret. It was going to get very quiet.

"Heh… When all's said and done, the memory of walking around town with a princess and a duke's daughter ain't half bad as a souvenir."

Feeling a wave of fondness, he made pleasant conversation with passing castle guards as he roamed around. As he turned a corner, however, a figure suddenly dashed across his view. He almost managed to convince himself that he'd seen nothing, but to the great dismay of his already-aching stomach, his conscience forced him to stop. Mustering up every remaining ounce of mental energy, he looked toward the figure.

Long hair the color of white gold trailed behind the creature as she jogged down the hallway. Though clad in noble dress, her mannerism evoked more the mischief of a child used to the streets. Connery recognized her.

That's…one of the girls Princess Mia brought with her. I think she's called Miabel?

He had a very bad feeling about this, the kind you got when you saw something that you knew you definitely should not have. Again, he was seized by the desire to pretend he'd suffered a momentary bout of blindness…

"Ah, scorching suns… I can't just ignore her…"

It'd stain the honor of Sunkland's knights if he walked away from a girl who'd gotten lost in the castle. They were upholders of justice; being kind to women and children was part of that.

I serve Count Lampron as a knight of Sunkland. I mustn't act in ways that sully the reputation of milord. He thought it again to himself. Then again for good measure. Only then did he walk toward her.

"Miss Bel…"

"Oh, Sir Connery."

She spun around at his voice and blossomed into a smile. Having regarded her with little more fondness than he had for nose warts, the sheer innocence of her expression stung his conscience.

"What might you be doing in a place like this? Have you gotten lost? I can take you back to the hall if you'd like."

"Oh, no. I'm actually on an adven—tour. I'm touring the castle. For studying purposes."

What guilt he'd felt toward her vanished in the blink of an eye. In his mind, he was shouting things like, *Did you seriously just try to cover "adventure" with "adven-tour"? You realize you basically just said the same thing, right?* and *Who the hell goes on an adventure in a castle? Are you out of your mind?!* Out loud, however, he said, "I see, I see. But there's a ball going on right now, and I suspect everyone expects you to be present. They'll be very worried to find you missing."

Connery pressed firmly on the bridge of his nose, willing himself to stay calm. Children, he reasoned desperately, were adventurous creatures. It was, therefore, natural for them to go on adventures. A castle like this presented the perfect opportunity. How could they resist? Besides, he'd been the same, hadn't he?

I loved my adventures too as a kid... I guess young noble girls are the same. Wait... Are they?

He abandoned the train of thought, suspecting it'd only leave him more confused.

"Anyway, let's head back to the hall, shall we?"

"Oh, um, actually... While I was adven—touring the castle, I saw General Dion and Keithwood, so I started following them. I was in the middle of doing that."

He chewed on the two names. The first was one of Princess Mia's guards. Connery hardly considered himself a veteran fighter, but even he could tell the man named Dion was on a completely different level.

King Abram was a beast with the sword during his prime, but even he might not have been a match for that Dion. I'm not even sure if any of our Sunkland knights could claim to be his equal.

Furthermore…

"Keithwood, you say…"

Keithwood, youthful attendant to Sion. Friend, confidant, and arrow to the prince's bow. The king's trust in him ran deep as well. For someone like him to be walking around the castle with someone like Dion Alaia…wasn't particularly strange, but Connery couldn't help but catch a whiff of something fishy.

Considering she's with the princess, it seems reasonable to assume that the Great Sage of the Empire saw something in her. That Citrina girl of the Four Dukes seemed like a smart cookie, so this Bel girl might have something up her sleeve too. Maybe she saw Keithwood and Dion together and something occurred to her.

The childish excitement she radiated seemed to indicate otherwise, but…

"Where are those two, by the way?"

"Uh, they're that way."

She started sauntering down the hallway. Connery followed her, his brows furrowing as he realized what lay in that direction.

Prince Echard's private room is that way…

The bad feeling came back, stronger and more unsettling than before.

Chapter 16: Time of Judgment, Friend or Foe...

Mia, along with Citrina, Esmeralda, and Rafina, received a summons to the King of Sunkland's personal chambers.

Rina's the one who administered the antidote. Esmeralda's the party's main guest. Miss Rafina's, well... She's the Holy Lady, so if she's around, it's sort of impossible not to include her too.

Neither Ludwig's nor Anne's presence were requested. Abel wasn't called either. It was understandable. Though he was treated, the king's health was certainly in no state for him to be meeting large groups of people.

Interestingly, Tiona had—perhaps unintentionally, due to her tending to the king during treatment—followed Abram out into the hall.

Maybe she's getting a change of clothes because her dress got dirty... But whatever. What's important right now is Echard. The worst-case scenario is him being identified as the culprit, which would almost certainly condemn him to death. I need to prevent that at all costs.

As she left the hall, she swiped up a nearby cookie and popped it into her mouth. Sugar intake, check. Brain stimulation, check. With her mental faculties reinvigorated, she laid out a plan of action: *The basic idea is to blame absolutely everything on the Chaos Serpents. It was someone connected with the Serpents who handed him the poison in the first place, so technically, it's not wrong to say they're the ones at fault. Given that, I think it's fine for Miss Rafina to find out.*

She was now armed with an effective excuse in case Rafina found out the truth later. A veteran of explaining herself, Mia knew it was always a good idea to have a spare excuse on hand.

Then comes the issue of "friend or foe." I need to carefully determine who's on my side...

This upcoming issue would not be as clear-cut as the situation in the party hall. Her friends were not guaranteed to take her side.

Mia was very much a proponent of the "see no evil, hear no evil, speak no evil" approach to dealing with problems. Were it up to her, she'd rather everyone shook hands, made up, and agreed never to mention the issue again. The poison came from the Serpents, so why not just shift all the blame to one of their shadowy assassins? That way, Echard could be a victim, deceived and exploited against his will. That seemed like a far more preferable interpretation for everyone. Alas, it hinged on the cooperation of people who weren't inclined to settle in such a fashion.

I guess none of us would be here if this was something we could just wave away.

Sion, for one, was unlikely to agree to her convenience-based approach to accountability. Abram, likewise. Heck, she doubted she could even get Rafina on board. Tiona was a bit of a wild card too.

The only people who'll definitely take my side are Esmeralda and Citrina...

Mia glanced at the pair of Etoilines. Citrina was no problem. As an ex-Serpent, she could be counted on to keep secrets and speak deftly. As for Esmeralda, Mia had absolute faith in her as well. Rather, she had absolute faith in Esmeralda's love for cute boys. Given Echard's charm, there was no way Esmeralda would say anything unfavorable to or about him.

Or me. Probably not, at least. We're friends, after all...

As a matter of fact, Mia had been more than a little moved when Esmeralda raised her voice in outrage. Her willingness to speak so bluntly to a hall of guests in Citrina's defense boded well for the reliability of her allegiance. She was, in fact, still fuming.

"I can't believe how rude they were!" cried Esmeralda. "Such impudence! Who do they think they are, accusing Miss Mia and Miss Citrina of wrongdoing! It's an outrage! Absolutely unforgivable!"

"Perhaps the excessiveness of their reaction can be interpreted as a sign of their loyalty. It shows how important His Majesty King Abram is to them," suggested Rafina in a pacifying tone. "They are accustomed to yielding all matters of judgment to their king, believing that since their king cannot err, they need only obey his command... Therefore, when forced into a situation where they must exercise their own judgment to discern good from evil and right from wrong, they panicked. Bereft of composure and guidance, they regressively clung to their original goal of attacking Mia, for it was all they had... In my opinion, that more or less sums up the events in the hall."

Huuuh. So that's *why they turned on us, despite the fact that it would likely worsen the problem. No wonder. I'd better make sure father never hears of this, though. Which means I need to have a very firm word with Esmeralda later.*

As Mia pondered the implications back home, Rafina murmured something highly concerning. "Not that it makes their actions forgivable in any way..."

Mia glanced Rafina's way to find her smiling. It was such a diplomatic smile that Mia broke out in a cold sweat.

Eeek! Miss Rafina's still upset! She's livid! *I-I'd better have a word with her too!*

"B-But you know," said Mia, figuring she'd better do something before things spiraled out of control, "King Abram will probably chastise them appropriately. I don't think we need to get too upset about it. If relations with Sunkland deteriorate, it'll leave an opening for the Serpents. And the poison that was used seems to have come from them in the first place..."

Mia veered the conversation as hard as she could toward their common foe.

Rafina's eyes widened with sudden realization. "The Chaos Serpents?"

"Yes, there is strong suspicion of their involvement. Right, Rina?"

Citrina nodded in response and explained her reasoning.

"An Equestri... Or rather, a man who looked like one... I see," said Rafina, pondering.

Seeing that Rafina's expression had grown pensive, Mia let out a relieved sigh. *Okay, good. She's more cautious now. That should keep her from thinking herself down a dangerous rabbit hole. Though, moons, I wish Ludwig were here. Not having access to his wisdom is really crippling. Anne too...*

The absence of her trusty subjects left her feeling a little helpless. She had neither of her right hands, man nor woman.

I don't know where the others stand on this issue, nor do I have any idea how Echard himself is going to react. I'll just have to deal with whatever comes, she thought as she approached the door of the king's chamber.

Bracing herself, she stepped in.

Inside, she found King Abram in his bed. No healers were in sight, save for an old physician standing by. Citrina's antidote had clearly done its job. Beside the king was his wife, along with Tiona, who'd changed into a new dress. Upon seeing Mia, Tiona let out a breath of relief. Evidently, the weighty atmosphere had taken its toll on her. She bowed and quickly joined Mia and her friends, passing by Sion who did the reverse to stand with his father. Soon after, he was joined by Echard, then Count Lampron and an aged man, who introduced himself as the chancellor. Their arrival rounded out the cast, for the king chose then to speak.

"Thank you all for coming here," said Abram, his voice still frail and fatigued. His gaze, though, was anything but, having recovered its usual sharpness. "First, allow me to apologize for the numerous discourtesies you suffered. Miss Citrina Yellowmoon, please accept my deepest gratitude for saving my life."

"There is no need for gratitude, Your Majesty. Your good health is a blessing to us all," Citrina replied. She regarded the king for a second, then turned to the nearby physician. "How is His Majesty's condition?"

"Thanks to your prompt treatment, the effects of the shadowbane have been mostly neutralized." The physician bowed deeply. "Please accept my deepest gratitude as well for saving our king."

The queen consort followed suit. Sion, Echard, Count Lampron, and the chancellor all lowered their heads. The solemn formality of this display elicited a rare moment of abashed uncertainty from Citrina. Being thanked by others was not something she was used to.

When the king straightened again, his expression had turned austere. "Now then... Echard, what do you have to say for yourself?"

The young prince's shoulders twitched visibly. His fists tightened in a futile bid to keep himself from shaking. "I am very sorry, father... I have nothing to say in my defense. This was the result of my own folly."

His voice, though soft, echoed with painful clarity throughout the room.

Chapter 17: Princess Mia...Rides a Wave in a Breakthrough

"I am...sorry, father..." With one last apology, Echard fell to his knees. His head crumpled forward. "I...poisoned the drink for my brother. It was me. I am entirely to blame."

"What?!" Esmeralda let out a cry of disbelief.

Oh, right. I guess I didn't tell Esmeralda, did I? thought Mia, belatedly realizing she'd kept Esmeralda in the dark.

Citrina took a step forward. "Excuse me, Your Majesty, I would like to request permission to speak," she said, waiting for Abram to nod before continuing. "If it were Rina— Ahem, if I were the one who gave His Highness the poison, I would do it without telling him it was poison. Or I would tell him it was only a minor toxin that would have no serious consequences on one's health. I find it questionable whether His Highness was aware of the lethal nature of the substance he employed."

"Nevertheless," Abram began in response, "the fact remains that he infused into the drink of the crown prince an unknown poison with the intention to do harm. That is, I presume, why Echard has not defended himself."

"It is entirely my fault. My actions are inexcusable," repeated Echard, his voice trembling and his head still only inches away from the ground.

Citrina's argument, though sound, meant little if the offender refused to acknowledge it. Conversely, even if Echard claimed ignorance, at this point, it would sound like nothing but an attempt to escape blame.

What Rina said is probably true, but...almost impossible to prove. Mia sighed softly.

"The poisoning of a king is unheard of in Sunkland's history... but if we were to follow precedents of most other kingdoms, it would be an offense punishable by death. In this case, the accused is a prince..." The king trailed off, his tone grave, as he glanced questioningly at the chancellor.

The chancellor nodded. "I'm afraid your suspicion is correct, Your Majesty. Even if the accused is a prince..."

"Abram..." The queen's face paled.

She took a step toward her husband, only to be stopped by a chillingly harsh gaze. The air itself about him seemed to push back, prohibiting approach. Suddenly, the king felt incredibly distant. The hints of affability he displayed during the ball were gone, along with any sign of compassion for his son. What remained was all his regality—and nothing but. There lay the king in all his unapproachable glory, pure and righteous, more justice than man.

"Even if it's your son, Your Majesty..." the chancellor said nervously, "It pains me to say, but giving him a lighter penalty is..."

Abram nodded, the motion slow and laden, as if his crown were made of lead instead of gold.

"*Especially* if it's my son, my good chancellor," he said. "The severity of the punishment must be of the highest order. If I allow my kin to enjoy undeserved amnesty, the very justice of our kingdom will crumble."

Uh-oh. I do not like where this is going...

The conversation had taken a very dangerous turn, and Mia was painfully aware. She just couldn't do anything about it.

There was no opening for her to get a word in. By now, it'd become clear to her that Abram had not called them here for their advice. They'd been brought in as nothing more than observers to bear witness to the fact that a fair and impartial verdict had been reached with regard to this awful matter. That justice had been upheld.

The talking had been done long before she'd arrived. Her role was simply to testify to the world the moral integrity of Abram's judgment and Echard's sentence. The young prince...would enjoy no reprieve.

I feel...nothing. No tide. No waves.

It did not, in fact, feel like she was even in the water. Abram's approach had rendered her a complete spectator. She could but watch helplessly from ashore. And she was joined on the coast by her friends, including Rafina. Even the Holy Lady's input was unwanted. Mia watched in speechless horror as the righteous ruler of Sunkland proceeded to raise his sword of judgment and, allowing no outside counsel or caution, bring it down upon the neck of his son. It was right then...

"This is wrong!"

...That a sharp voice split the stifling air. It trembled a little, but Tiona Rudolvon nevertheless looked Abram in the eyes, her gaze unflinching and determined.

"All this talk about stricter judgment and harsher sentences *because* he's family... It's crazy!"

It was not her place to speak. She had no right nor business. But she didn't care. She had something to say, and she was going to say it, propriety be damned! The sheer nerve Tiona displayed left Mia awed.

Wow, talk about not reading the room! But I like it! You go, girl!

This was fundamentally a Sunkland problem. On top of that, it was a *family* problem between King Abram and his sons. It had literally nothing to do with Mia, much less Tiona. The substantial degree of separation between them forbade intervention. No one wanted to hear what Mia and her friends had to say. So oppressive was the air that it felt like even the slightest utterance might invite an angry rebuke telling them to shut up and watch it play out. And so, they had.

But not Tiona. Tiona didn't give two damns about the air in the room. She chose not to read it. She knew it, felt it, and *rejected* it, unhesitatingly opting to say not what was appropriate, but what she thought was right.

It was, perhaps, inevitable. Tiona was the kind of person who, in the previous timeline, had been referred to as the Saint of the Revolution. Breaking down established customs was sort of her thing.

However, her audacity was not founded on recklessness but conviction.

"Family is precious, something you protect with your life."

Those were the words her father had on so many occasions spoken to her. Outcount Rudolvon had started out as an agrarian leader, gaining his noble status only later in life. He'd taught her that the duty of nobles was to safeguard the peaceful lives of those who resided in their domain. They were their people. Their *family*.

For Tiona, the people of her domain were her family. Was she then to judge all her people more strictly? Did they all deserve harsher sentences? The logic on display was one she could not accept. To her, family was something she would risk everything to protect— even her own life.

Her unyielding courage, like an arrow of pure will, bore a burning hole straight through the thick wall of exclusion that prevented their involvement. Through that hole—that breakthrough—Mia saw hope. She *felt* it. A wave rolled through the hole. It was yet small, reaching only her ankles, but she would ride it, for that was the Way of the Seamoon. No respected practitioner of the Flotsam would allow a wave to go un-limply-drifted, no matter its size or shape.

And so, Mia took a quiet breath and, ready to be swept away by the diminutive current, opened her mouth. "There is a flaw with your verdict, Your Majesty."

"A flaw, you say?"

Abram shot her a sharp glance. She flinched a little.

I-It's okay. I can handle this. It's not as bad as when Dion Alaia glares at me. Close, but not quite as bad...

The thought allowed her to keep her cool.

"Yes. One could also call it an injustice."

"Injustice?!"

Mia didn't know who let out the affronted cry, and she couldn't afford to find out. Allowing herself only a second to breathe and compose her thoughts, she quickly recalled the events of the previous timeline.

Tiona Rudolvon had been the leader of the revolution, but she was not, in fact, the one who'd sentenced Mia to the guillotine. It hadn't even been any of the revolutionaries. The one who'd decided Mia's fate was the prince of another kingdom, Sion. The reason was simple—to ensure distance between the punisher and the punished. Those who felt personal grievance toward her risked demanding a harsher penalty than was appropriate. It would twist justice into revenge.

It's so like him to be concerned about things like that. He had to make sure the whole affair looked righteous to everyone both inside and out.

Not that it helped Mia, though, considering her head still rolled! Anyway...

Oho ho, thanks for coming up with the idea, Sion, because I'm taking it for myself!

And so, Mia engaged in some shameless appropriation of intellectual property. Arming herself with the sword of rhetoric once wielded by her archnemesis Sion, she let out a fierce battle squeal and swung it at Abram!

"Your Majesty, I must remind you that you...are the victim. You have suffered through this incident. Would it not be possible, then, to interpret the increased harshness of your judgment as the undue exercising of your power to square a personal grudge against the offender?"

She did not beat around the bush. He'd hit them with "what if people think I'm being unfairly lenient because he's family?" So she struck back with "what if people think you're being unfairly harsh because you're the victim?" She matched him tit for tat, unfairness against unfairness. Suspicion ran both ways, so she offset one possible perception with its equal and opposite.

"By the ignorant, at least," she added. "But ignorant gossip is still gossip."

The implication, of course, was that *she* didn't think so, but some other people might. After all, this was Mia. She wasn't going to pick fights without making sure she could deflect retaliation elsewhere. In the process, however, she successfully snatched the banner of justice out of Abram's hands.

Silence followed, during which Abram closed his eyes. After a pensive moment, he broke it. "Very well. Your argument proves compelling, Princess Mia, and I believe it deserves consideration. What, then, do you suggest I do? What sentence should I pronounce?"

"Simple. Nothing, Your Majesty," answered Mia. "You should pronounce nothing, because you have a fine son who can do so in your place." She turned to Sion. "It is my belief that Prince Sion is most fit to pass judgment on this matter."

His gaze met hers, and she held it. Maybe…she'd just condemned Sion to sentencing his own brother to death. Maybe she'd just pressed a blade into his heart, and all that remained was for the flesh to give way, and a lasting wound to form. Even so…she believed in him.

She believed, because she'd seen his regret in Remno, and she'd seen his resolve at Saint-Noel. She'd heard him swear that he'd earn his own redemption. Sion Sol Sunkland was her friend, and she had faith in him.

I'm counting on you, Sion!

She gave him an expectant look…

It's all yours now!

…And proceeded to off-load the problem onto him wholesale!

Chapter 18: Swoosh, Swoosh!

"Uh… Me?" said a dumbfounded Sion.

What in the name of the sun is she thinking?

He stared at Mia, who gave him a vigorous smile, as if cheering him on. As he regarded her expression, it clicked.

I see… The chance I've been looking for, she's giving it to me… To earn my own redemption.

He'd located the missing Wind Crow agent, Bisset, in Tearmoon, but he hardly considered himself sufficiently atoned. Though he'd continued looking for a way to make up for his mistakes, the last thing he expected was to find it in a situation like this. The events in Remno flashed across his mind.

"No one lives perfectly. That is why we forgive, so that we may all have chances to make amends."

Mia's past words echoed in his ears. Chances indeed. She'd given him one through that kick of hers. It had driven the memory of his failure through his flesh into his heart.

Justice…and fairness, huh…?

How easy they were to speak…and how difficult to uphold… With a deep sigh, he closed the mnemonic locket of failure in his mind and exited his thoughts.

"Father," he said, looking directly at the king, "if I may be so bold, I ask that you entrust the adjudication of Echard's case to me."

Abram silently regarded his older son, then nodded. "Very well. I hereby leave this matter in your hands, Sion."

Sion closed his eyes and breathed out. He turned back toward Mia and her friends.

"I need information. Miss Citrina, you mentioned earlier that you know where the poison came from. Could you explain in further detail?"

Oh? The first thing he does is ask others for advice? Interesting. Mia privately lifted an eyebrow at Sion. She'd expected him to immediately start impressing his own opinions on everyone. Instead, he was proceeding with far more caution. *Not bad. That's a smart choice on his part.*

For Mia, who strove to become the ultimate yes-man, Sion's inquiring attitude resonated greatly with her. She nodded with haughty approval.

"May I?" asked Citrina, glancing toward her.

Mia considered the meaning of her request.

I see. She's concerned about potential Serpents among us.

Aside from her friends, they were currently in the presence of King Abram, Echard, Count Lampron, and the chancellor. How much she could safely say about the Chaos Serpents was certainly a valid question, and a question to which she did not have the answer. So, she pointedly glanced at Rafina, performing the metaphorical equivalent of a deflecting twirl that sent the query careening toward someone else.

Swoosh! Question redirected.

"Good question..." After a pensive moment, Rafina answered, "How about using what happened to the Wind Crows as an example to explain?"

Mia struck her hand in agreement. The Sunkland royals were of course aware of how control of the Wind Crows had been partially hijacked during the Remno incident. Framing the current incident in a similar vein seemed a safe way to provide information without leaking anything crucial to any serpentine ears that might be listening.

"Just to be safe, though…" Rafina murmured as she closed her eyes and folded her hands before her chest in prayer.

She recited a verse from the Holy Book, her voice lyrical and resonant.

Blessed be. Blessed be. Glory to our land and home.
Pray holy wisdom for the sword-bearing king.
Blessed be. Blessed be. Glory to our land and home.
May he rule with justice and bring peace to man.

The sudden psalm by the Saint of Belluga left the room stunned, but only for a second. Soon, all eyes had closed. Only after her voice had faded did Lampron politely ask, "Excuse me, Lady Rafina, but might I ask what that was for?"

"Important decisions must be made with a calm heart. Before the Lord, we find peace, and with it, wisdom and truth. So, I spoke a passage from scripture. May my prayer allow us to make the correct decision."

She favored him with a gentle smile. Her eyes, though, remained sharp, carefully appraising the members of the room. After inspecting each person in turn, she said, "I think…we should be fine, as long as we speak with care."

"I see…" Mia nodded as she pointedly glanced at Citrina. "Well, there you have it."

Twirl and deflect. *Swoosh!*

Like a dutiful courier, Mia deftly ferreted the messages back and forth, making sure to stay out of the actual conversation while she did. She heard the message, relayed it, and then she shut up. Discretion was the entirety of her valor.

"Understood," said Citrina, stepping forward. "Allow Rina— Err, allow me to explain. As I'm sure you're aware, Sunkland's intelligence agency, the Wind Crows, was previously infiltrated by suspicious actors. We suspect that the one who supplied His Highness Prince Echard with the poison is connected with those infiltrators."

"What?!"

The revelation left much of the room speechless.

"Based on my investigation," she continued, "a suspicious person whose traits resemble those of the Equestrian Kingdom was seen with some frequency at the open market. This person is likely the offender we're looking for, because during my investigation, there was an attempt on my life."

"No! Inside the capital?"

"An Equestri, you say?"

Count Lampron and the chancellor both expressed their surprise. Abram, meanwhile, remained still, his eyes closed and ears open.

"Miss Citrina Yellowmoon, are you certain that the offender is someone from the Equestrian Kingdom?"

"To be precise, it was someone whose physical appearance resembled someone from the Equestrian Kingdom. I do think it is rather strange for someone to walk around in such conspicuous attire...but the fact stands that such a person was seen going in and out of the open market," Citrina replied before hastily adding,

"Our foes are experts at sleights of hand. They can, for example, hide the poison in an envelope and place it in a coat pocket unnoticed, or, say…slip it into a bag of purchased goods. There are countless ways for them to deliver the poison. Even if the prince was never left alone, they would probably have attempted an approach."

My, Rina seems a little nervous. I wonder what's gotten into her? Mia tilted her head quizzically.

"We are dealing with master manipulators," said Citrina. "I have no doubt it is very easy for them to exploit any anxieties Prince Echard might harbor to coax him into poisoning Prince Sion. Like I said earlier, it is entirely possible for them to have handed over a substance without even explaining that it was poison."

Though she ended on a conclusive note and began stepping back, she paused to add one more statement.

"Forgive my verbosity, but I should also mention that in using Prince Echard as their instrument, our enemies have likely factored his resulting punishment into their calculations as well. Should we adjudicate this matter exactly according to Sunkland customs, we may be playing right into their hands. That is all."

With that, she withdrew, but not before sparing a look of mild pity for Echard.

Rina… She must see her old self in him. It occurred to Mia that for the young Yellowmoon, Prince Echard's plight may have hit a little too close to home.

Sion didn't say a word during Citrina's briefing. His silent, close-eyed contemplation continued long after she finished. Finally, he looked at Rafina.

"Miss Rafina… May I hear your thoughts?" he said, choosing to ask the Holy Lady for advice.

The moral framework of the Central Orthodox Church was shared by almost every nation on the continent. Since everyone referred to the Holy Book to judge good and evil, it was natural to seek Rafina's opinion.

"My thoughts…"

Her gaze grew distant, as if she were peering through layers of fog and mist to ascertain some faraway truth. After a long pause, she said in a quiet, ruminative tone, "Those who have power must wield it correctly. Therefore, between the powerful and the powerless, the former must be judged with a higher, stricter standard. This… I believe is true."

As the Holy Lady, Rafina had no tolerance for tyranny. Those who'd been bestowed with power by God had a duty to live up to that gift through their conduct. Her position on this matter could not and would not ever waver.

"However, this current matter…is not one of power abused. Furthermore, the victim is the father of the perpetrator. It seems to me, then, that we should judge this through not the lens of noble duty but the common ethics of man. The Lord has taught us through the Holy Book that since time immemorial, justice should be upheld through the principle of reciprocity. He who robs an arm shall have his arm severed, and he who robs an eye shall have his eye gouged…" She paused, sweeping her gaze slowly from face to face, before finishing in a solemn tone, "And suffer no further. The principle defines both extent and limit."

The ancient principle of an eye for an eye demands equal injury as recompense. No less—and no *more*. With her position stated, Rafina quietly turned toward Abram.

"Therefore, if I were to judge the justice of the impending verdict, then I would be concerned with only one question. Did His Majesty lose his life?"

In other words, her conclusion was that if one judged the incident only by the objective events that took place, then putting Echard to death would be too grave a punishment.

"That being said," she continued, "my critique applies only to the appropriateness of the punishment. It does not absolve anyone of guilt. The tenets His Majesty spoke of are in no way irrelevant. In addition, I do believe we should consider the motive behind the poisoning as well. But…"

It was at this point that Rafina found herself of two minds. Her past self would doubtlessly have deemed Echard's actions deserving of capital punishment. As a member of the royal family, he'd behaved in a fashion egregiously unbefitting of his station, demonstrating a lack of the fundamental qualities necessary for correctly wielding power. The current Rafina…quietly placed her hand over her chest.

"Prince Echard is still young. His complex toward his older brother is understandable, if not commendable. It is a very human failing. I find myself wondering if we would be better served not by his death but his betterment, so that he might one day acquire the prudence and discipline that would qualify him for his station."

As she spoke, she recalled that unforgettable day in Saint-Noel when Mia wielded the hammer of justice. Rather than strike down the offending Tearmoon nobles, she'd propped them up, giving them a chance to atone for their sins. She'd fostered their growth… and grow they did.

Surely, it's the same this time. She's doing this for Prince Echard. And now, I think I finally understand a little of how she feels too.

It made her glad, knowing she could empathize with her friend. She found herself wishing, earnestly and fervently, that Echard would be given a chance to make amends.

Mia, while listening to Citrina and Rafina answer the questions she'd *swooshed* to them, kept sneaking glances at King Abram. Throughout the exchange, she found his expression unchangingly stern.

Hm, well, he's a tough nut to crack, isn't he? After hearing those two talk, I thought for sure he'd be all ready to forgive Echard... I mean, I'm convinced. He probably just needs one more push. If only there was another wave...

As if answering her call, a knock sounded on the door.

Chapter 19: The Miabel Dialogue: What Is a King?

"Excuse me, Your Majesty. Keithwood urgently requests an immediate audience. Should I show him in?" asked a guard who stepped into the room.

After receiving permission from the king, he gestured at the doorway. In walked Keithwood, Dion, and an oddly nervous and sweat-browed Connery, all of whom...were led by Bel.

"My, Bel? Where have you been all this time?"

"As a matter of fact, Miss Mia, I went on an adven—tour of the castle!"

That's just about the least effective correction I've ever heard. She might as well have said "adventure."

Mia shook her head at her granddaughter's egregious clumsiness with words.

She really needs to be more mindful of what she says, or she's going to have a lot of problems down the road. At the same time though, it doesn't seem to have prevented her from getting along with Dion, which is something I'll never understand...

How the girl managed to interact so casually with the man, who in Mia's eyes was always one slipup away from lopping her head off, never failed to boggle her mind.

Keithwood also afforded Bel a wry smile before turning toward Abram and lowering himself to his knees. "It is a great relief to see Your Majesty well."

"A relief we all owe to Princess Mia and these fine young ladies," replied the king, who smiled affably at Tiona and Citrina. "But let us not dawdle. Speak, Keithwood. What urgent matter brings you here?"

"Yes, Your Majesty. I received a tip from Princess Mia and, gauging the risks of inaction to be significant, conducted an unauthorized search of Prince Echard's room. I regret the impropriety but believe it was necessary given the circumstances."

Abram closed his eyes, his expression pensive.

The ensuing silence prompted Keithwood to continue. "I apologize for acting independently. I could not find the chance to seek your instructions."

"And no one can expect you to have. It is a stroke of pure and tragic misfortune that Echard chose to act on this day," Abram finally said with a long sigh.

Mia looked from the king to her granddaughter. "And why were you with them, Bel?"

"Oh, yes, about that…"

Thus, Bel began to tell her tale, in which she went on an adven— tour of the castle.

"This way."

Bel led Connery through one castle corridor after another. Normally, she'd have been stopped by guards long ago, but Connery's presence had functioned as a permit of free passage. The captain's work had acquainted him with much of the castle's sentries.

As he followed, Connery wondered if this was all a big mistake. Keithwood's behavior was, however, undeniably peculiar.

It was feeble justification for him entertaining the girl's exploratory quest through the castle, but it would have to do for now.

"Oh, by the way, Sir Connery, have you been working under Count Lampron for a long time?" asked Bel.

He sighed at her eager curiosity and said, "Yes, I suppose so. I've served milord since I was a young lad. I must admit, though, young Connery had no idea he would eventually be acquainted with a prince."

"Oh, I see. That means you've known Prince Echard for a long time too, right? Count Lampron was his mentor for a while, wasn't he?" said Bel, her head tilting with spontaneous wonder. "Can I ask you a question, then?"

"Go ahead."

"What is a king?"

Connery froze, his mind struggling to grasp the meaning of the question.

"A...king?" he said, blinking in bewilderment. "Do you mean His Majesty? King Abram?"

"Mmmm, no, that's not what I mean..." She pursed her lips for a while before rephrasing her question. "I'm curious about kings and emperors. People who rule other people. Princes and princesses too. I want to know what they're like."

"Ah, I see." Connery nodded. This girl, he figured, had probably developed an interest in royalty as she got to know Princess Mia and Prince Sion. The context of her question was now clear to him. Unfortunately, that didn't change the fact that it was still a *hell* of a question, and he struggled to produce an answer. "Hmm... Well, I can't speak for others, but to me, a king is...something like an agent of God. A proxy, almost."

"A proxy?"

He nodded firmly. "We who live on this continent believe in God. Therefore, all of us base our moralities on the teachings of the Holy Book. However, not every problem can find a solution in the Holy Book. Sometimes, we're faced with difficult choices for which it has no advice. In those cases, the king is the one who makes the decision. In my opinion, a king is someone who acts on behalf of God, making moral judgments using the divine authority entrusted in him. That is why we place our absolute faith in His Majesty."

"So that's what a king is in Sunkland... Hmm..." Bel crossed her arms and nodded in thought. Soon, however, she let out a squeal. "Eeek!"

Connery spun toward her to find her being pulled away by the arm.

"Halt! What do you think you're doing?"

He rushed to help her but immediately backed off when he realized the identity of her captor.

"My duty, I'm pretty sure," said the sharpest of Princess Mia's swords, Dion Alaia. He lifted an eyebrow. "What about you?"

To his side was Keithwood, who also wore a puzzled expression.

"Sir Connery? What are you doing here?"

Chapter 20: Princess Mia...Is Left Bereft!

Connery let out a short sigh at the sight of the two men. "Looking for you, I believe. The young lady here said she saw the two of you walking around."

He shrugged inwardly. If his cover was blown, then so be it. Not that he was trying to be sneaky or anything. He just figured he'd follow her and see what the two men were up to.

I guess that's as far as I'll get with the shadowing. Time to take the girl with me and leave.

He'd kept an eye on the girl during her "tour" of the castle. His duty here was done. The thought made him relax—perhaps a little too much, as he was blindsided by the next development.

"I see... You know what? This is actually perfect," said Keithwood. "It would have caused some problems down the line if the two of us went in by ourselves. With you here, though, we'll have the testimony of Count Lampron's guard captain."

Connery had hoped for a quick exit, but fate wasn't about to let him off the hook that easily.

"Testimony? I'm...not sure what you mean."

"Testimony," said Keithwood in the most casual of voices, "because we're going to search Prince Echard's room right now."

"Huh?"

As Connery processed the meaning of what he'd just heard, a sinking feeling settled in his gut. He had, he realized, just inserted himself into the wrongest place at the wrongest of times.

"Wh-What do you mean? Ha ha ha, I'm not great with jokes, you see. I seem to have missed the humor. In fact, I don't think it's very appropriate at all. It's not like you to make such irreverent remarks, Keithwood."

His futile laughter sounded all the emptier when Keithwood's expression remained upsettingly sober. The man wasn't joking. Connery turned pleadingly to Dion, who *was* smiling but somehow looked scarier doing so. It immediately occurred to Connery that he was witnessing not the smirk of someone appreciating a crude joke but the grin of someone who thrived on trouble and danger. Had this man charged alone against an army, he'd probably still be smiling. In pure desperation, Connery turned to his last hope, the girl whom the Great Sage of the Empire had seen fit to bring with her.

"Wow..." said the girl. "We're sneaking into a prince's room? That sounds like an adventure! Plus, I get to do it with the Libra King's loyalest of knights, Keithwood! And General Dion too! This is amazing!" Bel's eyes glowed with excitement.

Nope. No hope there. I guess we're doing this then... thought Connery, feeling five shades bluer than he had a minute ago.

"It's a bit dangerous for Miss Bel to come with us...but there's no time. We'll just have to risk it. Sir Connery, please follow us and protect Miss Bel. Also, put this on," said Keithwood as he held out a mask.

"This is..."

"Cover. Just in case. Better not to let your face be seen."

"This reminds me of a rumor I heard. Apparently, there's a masked duo going around taking out small groups of bandits in the local region."

"As you know, milord has a strong sense of justice. It…keeps me fairly busy."

Keithwood shrugged, but Connery couldn't help but feel a tinge of pity for the attendant.

Thanks to Keithwood's meticulous knowledge of guard positions and patrol routes, the group managed to reach Prince Echard's room without too many problematic encounters. The closest call they had was when Bel had tripped and fallen with a shriek, summoning a bunch of guards that Keithwood and Dion promptly engaged. What had ensued was less a fight than an exhibition of the pair's overwhelming skill, incapacitating the guards without causing so much as a wound, never mind a death. With expert precision, they'd relieved the guards of only their consciousnesses, nothing more.

After the battle, Dion eyed Bel, who let out an embarrassed laugh that elicited an exasperated sigh from the knight. "Bloody hell… You remind me of a certain princess in a certain forest." He then looked at Keithwood. "Gotta say, though, you've got one hell of a sword arm. Prince Sion's a natural, but you ain't half bad yourself."

"I appreciate the compliment."

"What do you say we go a few rounds? It'd be a nice souvenir for me."

"Ha ha, no thanks. I can't see myself lasting even three seconds. I'll get you a proper souvenir instead." Keithwood chuckled genially, turning to hide the sheen of cold sweat on the back of his neck. Make no mistake, Dion Alaia was a monster. He could feel it through the man's aura, and it made his hair stand on end.

Forget three seconds; it'd take a *monumental* amount of grit just to draw his sword when every fiber of his body would be screaming at him to turn tail and run the second Dion stood as his foe. The sheer sense of terror was...familiar, in fact. He'd felt the same way when faced with Mia's cooking.

Just like how it's imperative that Princess Mia is never allowed to cook, and especially not mushrooms... It's equally crucial that Dion Alaia never faces us as a foe. If it ever looks like we might go to war with Tearmoon, I'd better do everything I can to avert it... Ugh, nothing is ever easy.

He grimaced as he mentally greeted his old friend, the headache.

After slipping into Echard's room, Connery couldn't help but utter an admonishment. "Keithwood, I must remind you that even someone in your position—"

"Isn't allowed to do this. Yes, I am well aware." Seeing the guard captain's grave expression, Keithwood smiled wryly. "But special times call for special measures. And this is a very special time, because the welfare of the royal family is at stake."

"The...royal family?"

"Apparently," said Dion, taking over from Keithwood, "a very suspicious fellow was spotted speaking with your second prince. And probably handed the boy some poison."

"Wha—? P-Poison?"

"Yep. Or so goes the rumor, anyway."

Connery blinked a few times, then shook his head. "Figures. So it's a rumor. That certainly doesn't justify this behavior—"

"It's real credible, though," said Dion, cutting Connery off. "The fellow was seen hanging around the open market, where he likely passed the poison to the second prince. Does any of that ring a bell?"

Connery's cheek twitched. "Th-The open market, you say..." There was a slight tremble in his voice. His eyes began to dart left and right. Connery was not a man who could keep secrets.

"Sir Connery, is something the matter?" asked Keithwood, noticing the change in his mannerisms.

"No. It's, uh..." As he fumbled for words, Dion lay a firm hand on his shoulder.

"Is that the peal of recognition I hear? If you know something, honesty will probably serve you much better. Just saying."

"I, uh... Well..." His gaze wandered to Bel, who tipped her head curiously at him. Her big, unsuspecting eyes dealt him a decisive blow. "You see..."

He came clean. Connery was not a man who could lie with a straight face in front of innocent children. In general, he was just a decent, honest fellow.

"A while ago, when I accompanied His Highness to the open market, there was a short time when I lost sight of him..."

Dion burst out laughing at his confession. "Ba ha ha! You wouldn't last two seconds in an interrogation, would you? You're a good man, Connery, and I appreciate the honesty. But do try to keep a tight lip around other people, okay? For your own sake."

"I...should, shouldn't I? But..."

"No, like, seriously, just keep your mouth shut. Our princess isn't very fond of seeing heads roll. I'd rather not give her any nightmares."

There was a soberness to his tone that compelled Connery to nod.

"All the more reason, by the way," continued Keithwood, "to incorporate you into this operation. You'll be helping both yourself *and* His Highness."

After a long silence, Connery said, "All right. It doesn't seem like I have much choice. Count me in." He let out a resigned sigh as he tried to remember more details of that day. "To the best of my memory, I cannot recall His Highness holding anything. Whatever we're looking for, it probably can't be too big."

Echard's room was impressively spacious. Having been built for war, Solecsudo Castle prioritized function over luxury, and its inner chambers were by no means large. Unless you put three of them together.

The first of the sub-rooms was a miniature library, with rows of shelves holding a great number of books. It was also outfitted with a desk for reading and writing. The second sub-room had religious paintings adorning the walls. Judging by the presence of tableware, it was likely used for activities such as afternoon tea. In the third, there was a gigantic canopy bed.

"This is one hell of a room to look through..." said Dion with a sigh as he scanned the chamber. "And we don't even know what we're looking for. Hell, maybe the kid's keeping it on him. How're we supposed to find the thing?"

His grumbling prompted Keithwood to shake his head. "I doubt he'd bring it to today's party, considering he'll be the center of attention. He could have thrown it away, though, so there's a good chance we won't be able to find anything. Still, we— Uh, Miss Bel? What are you doing?"

Bel was on all fours, peeking under the bed. Keithwood gave her an exasperated look.

"I remember Rina telling me that noble boys hide things they don't want other people to see under their bed..." she said, looking over her shoulder at him with a guiltless giggle. "Rina's so smart.

She knows everything. Apparently—and this is something she told me too—even if you don't know what they're hiding, all you have to do is say 'I know what you did,' and they'll panic and tell you all sorts of things. And there's more…"

Connery called up a mental image of the girl named Citrina. She was certainly sweet and lovable, but he remembered feeling a hint of something uncanny about her.

Makes sense. That girl's probably got something up her sleeve. I'd expect nothing less from one of Princess Mia's aides.

He watched as Bel stood up, arms and brows both knitted in thought. She stared at the bed. After a span, she pursed her lips and thrust a hand under the pillow.

"Ah!" With a cry of surprise, she retracted her arm, revealing something in her hand. Keithwood leaned in to take a closer look. His brows furrowed.

"A troya? What's a charm like that doing here?"

Bel held up a finger, wagged it at him, and explained with great pretentiousness, "I've made troyas like these before. You start by rolling up some stuffing for the stomach, then you weave the thread around it. That way, when you're done, you can take out the stuffing, and there'll be a pocket inside." She pulled open the belly of the equine-shaped charm. "See? You can hide stuff in here," she said, extracting a small vial filled with black powder.

"So you found this in Prince Echard's room…" said Mia, exhaling with a tinge of regret.

If only Keithwood had found this before today's party. This whole mess could have been averted…

It was, however, no use crying over spilt milk. Especially when the milk excused the spill. The poisoning justified their unauthorized search of Echard's room. Without the incident, they'd simply have intruded upon the privacy of a prince. After all, there was no definite knowledge of his possession. Mia knew for certain, of course, but she'd have to invoke clairvoyance for her testimony, which was questionable at best in a legal context.

Yeah, the cause-and-effect situation isn't working in my favor. At least no one actually got assassinated. That's worth giving thanks for, thought Mia.

She figured Bel's discovery, though new, would largely be irrelevant to the proceedings. They knew there'd been a poisoning, and they knew what poison it was. The only thing this changed was that they'd found the actual powder.

"Could I take a look?" asked Citrina, stepping up.

She took the vial and gave it a quick shake.

"I see. If I may be so bold, I believe this is circumstantial evidence that Prince Echard did not have murderous intent."

"What do you mean?" asked a surprised Sion.

"Earlier, I asked Prince Echard how much poison he'd put in the wine glass. His answer was one pinch." Citrina held the vial up to the light, illuminating its contents. "As we can see, there is still a great deal of powder inside, meaning it was a conscious decision of his to use only one pinch. Had he intended on murder, he'd surely have put in more. When it comes to poison, there's no reason to risk the victim surviving due to too low a dose. Especially if he intended on delivering the poisoned drink personally during the party, since the commotion that would ensue meant he'd only have one chance. Therefore, I believe that the contents of this vial disprove murder as his motive."

Mia found herself greatly enlightened by this explanation. The vial resembled a sugar shaker, allowing her to apply a far more familiar logic to the situation. With a shaker half full, she'd feel a desire to use it more sparingly so it doesn't run out. Her shakes would naturally become gentler and fewer. Give her a full shaker, however, and she'd dump a good cube's worth into her tea. After all, the way she saw it, who wouldn't prefer their tea to be overly sweet rather than not sweet enough?

Poison was undoubtedly the same. Had the vial held only a tiny bit of powder, she could see Echard using only a pinch, but with so much in the vial…

He had tons, but only used a little… Obviously, that means he felt it'd be a problem if he put in too much. Admittedly, he could have been hoping for a subdued reaction to avoid exposing himself, but even then, one pinch seems too little… Hm, this argument is actually pretty convincing.

"With so much on hand, it would make sense to try it first on a mouse or something. I would, at least," said Citrina, the casualness of her tone at odds with the content of her remark. "That way, I'd know what it does. But Prince Echard almost certainly didn't even do that much. The imprudent nature of his actions paint the picture of someone acting on impulse. Someone who didn't care if he was found out afterward. After all, if you wanted to kill someone, you'd try your best to keep your involvement a secret, right? And even if you didn't care about being seen, you'd at least make sure you use enough to guarantee the victim's death."

She favored her audience with a sweet smile. It made the morbid nature of her analysis all the more unsettling. Then, she presented her conclusion, her tone all but screaming "Q.E.D."

"Therefore, it seems clear to me that Prince Echard acted on impulse, not premeditation. Furthermore, he did not believe this to be poison, nor did he intend to use it during the party. It was a combination of the poison's coincidental availability and a whim that forced his hand."

There was something oddly compelling about her argument. Perhaps it stemmed from her familiarity with the subject. Being an expert, she had an intimate understanding of both the tools and the psychology of those who employ them.

Mia nodded in agreement. She'd applaud if she could. Thanks to Citrina, there was now a legitimate degree of doubt surrounding Echard's motive.

Mmm, this is good. First, Miss Rafina, then Citrina. The tides are changing in favor of a lighter sentence. Surely, even Sion can't ask for his death in this atmosphere!

She let out a breath, figuring all that remained was to wait for Sion to concede a milder verdict. Which was why she failed to correctly parse the subsequent question.

"What do you think, Mia?"

And there it is. Time for the final answer. Go for it, Mia. Tell Sion what he should say. We're all waiting for you to wrap this up, Mi— Wait... Mia?

Only then did Mia realize that after the sequence of expert opinions, Sion had made no attempt to take control of the conversation. He remained withdrawn, watching her like a complete bystander. *Her!*

"...Huh?"

Her jaw would have dropped if it weren't frozen in shock with the rest of her body. Every pair of eyes in the room was focused on her, waiting for *her* verdict.

Huh? W-Wait, me? Uh... What do I...?

She drew in a trembling breath and prepared to speak. As she opened her mouth, there was suddenly an odd discomfort in her throat. It felt dry and scratchy. Her breath left her not as words but a choking cough.

What is—? No... It can't be... Is this poison?!

It definitely wasn't. It was just the cookie she'd swiped when leaving the ballroom. Its dry, crumbly remnants were mounting an insurgency in her throat.

Left bereft of her voice, Mia found herself in her darkest hour.

Chapter 21: A Delivery from a Loyal Subject

Let us return to the ballroom.

Calm had descended upon the once-restless crowd, but a vague sense of anxiety lingered in the air. It was into this atmosphere that an out-of-breath Anne returned.

"Ah, good. You're back," said Ludwig. "Was there a problem? You were gone for a while."

He regarded her, puzzled by her evident exertion. The guards she'd gone to find had already stationed themselves outside the hall's entrance. If anything were to happen, they had orders to force their way in immediately. It didn't look like they'd be needed, though. Sunkland's soldiers were doing a good job of maintaining order, and the people in the hall had regained their composure.

Ballroom security is being handled by Count Lampron, I believe? His men are well-trained.

What concerned him more, however, was Anne. According to the guards, after instructing them to gather outside the hall, she'd rushed out the castle. Her errant behavior had left him worried.

"Um... Would you happen to know where milady went?" asked Anne. "I thought she might be thirsty after so much dancing..." She held out a bottle. "So I went to get some juice from the innkeeper who knows Lady Rafina." Sweat streamed down her forehead. She wiped it away with a smile and added, "The drinks here in the hall are probably fine, but..."

Ludwig nodded, sympathizing with her concern. A drink for the king had turned out to be poisoned. It was certainly possible for other drinks to be tainted as well. If there was even the slightest chance that Mia might have consumed something harmful...

Clearly, Anne had decided that the risk, however small, was worth a minor marathon.

"Miss Anne, your dedication is a marvel to behold."

Her unwavering loyalty, though worthy of his admiration, also elicited a hint of envy. She'd identified a potential source of harm to Mia that had completely escaped his notice.

It's reasonable to assume that Her Highness would be thirsty after dancing. However, it was best to avoid consuming the drinks in the hall. After recognizing Her Highness's needs and assessing the situation, she looked for an optimal solution, then promptly acted on it. She is truly a model attendant.

Ludwig had not, of course, seen Mia popping totally-could-have-been-poisoned cookies into her mouth on her way out of the ballroom. With that said, even if he *had* seen, he'd probably have attributed some sort of Ludwig-esque explanation to it. Instead of, you know, simple thoughtlessness.

Anne smiled bashfully at his compliment and shook her head. "I have a long way to go before becoming a worthy maid to milady." She glanced at the bottle of juice. "I hope it helps a little. I mean, stuff like this is all I can do for her..."

"And it is, in my opinion, enough. So long as we do our very best to assist Her Highness, we will surely be of use to her. She is not one to let effort go to waste. I have no doubt that every bit of help we provide will be incorporated into her plans," said Ludwig with a classic finger-to-glasses gesture. "Let us continue to aid her, as we have always done."

Anne gave him a heartfelt smile. "Yes. Let us. Thank you for your kind words."

The two loyal subjects nodded at each other, feeling a deepening camaraderie as fellow vassals of their beloved princess.

"Now, I apologize for the sudden change of topic," said Ludwig, "but could you see to Her Highness on your own? Prince Abel and I have found ourselves a tad...occupied."

"Do you mean you have to keep an eye on the people here so the culprit doesn't escape?"

"That is part of it, yes, but..." He cautiously scanned the surroundings before continuing. "It looks calm in the hall right now...but it's actually a little dangerous here."

"What do you mean?"

"As you might have guessed from the fact that I asked you to bring our guards, there's no guarantee the hall won't descend into a state of panic again. For the people of Sunkland, King Abram is a spiritual pillar. Right now, the nobles and the guards are all relatively calm, but if emotions run high again... Someone needs to be able to keep things under control." Ludwig glanced at Abel. "Admittedly, I'd prefer for Prince Abel to be somewhere safer as well, but..."

"I appreciate the thought, Ludwig, but I assure you, I'm fine," said Abel with a good-natured grin. "Not to brag, but I'm pretty sure I've got more experience taking punches than you. Plus, you're one of Mia's most important subjects. I can't let you stay here by yourself. Besides, if I can help keep things tame here, then I'd be doing her a big favor. And I'm sure she doesn't want to see any unnecessary blood being spilt either." He shrugged casually and added, "Again, not to brag, but between a Tearmoon commoner and a Remno prince, I think the latter has a bit more sway over people."

Ludwig let out an amused *hmph*. "Well then. There you have it," he said, turning to Anne. "Could you see to Her Highness then?"

"Understood."

She nodded and turned to walk away, only to pause when Ludwig spoke again.

"Oh, before you go… Could I ask you to deliver a message for me?"

The princess he served was caught in the middle of a political and diplomatic storm, and he couldn't provide any direct help. That made him a little upset, so he chose to at least provide some words.

"Please tell Her Highness this: 'Please go ahead and do whatever you deem necessary, because we'll handle the rest.'"

Anne held his gaze for a moment, then nodded. "Understood. I'll make sure to relay it word for word."

With that, she left.

While searching for Mia, she was fortunate enough to run into Keithwood, who led her to the king's chamber. She patiently waited outside for the talk to finish, but upon hearing Mia cough, she hurriedly entered the room.

"Excuse me, milady."

Chapter 22: Princess Mia...Finally Decides on Revenge!

Uh-oh. This is bad.

She continued to cough as the slow, familiar feeling of panic began to set in again. She was almost done. Her fingers had almost touched the finish line. But at the very, very end, the hot potato ended up in her hands. Now, as the last speaker, she had to deliver the most important message. And with her throat scratchy, to boot!

Wait... I might be able to turn this into something good. If I just keep coughing like this, maybe someone will speak in my place.

There *was* a wave! She just had to realize it. Just as she was about to jump on the dubiously helpful current, she heard a knock on the door.

In came her loyalest of subjects, Anne.

"Excuse me, milady. I thought you might be thirsty after dancing, so I brought you a drink." She held out a platter, on which stood a glass of juice.

"My, Anne, what perfect timing! How thoughtful of you— *Hack!*"

Despite her pharyngeal discomfort, Mia eyed the glass with hesitance. The juice seemed delicious, but if she drank it, it would surely soothe her throat. Without her cough, she'd be forced to speak. Decide, rather, on what to do with Echard.

Hnnnngh, there's no way to get myself out of this. I should have thought about this while everybody was still talking. If only I'd known...

She took the glass from Anne, brought it to her mouth, and tipped it ever so slightly. The slower she drank, the longer she could stall. A refreshing flavor spread across her tongue, tart but pleasant. Her nose was tickled by a citrus aroma. She savored the experience.

This tastes like a sip of morning dew gathered from a flower growing deep in a forest just waking to the warmth of spring... The refreshing sweetness reminds me of the mushrooms of—

She caught herself before she added "juice" to her list of would-be connoisseur types.

Okay, get a hold of yourself. This is no time to wax poetic. I need to figure out something clever to say that'll convince Sion and King Abram to ease up on Echard's sentence...

Her brows furrowed in thought, then unfurrowed in surprise when Anne spoke again.

"Milady, I have a message for you from Ludwig." Anne's expression was utterly serious.

"My... What is it?"

"He said, 'Please go ahead and do whatever you deem necessary, because we'll handle the rest.'" Anne slowly placed her hand over her chest. "I...am of the same opinion, milady. Whatever you think you need to do, go ahead and do it. Whatever happens after, we've got your back."

"Anne..."

She uttered a soft word of thanks to her maid—and to four-eyes, though she kept that one private. Her eyes closing, she recalled Anne's final act of loyalty, so long ago, as well as Ludwig's dogged determination to save the empire. She heard an echo of his "I'll do something about it"—the phrase he said to every problem that arose, never showing so much as a grimace...

Wait, he did grimace, actually. He grimaced a lot. And scowled. And glared. Oho ho, how terribly nostalgic. She chuckled softly. *We sure traveled a lot, didn't we? Up and down the empire. I mean, I did most of the work, but I guess I have to give the stupid four-eyes some credit. He helped too. A six-four split between me and him, I'd say...*

In actuality, it was more like two-eight. Then again, she was a straight up burden at times, so maybe one? More than zero, though, for sure! She *did* help! Sometimes!

Alas, her efforts had not been destined to bear fruit. The seeds she and Ludwig so tirelessly sowed...had died in the soil.

Huh. You know what? Thinking about this is ticking me off. I worked so hard. It's not fair!

A wave of roiling anger rose up through her chest. She was gripped by something between frustration and outrage. At that moment, it occurred to her that this might be her chance...to get some revenge.

That's right... This kind of opportunity doesn't come around often. I should get some payback! All right, it's time to even the score!

Her goal established, Mia found her mood instantly refreshed. She took one more sip of juice, just to make sure her throat was in perfect condition.

"Thank you, Anne. The drink is much appreciated."

She returned the glass to the platter and turned to face her audience again. They waited in silence for her to speak. With what she assumed was stately grandeur, she turned up her chin and huffed an indignant breath out her nose.

"We, as people," she declared in a solemn tone, "must all reap what we sow..."

That was a lesson she'd learned firsthand, an eternal truth she wouldn't ever forget.

"Whether the seeds are good or bad, whether they sprout into fortune or tragedy, we must still reap them with our own hands. That is how the world works. Wouldn't you agree, Your Majesty?" She glanced at Abram for confirmation.

The king's eyes gleamed with wisdom. "Yes. That is indeed the way of things..."

Upon hearing him affirm the correctness of her statement, an intense emotion flared inside her—anger. She was *angry*. And why wouldn't she be? It was so unfair! So, if she just happened to sow a bad seed, then she'd have no choice but to reap whatever awful disaster sprouts from it? Even if she knew it was going to ruin her life? No second chances. No making amends. Only her inevitable destruction.

That can't be right!

It was a repudiation of everything she'd done to change the course of her life. She'd gone so far as to *leap back through time*, for heaven's sake. To be told all that hard work was for naught... That infuriated her.

So, she sought her outlet in revenge. Lighten Echard's sentence and call it a day? Everyone shakes hands and never mentions this again? No! Such evasive solutions would no longer appease her. She demanded satisfaction! Of the payback sort!

"It *is* certainly true that one must reap what they sow..." she said, eyes closed and voice infused with oracular solemnity. "But the time for reaping is not now."

She paused, lending a sense of finality to her statement before continuing.

"All flowers, no matter their shape or essence, start as a seed. Once the seed is sown, it must sprout, grow, and blossom before bearing the fruit of consequence. But that process takes time. Time...

that we should afford Prince Echard. The day will come for him to reap what he has sown, but it is a day that we should *let* come, no?"

Her petition was for time.

"So, you're suggesting…a suspended sentence?" asked Sion.

Mia gave him a took-the-words-right-out-of-my-mouth nod.

"That is *precisely* what I am suggesting."

Just getting the time wasn't enough, though. That time had to be put to use.

"Furthermore…" She proceeded to define the purpose of the reprieve. "If he goes on to sow more seeds… Different ones. *Good* ones. And many, many of them, then perhaps…"

Her gaze grew profoundly distant, as if she were looking through time itself at some irretrievable past, seeking the figure of a loyal subject she could never see again.

"Perhaps even seeds of guilt can be made to expire in their shells, never to bud…"

Her voice trembled a little, the way it did when one prayed for something with all their heart. Within her words was an earnest plea that the Mia of a bygone timeline had desperately mouthed to the heavens. A wish. A hope. One she'd shared with eyes so nostalgically quadrupled. Together they'd struggled, knowing with painful clarity that they must reap the seeds of ruin sown so deeply within Tearmoon soil but nevertheless searching for a way to keep them dormant. With tireless effort, the Mia of yonder had sought—in ultimate vain—another outcome, one where the seeds would rot unsprouted into the earth.

She'd sought redemption. Perhaps it was foolish of her to do so. Perhaps redemption does not exist, and the reaping of seeds sown was as absolute as the cycle of the sun and moon.

But that's absurd! Just because I made one mistake, I'm destined for destruction? With no chance to make up for it? Unacceptable! That can't be how it works, and I'm going to prove it right now! Using Prince Echard!

Mia had a dream. A dream where Echard returned to Sunkland atoned and triumphant. A dream where people cheered his many redeeming deeds, relieved that his death had been averted. It was also a dream about herself...of a past cut short, and a future that might have been.

She was going to make that dream a reality. And when she did, she would finally point at those damned seeds and say to them what she'd been meaning to for so long.

"Serves you right!"

To stand over their desiccated corpses, their threatened consequences forever rotted, and *laugh*. That would be her revenge.

I was denied a second chance...but this time, I'll give it! I'll give out so many! Everyone gets a second chance!

Cause and effect could go eat dirt. There would be no reaping, because instead of a scythe, she'd brought a hammer!

"I see... So that's the opinion of the Great Sage of the Empire..." murmured Sion. He smiled. "Every time, Mia, you're..."

He trailed off, the unspoken sentiment lost to the infinite void of thoughts unvoiced. With a short sigh, he turned to Echard.

Chapter 23: Sion's Decision

"Echard, your sentence is as follows."

Sion looked down as his brother looked up. They held each other's gaze.

"What you did, this heinous act of poisoning the king... It cannot be forgiven. However, Miss Citrina has highlighted the possibility that you did not intend on murder. You might not have even known the substance in your possession was poison. Is what she suggested true? I need answers, Echard, and I need to hear you say them in your own words."

His piercing question was met with only a shake of Echard's head.

"I...have nothing to say."

The younger prince chose silence. It was, perhaps, an attempt to defend what he saw as the last vestiges of his integrity, driven by the misguided ego of youth. Speaking the truth, he figured, would be taken as pleading for his life. He had erred, but he would not grovel. He would face the consequences of his actions with dignity.

Echard *welcomed* punishment. His regal status in a kingdom founded upon justice colored his beliefs. So great was its influence that he felt only through this sentence would he—for the first time in his life—be legitimized as a prince of Sunkland. He couldn't afford to stain the noble legacy of Sunkland by twisting its justice to save his own life. That, at least, was a line he would not cross. In his death, he saw honor.

It was a juvenile honor, and one Sion would not grant him.

"If there is indeed someone who gave you the poison—someone who tempted you with deceptive words—then your silence will lead to their escape. You will be abetting and enabling a felon. More victims may fall prey as a result. If the allegations are true, Echard, then there is a cost to defending your honor. A grievous cost that invalidates the very honor you wish to defend. It is not how royalty should behave."

The words Sion spoke to his brother were the very ones he'd wrestled with himself. After his failure in Remno, he'd also fallen prey to the logical trap of righteous penance, believing it shameful to avoid penalty. He'd longed for his punishment, just as Echard did right now. When he'd stared down the blade of Abel's sword, he'd welcomed the notion of its cold metal biting into his flesh. Having espoused justice with such zeal for all his life, he'd deemed it the only fitting way to take responsibility for his blunder.

The Great Sage of the Empire had disagreed. She'd delivered a much-needed kick to his rear that dislodged his embedded head. Having freed him from his self-absorbed fixations, she'd then told him not to flee to death but to bear the shame of his failure in life. And, with the disgraceful memory forever etched in his soul, to redeem himself.

Even now, Sion still felt a deep shame. He thought himself unworthy to speak of such noble concepts as justice and fairness. But he must, because Echard needed to hear it, and because to do otherwise would be an even greater injustice. Silence, in this moment, was equivalent to surrender. Not only would it not serve Echard's interests, he would be straying from the path of redemption

Mia had shown him. He needed to act. To do *something*. But what was the right thing to do? Where did justice lie?

Justice lay with the king, whose power was temporarily vested in him. What, he asked himself, *is* a king?

"Sion…" Echard whispered his name.

He caught a brief glimpse of his young brother's face, on the verge of tears, before it was cast down. Slowly, ever so slowly, words trickled out of the boy's lips.

"It's…true. I know this will sound like an excuse, but a man I do not know came to me at the open market. It was him who gave me the poison. I was told that it would cause mild abdominal pain."

Echard's voice was unsteady. At times, it faltered, only to resume with greater hoarseness. The princely mask fell, revealing the frightened, vulnerable boy underneath.

"It was reckless of me… I know that now. Without testing its effects, I tried to have you drink it," he said, not meeting his brother's eye. "I…do not know what drove me to do so."

There was a sense of genuine perplexity to his tone as he continued.

"I think…it was bitterness. I have always felt inadequate compared to you. The feeling grew and grew until I could contain it no longer. That was when I saw the poison. It whispered to me. It told me to put just a little bit in. It assured me that no true harm would come and that I would feel better after I took you down a peg. And I…listened. I fell for its temptation." Echard bowed his head to the ground. "I yield my fate to your judgment and accept whatever punishment you deem appropriate. Please do not let my mistake stain Sunkland's legacy of justice."

Then, with some hesitance, he added one more statement.

"Also, about the person who gave me the poison... He looked like an Equestri, but...something was off. I am not sure what, but that was my impression. It did not seem like someone merely donning an Equestrian costume, but something about the man did not resemble the Equestris I know."

"His smell, perhaps?"

All eyes turned toward the sudden speaker to find a narrow-eyed Rafina.

"His smell?" asked Echard.

"Yes. I heard that in order to keep their horses safe, those of the Equestrian Kingdom apply a certain type of scented balm to their bodies that wards off carnivores. You wouldn't notice it if you weren't paying attention, but perhaps that man you met was lacking that special scent."

Echard frowned in thought. "That...is possible." He nodded. "I think you might be right."

"Well spoken, Echard. I commend your honesty," said Sion, causing Echard to straighten. "As you are clearly aware, your actions are not excusable. It is a serious offense that might have thrown the kingdom into chaos. Had father succumbed to the poison, I would have had no choice but to sentence you to death. Even his survival cannot absolve you of guilt. I must condemn you, or justice will waver."

Righteousness in Sunkland was pure and holy. The color of unsullied virtue. It allowed no smear, no blemish. For it to stand, all sin must be punished.

"However, I have listened to Miss Rafina's thoughts, and I have heard Princess Mia's words. I find them compelling. I believe that reprieve is the correct course of action. You shall therefore receive a suspended sentence."

It was, for all intents and purposes, full approval of Mia's argument.

"A suspended sentence… But—"

"But make no mistake," said Sion, assertively cutting his brother off. "Your sentence is only suspended; it is by no means void. And until the suspension expires, your involvement in this incident will be kept secret."

"Will that satisfy public opinion though?" asked the chancellor, his expression concerned.

Sion laughed. "The person responsible for this is connected to a group that had the means to twist the Wind Crows into serving their interests. Sneaking into the ballroom and slipping some poison into a drink seems well within their capabilities."

In stating so, he was effectively declaring his intention to attribute the incident to the Chaos Serpents. It was, in fact, his only option; framing an innocent individual was beyond the limits of his moral compass.

"With that said…" He then frowned. "Echard, you cannot be allowed to remain in Sunkland. I shall send you abroad."

While Echard's sentence was suspended, the Serpents might attempt contact with him again. If he stayed in Sunkland, any such contact risked being seen and inciting a public outcry demanding fair trial. Furthermore, asking him to perform good deeds to atone for his sins would be difficult within the kingdom's borders; his status as prince made most undertakings trivial. The undue ease would neither earn his redemption nor satisfy his own conscience.

What Sion wanted was for Echard to grow as a person. It seemed more prudent, given the circumstances, to send him to some faraway place and let the rigors of the unfamiliar refine his mettle. Wherever he was sent, however, would have to be a nation they could trust. Otherwise, he might end up being a national liability, exploited by foreign actors with ill intent. Belluga, under Rafina's watchful eye, seemed promising...

"In that case, allow me to help. On behalf of the Greenmoons, I extend our invitation."

An answer came from the most unexpected of places. Esmeralda Etoile Greenmoon, feeling it was finally time for her to shine, strutted to center stage.

"The Greenmoons? I'm not sure if—"

Sion's uncertainty was overridden by Esmeralda's assertiveness.

"My, Prince Sion," she said with a smug smile, "have you forgotten that *I'm* Prince Echard's fiancée? I believe I have every right to welcome him into my household."

The first to respond was the organizer of this event, Count Lampron. "Given the circumstances, Miss Esmeralda," he said, flustered, "I do believe this marriage proposal is—"

"Excuse me?" She cut him off, then shook her head with a knowing smile. "Do you mean to embarrass me, Count Lampron? After such a ceremonious announcement of our marriage to so many people, we cannot *possibly* renege on the arrangement."

Her rebuke allowed no argument, since it was Sunkland's fault that her honor was now at stake.

"Fortunately, we Greenmoons have many connections within other nations, just as we do with Sunkland nobles like yourself, Count Lampron," she said as she turned toward the queen. Her smile softened. "If he stays with us, not only will we help him expand his horizons, it will also be easy for him to visit home."

"Lady Esmeralda... How thoughtful of you..." The queen was moved by her words.

So was Mia, though given her mumbled "Not bad, Esmeralda," her emotion was perhaps more cynical.

Sion, meanwhile, was made to recall his last summer. The time he'd spent on the Greenmoons' yacht sailing through the Galilea Sea, along with the adventures that followed… They had indeed been invaluable experiences that fostered growth. A chance to see more of the world would surely do Echard more good than harm. So, he looked at his father, then his mother, and finally Esmeralda.

"In that case… I'll leave my brother in your care."

Seeing Sion lower his head, Mia let out a breath she'd been holding for a long time.

Phew, I think this case is finally closed. Things worked out pretty well for everybody, I'd say. Esmeralda has a cute future husband, and she even gets to take him home. She must be happy. Granted, we'll have to make up some official excuse to bring him to Tearmoon, and Duke Greenmoon probably has to be filled in about what's actually going on. That'll probably make it hard to have an actual ceremony…

That wasn't all. She glanced at Echard.

We didn't do anything about Prince Echard's hang-ups. If anything, all this thoughtfulness is probably making his inferiority complex worse.

Some problems still existed, yes. But *most* of them were solved! And that was enough for Mia, because it meant that at long last, her job was done. Surely, she could exit stage left now.

Something, something let her guard down; something, something took her by surprise.

"Oh, there's one more thing," Sion said all of a sudden. "Something that…must be done. Could someone ask Prince Abel to come here?"

Oh? I wonder why he wants Abel's presence.

Mia gave him a quizzical look, to which he laughed.

"Echard, I'd like to show you something."

The younger prince had for the past while been watching the proceedings with a resigned glaze to his eyes.

It didn't happen... Sion didn't sentence me to death...

Aided by the advice of the Great Sage of the Empire and her friends, Sion decided to give him a suspended sentence. It was undoubtedly the most lenient of options available to him, an optimal solution that required an enormous effort of ingenuity to reach. To the young boy, however, Sion's needle-threading miracle of mercy only inflamed his self-pity. So removed was his reality from the fear of death that even the salvation of his life failed to evoke sufficient appreciation.

Again, Sion's the bigger man... I tried to hurt him. Maybe even kill him. And what does he do? Show me compassion.

For Echard, his brother's overwhelming forbearance only made his own pettiness more apparent, filling him with a deep sense of defeat. The psychological chains binding him were thick and not easily unraveled. Day by day, their asphyxiating links would eat further into his soul.

Just then, a voice was heard outside the room.

"Excuse me. Prince Abel is here."

Echard turned toward the door to see it open, revealing his brother's friend and second prince of the Remno Kingdom. The sight of Abel revived a long-forgotten memory.

Yes, I have seen him before. He was here for a sword bout with Sion... I'm pretty sure Sion wiped the floor with him. And they somehow became friends after that? I wonder what kind of person he is... he thought, feeling the slightest hint of curiosity.

After walking into the room, Abel first regarded Abram and let out a breath of relief. "Your Majesty, it is good to see that you have recovered. What happened back there gave me a serious scare."

"Thank you for your consideration, Prince Abel. I regret making you an involuntary audience of this shameful state of affairs. Please accept my sincerest apologies."

"Apologies? There is no need for you to apologize, Your Majesty, or even concern yourself with such things. You are an indispensable individual for this continent, and your health is of the highest priority. Please take some time to rest," said Abel before turning to Sion. "By the way, why have you called me here?"

Echard wondered the same thing. No part of the conversation had implied the necessity of Prince Abel's presence.

"Right. About that. First, let me thank you for coming on such short notice," Sion answered before bowing his head. "As a matter of fact, I need to ask you a big favor."

"Oh? Go ahead. I do hope it's something I can actually help with," said Abel, head tilted quizzically.

"It is, and you're the only one who can. You see, my little brother Echard is going to be leaving Sunkland."

"Is that so?" Abel, eyes narrowing, glanced at Echard. "That's rather…sudden."

"It is. And to that end, I'd like to send him off with a parting gift."

"Oh? And what might that be?" asked Abel, still not following.

Echard was equally lost. What in the world was Sion up to? Feeling a tad uneasy, he regarded his older brother, who noticed and regarded him back.

"Echard, there's something you should know. Something that will keep you moving forward in the future. And I'm going to show you what it is right now."

With that, Sion turned back toward Abel and said in the calmest of voices, "Abel Remno, I ask that you draw your sword and

163

face me in a bout—" He paused mid sentence and shook his head. "A bout? No, not a bout… A duel."

Sion straightened and, with a hand to his chest, addressed his friend again.

"Abel Remno, I challenge you to a formal duel for the Great Sage of the Empire, Mia Luna Tearmoon."

For a few seconds, the room was gripped by deafening silence.

"Huh?"

It was broken by a silly-sounding voice. The person it belonged to shall remain unnamed. Though not Echard, he shared the voice's consternation.

What?! Has Sion lost his mind?

"Are you serious?" For a second, Abel was stunned, but he soon collected himself. "I…suppose you are. You don't seem to be joking."

"I am not. Besides, you'd kill me if I were."

They traded sober gazes.

"I see… Well, given the stakes you have set, I find that I have no choice but to accept. Do know, however, that you have forced my hand, and I will fight you with all my heart and soul."

"I do know, and I wouldn't have it any other way. Bring your A-game, because I sure will." A fierce smile spread across Sion's lips, the likes of which had never been seen. "You see, I decided that I've had enough of showing restraint. From now on, I'm going to be honest with myself."

"Oh yeah? Now that's music to my ears. Here's hoping this was worth the wait." Abel proceeded to match his expression.

"Um, Sion? What's…going on?" asked a bewildered Echard.

Sion flashed him a grin. "Like I said, this is my parting gift to you. Watch carefully, because it's something I'd like you to remember." He then turned to Count Lampron. "Our guests in the ballroom are probably expecting an explanation of some kind.

I'll speak to them personally, but in the meantime, Count Lampron, could you go ahead and get the place ready?"

"Certainly. But, Your Highness, what of this…duel you speak of?"

"We can deal with that after the explanation." He glanced at Abel. "Is that okay with you?"

"I don't see why not." Abel nodded agreeably. "I'm ready whenever."

The previously unnamed individual looked from one prince to the other. "*Huh?!*"

Again, Echard heard the silly-sounding voice.

Who could it possibly be?

Sion challenged Abel to a duel. Mia responded with…confusion!

Huh? I-I don't— What is going on? They're dueling for me? What does that even mean?

Utter confusion, in fact!

Her mind completely failed to wrap itself around the sudden turn of events.

S-So, Sion challenged Abel to a duel for me… But for that to make sense, Sion would have to have feelings for…

While she wrestled with her consternation for control over her mental faculties, the situation continued to develop.

"All right, then. Please get some more rest, father. I'm off to reassure our guests in the hall."

"Very well. I'll leave it in your hands, Sion. Oh, and Miss Rudolvon… I'd like a few minutes with you. Would that be okay?"

"Certainly, Your Majesty." Tiona nodded meekly.

With that, Mia and co. followed an eager Sion to the hall, leaving Tiona with King Abram. The whole way, consternation continued to hold its ground against Mia's offensive.

"Milady, are you all right?" asked Anne, concerned by her mistress's visible unease.

"I-I'm not sure. I have no idea what's going on right now."

"Ha ha ha, I see that the Great Sage's wisdom doesn't extend to the hearts of young men," quipped an amused Dion. "Don't say that to Prince Sion, by the way. I don't want him K.O.'ed before the duel even begins." He shrugged and added, "It was a confession of love, in case you're wondering. A pretty blatant one at that."

"Th-That's impossible. How can Sion of all people...? He must be up to something! I *know* he is!" Mia argued in a half-daze as consternation threatened to rout her entirely.

Soon, they arrived at the hall, in which Sion was immediately bombarded by questions from Sunkland nobles.

"Your Highness, how is His Majesty?"

"Has His Majesty recovered?"

"Who is responsible for this terrible act?"

He faced them and said in a commanding voice, "Still yourselves. His Majesty is enjoying some quiet repose in his chamber. He is conscious and coherent. I was told by the physician that he will recover with rest." Then, he turned toward Citrina and bowed low enough for everyone to see. "And it is all thanks to you, Miss Yellowmoon. On behalf of Sunkland, I offer you our sincerest gratitude...as well as our deepest apologies for the discourtesy you suffered earlier."

Following his example, the accusing nobles voiced their apologies in turn.

"Please forgive me. I lost my composure. My behavior was inexcusable."

"We are truly grateful for your help in saving His Majesty's life."

Citrina favored them with a sweet smile. She was about to quip when she caught the sight of Bel out of the corner of her eye.

CHAPTER 23: SION'S DECISION

Reconsidering, she traded sarcasm for propriety and took a step back. "It's okay. In a situation like that, it's perfectly understandable for you to lose your composure."

"Wow, Rina! What did you do?" asked an astonished Bel.

Citrina blinked at her friend, then smiled. "Tee hee, nothing much." It wasn't as sweet a smile, but it came from the heart.

Meanwhile…

"So, the scoundrel who poisoned His Majesty's drink… Do we know who it is?"

"We're currently investigating the matter… But there have been reports of a suspicious person sneaking into the castle. We suspect this individual is the one who slipped the poison into the drink," said Sion.

"A suspicious person?!"

"Apparently, this same person was seen going in and out of the open market… Also, this is something I'd prefer to keep out of the ears of foreign guests…" Sion lowered his voice. "But the suspect is connected with the group that previously infiltrated our intelligence agency."

"Sun have mercy…"

This final revelation left the nobles speechless. Being acutely aware of what had happened to the Wind Crows, the invocation of that incident was enough to impress upon them the competence of the assassin. Meanwhile, foreign dignitaries, who knew little of the details, could only furrow baffled brows at the unsaid implications.

"But that means the assassin infiltrated the castle… Is that truly possible?" asked one of the nobles.

Before there was a chance to answer, a soldier came running into the hall.

"Pardon my intrusion, Your Highness. I have an urgent message."

167

Out of breath, he hastily whispered something into Sion's ear. The prince's eyes went wide for a moment, and he eyed Keithwood.

"Ah, I see…" he murmured, happening upon some private realization. Nodding, he turned to address the crowd again. "I have just received word that one of the castle guards has been discovered unconscious, likely incapacitated by the intruder we are speaking of."

"What?!"

Various voices of astonishment rose within the crowd. They belonged not only to Sunkland nobles; foreign guests were equally stunned. The rigorous standards to which Sunkland held its soldiers was no secret. Furthermore, these were castle guards, whose allegiance to the king was unshakable. Drawn to the strength of Abram's character, these were people who felt a personal devotion to him and trained tirelessly and passionately to safeguard his well-being.

One of these elite soldiers had been incapacitated—not killed, but rendered completely unthreatening. That alone would speak volumes about the overwhelming skill of the trespasser, but they had somehow also managed to evade discovery while doing it; no other guards reported seeing even a shadow of this mysterious agent.

"As a matter of fact, there were *four* intruders," said Sion, speaking as if he hadn't already ascertained their identities, "and we have no idea how they managed to enter the castle. It's possible they disguised themselves as guests for this occasion. In any case, there is a need for further investigation."

"Does that mean…we'll need to call one of the dukes back from the border?" asked an anxious noble.

The political power balance in the Kingdom of Sunkland was different from that of the Tearmoon Empire, and its structure was shaped by the kingdom's fundamental policies. The goal was for the righteous rule of the king to ensure peaceful and prosperous lives for his people. Given this vision, what was something that couldn't be allowed to exist? Persistently unrighteous rule in areas that, drawn by the promise of a just ruler, had voluntarily incorporated themselves into the kingdom. Such situations would shake the very foundation upon which Sunkland stood. As a result, it was necessary to dispatch the most trusted and competent of rulers to the newest of the kingdom's lands, which lay along its borders.

Thus, it became custom in Sunkland for regions around the capital to be populated by those with personal loyalty to the king while royal relatives and more capable members of the peerage governed the kingdom's frontiers. This also meant that if a crisis ever struck the king, there was a need to recall the powerful nobles to the capital.

"No, that will not be necessary. As I previously stated, His Majesty should be able to return to the usual affairs of government after a few days of rest," said Sion before flashing his audience a wolfish grin. "Besides, revenge is sweetest when delivered personally. I think it's best for His Majesty to direct the investigation and subsequent retaliation himself. Wouldn't you all agree?"

That got the nobles excited.

"Very true, very true! Your Highness is right!"

The statement also calmed the foreign guests, who were glad that, for the moment, no further escalation would occur. Sensing the shift in the hall's atmosphere, Sion then said, "Now then, with things the way they are, we can hardly continue the ball as is. At the same time, it would do our guests a great disservice to have them leave in such an unsatisfactory fashion. To that end, I propose a final event. Consider it both an apology and a closing performance to send everyone on their way."

The prince walked over to his Remno counterpart. "As a matter of fact, I am joined today by my friend, Prince Abel of Remno."

He introduced Abel to the crowd, then donned a stage actor's smile. "Together, we intend to put on a show of our swordsmanship in a bout against each other. We hope this will prove entertaining for you."

At first, this got a few puzzled looks from the Sunkland nobles. Soon, however, they caught on to what they assumed was the point of the performance. Normally, this would be no time for diversions. There were tons of things that needed doing, and though the king was no longer in any immediate danger, it was hardly appropriate for his subjects to immediately begin indulging in entertainment. While protocol called for a sober approach, the problem was how that would *look* to others. An overly cautious attitude would instead foment unease among the guests.

Sion's performance aimed for the opposite effect—to project an abundance of composure and confidence with the implication that Abram was not only of sound health but had the mental wherewithal to attend to the enjoyment of his guests. Or so the nobles assumed. Framed thus, the prince's situationally dissonant attitude was in fact a prudent one. Also, they figured there must be some truth to his nonchalance—that the king was indeed in reasonably good condition. In that case, they might as well relax and enjoy the show the future king was about to put on for them.

The air in the hall began to buzz with energy. Abel regarded the increasingly animated spectators and shook his head. "I know you want to settle this once and for all, but this is one heck of a place to do it. You're more of an exhibitionist than I thought," he quipped wryly as he took off his coat and began rolling up his sleeves.

"There is perhaps a bit of exhibitionism, but mostly, I just figured this would be an excellent opportunity to show everyone how incredibly skilled you are with the sword, my good friend," said Sion.

"Goodness. So this stage is meant for *me*. Well, I'd better try twice as hard so I don't suffer a humiliating defeat."

Abel swung his unsharpened practice sword around a few times and walked to the middle of the hall, where the large open area that had been reserved for dancing now served as a perfect ring.

"Hah, as if you had any intention of losing in the first place." Sion let out a hearty laugh and pointed his own sword at his friend. "All right, then. Like you said, let's settle this once and for all."

Thus, the curtains fell once more, setting the stage for the last scene. The climactic battle drew near...

"Huh?"

...But the heroine, mentally speaking, had barely made it past Act I.

What is Sion trying to show me? wondered Echard.

He couldn't make heads or tails of his brother's actions. Why did he propose a sword duel at a time like this? What was the point of watching him duel this other prince? Sure, everyone would get to see—as if anyone wasn't aware already—how much of a genius he was, but then what? Was this some subtle form of revenge?

Sion Sol Sunkland was a prodigy swordsman. Everyone knew that. His opponent was Prince Abel, a relative nobody in comparison. They were going to watch Sion pummel this poor prince—for the second time, if Echard's memory was correct—into pitiful submission, and *that* was supposed to be his parting gift?

Maybe he is *trying to get back at me or something...*

Was it a show of force to remind Echard who was destined to inherit the throne? To break his will for good? That was the simplest explanation, but it didn't seem like something his brother would do.

What, then? What is *this?*

No answers were forthcoming as he watched the two princes brandish their swords at each other.

"All right. Let's do this," said Abel, his voice bold and composed.

He lifted his sword high above his head and held it there. It was the same overhead stance as always, unchanged, unwavering.

"Still that stance, huh? You've been using it ever since that day during the swordsmanship tournament."

"It's the only one I know. I'd love to switch it up, but unfortunately, I wasn't gifted with your talent or smarts."

Sion grimaced at the comment. "I don't know about that... Talent's one thing, but lately, I'm starting to doubt just how much smarts I actually have..." He let his sword arm drop, keeping it relaxed as he held his blade parallel to the ground in a low stance. "I... will use the same stance as that day."

"Ah. I see... We've crossed swords more than once since then, but I suppose that makes today's bout the official continuation of that match."

"And, there's no rain. Nothing to get in the way. We can fight to our hearts' content. So let us dance this dance to the very end."

At that, the smile vanished from Abel's face. His expression fully sobered. He drew a deep breath, waited a moment, slowly let it out...

"En garde!"

...And with a daunting yell, dashed up for an attack.

It was a familiar sight for the Sunkland nobles. Prince Sion's swordplay had the brilliance of genius. He waited for the offensive and weathered it to gauge the extent of his opponent's abilities before maneuvering them into giving him an opening, which he would promptly exploit. From there, he would dismantle his opponent with expert precision. To witness Sion in battle was to witness domination. He fought with the poise of a king: unshaken, unstirred, ever ready.

It was therefore understandable that the spectating Sunkland nobles were expecting a similar performance. They knew the story. They knew its beats. They needed only to witness it play out again.

Their assumptions didn't even make it past the prologue.

With his very first strike, Abel declared a new narrative. There was no pretension to the stroke, no trickery or innovation. It was simple. Laughably so. Those unlearned in swordplay jeered his inexperience. They saw his dash as the impatience of youth, or perhaps amateur nerves—the hasty reaction of failed composure in the face of a mighty opponent.

Dion Alaia laughed. Not to heckle, however, but to commend. "Mmm... Not bad at all. A sure stroke bespeaks a strong mind. That's the mark of a good swordsman."

As if attesting the truth of his statement, Abel closed the gap with a single lunge, his front leg stretching far before planting itself into the ground with an echoing thud, the momentum concentrating on the edge of his blade as he swung it down toward his opponent.

It was a textbook motion—true to form in every way, except honed to a T. His sword flowed with the smooth grace of water...and struck with the bone-crunching power of a towering cascade.

The sound of clashing metal split ears, raised hairs, and shook the very room. In the stillness that followed, time itself seemed to stop. People held their breaths as the slow realization dawned upon their reeling minds.

This was no diversion.

Having seen Abel's downward stroke countless times, Sion had braced and caught it head-on before pushing into a bind. With their swords locked, he grinned.

"Impressive... Your go-for-broke skull smasher seems to be hitting even harder than before."

"Not hard enough, apparently. I'm trying to get good enough to remove some of the go-for-broke-ness from it, at least so I can reasonably fend off one of those assassins from the other day by myself," said Abel. "Against *you*, though…"

A vein on his temple popped, and he doubled the force on his blade. With all the frightening intensity of a boulder bearing down on a hapless victim, he threw himself against his foe…and smashed into what felt like a brick wall.

Sion did not budge. He met the oncoming force like the mighty ramparts of the castle in which he stood.

Abel, his balance askew from the failed push, stepped back to steady himself. As he withdrew, he preemptively swiped his sword crosswise to prevent a counterattack from Sion. However…

"Getting hasty there, Abel. A recklessly wide swing leaves you open."

The preemptive strike had been further preempted. Sion, having anticipated the retreating attack, moved forward in unison and struck down Abel's outstretched sword.

"Ugh!" Abel grunted. His arms buzzed with shock from the impact, no less devastating than his own crushing blow. In a split second, it all dawned on him. Sion, he realized, desired to throw his naked strength against Abel's. This was to be a duel not of technique but heart, soul, and raw willpower.

"I see… Because Mia's on the line. So this is the kind of fight you want, is it?"

"What other kind will suffice? Would you sincerely concede if I took her from you through finesse and attrition?"

The nonchalant confidence in Sion's voice went beyond mere haughtiness. In his eyes, Abel saw not bravado, but the cold, unshakable will of genius reforged. Of a man whose greatness, once errant, had been refined by pain and experience. And for the first time in a long while, Abel felt true fear.

A petrifying chill shot down his spine, demanding to know how it had been forgotten. How, faced with the physical incarnation of brilliance that was Sion Sol Sunkland, he could have afforded even a drop of insouciance. Was it their training sessions? Their handful of battles fought at each other's backs? Did those justify his undeserved hubris before the goliath, its shadow over him so constant the darkness had begun to slip his mind?

"Sweet steel of heaven… I'd better fight like my life is on the line," he said through gritted teeth.

"Your life," Sion replied, "and more. Fight me like you mean it."

Abel's expression sobered anew.

The battle had only just begun.

Abel tightened his grip on his sword. A breath later, he exploded into motion, attacking with a flurry of his trademark strokes.

Sion met them. No evasion, no parrying. He slammed his sword into each oncoming strike, sending it back with arm-numbing recoil. His grimace darkened with every successive blow. His lips peeled ever more into a pained snarl. But he did not give way.

Against Abel's devastating cascade, Sion exploited no opening, no flaw of stance. He countered barrage with greater barrage.

"Augh…" Abel growled. A blur of swords lashed out at him, colliding with the flesh of his arms and legs. He forced through the squall, the pain, and instead stepped forward.

"I'm not done yet!"

He could afford no retreat. To back down was to prove the superiority of his foe's strength. If he couldn't win through brute force, he couldn't win at all. With that thought hardened, he pressed on.

"Forcing your way through? Think again!"

Sion matched his ferocity, closing their distance farther. For neither combatant was concession an option. The second he'd challenged Abel to this duel, he'd burned all the bridges behind him. There lay only the oblivion of defeat. His mind was set. Forward, and forward. Nothing else. Bracing for grievous injury, he took another step.

Their duel transcended form and technique. It pitched sheer resolve against raw will. Seeing the passion of two princes smash so violently into each other, Dion let out an exhilarated whoop.

"Damn, now that's what I call a fight! So young, these two. Didn't think they'd ditch the fencing manual for a wrestling match with swords, but I like it! Gotta give it to Prince Sion. For all his tricks, he sure can hold his own in a clash. Genius indeed. Still green in my opinion, though."

Dion's commentary made Mia frown.

Sion...doesn't seem to be himself today.

Abel was as straightforward as always, but Sion was fighting him the same way. Sion, who'd always been the infuriatingly unflappable hero of the scene...was, no matter how she looked at it, swinging his sword with reckless, impassioned abandon. She tried to make sense of it, but the more she thought, the more confused she became.

This was, by the way, a new confusion. When the duel first began, she had in fact regained some semblance of rational thought.

Aha, I know what you're doing. You want me to reject your advances in front of everyone.

She'd come up with a whole explanatory scenario in her head. Sion, after beating Abel, would theatrically profess his love for her. She was supposed to turn him down, and in doing so, cheer Echard up. It was a commiseration through mutual tragedy kind of thing. Of course, for this to work...

Wait! Doesn't that mean I have to reject Sion in front of all these people? Sweet moons!

The realization had sent her into a bout of panic. Her stomach had churned uncomfortably at the mere thought of publicly giving Sion the elbow.

How am I supposed to turn down an advance by the prince of Sunkland in his own castle?! Hnnngh... Sion, you nasty, nasty person! You sure gave me one heck of a villain's role to play! I guess you'll never change! Hmph... Honestly, I wish Abel could somehow beat you. It'd be so much easier that way.

But that was mostly just a pipe dream. So, she'd spent most of her time thinking of inoffensive ways to deliver her message when Sion inevitably won. As the duel went on, though, things began to change. She noticed that Sion wasn't his usual self. Furthermore...

"Princess Mia, I implore you to watch milord carefully. His sword, especially, and what he is conveying through it."

She turned toward the voice to find Keithwood standing beside her.

"I've never seen milord lay his emotions bare like that. He fights for you, Princess Mia. Every swing and stroke is a message to you," he said.

That was the deciding moment. Keithwood, most loyal vassal of Sion's, just said so. It must be true.

The way he's fighting, it's as if something important is on the line... And that something...is me? He's fighting Abel for me?

She now knew the truth, and because she did, she could no longer wish so flippantly for Abel's victory. She wanted him to win, of course. That hadn't changed. But to look at Sion and eagerly wish him defeat... That was now beyond her too.

Wh-What is this? Something must be wrong with me. How come my chest feels so tight?

Her heart thumped with bewildering intensity. She wasn't sure when it had last beat this hard. At the guillotine, perhaps. And for good reason, for this was a historic moment.

Mia—yes, *that* Mia—had, in that moment, become an actual heroine! A real, bona fide heroine with princes fighting for her affection! Never before had such a thing happened!

Wh-What am I supposed to do in this situation? Anne... Oh, Anne— Gah! It's Bel and Rina beside me right now. Where's my romantic counselor when I need her?!

While Mia descended into further confusion, the duel continued.

Once, twice, thrice.

Swords clashed, and sparks flew. Every grating ring of impact took with it another piece of the two princes' stamina. Though dulled for practice, the swords were no less weapons, and every hit left its mark on the victim. Injury and fatigue accumulated exponentially through their unrelenting exchange. Yet they continued, the pace of their strikes somehow accelerating until it seemed the blades themselves would shatter. Then, they parted. With baffling concordance, they both drew back.

"Scorching sun... Knowing how you were before...you've come a long way, Abel. Good for you. And I mean that in the best way possible," said Sion, breathing with his shoulders. "I can hardly believe you're the same person."

Abel adjusted his grip on his sword, then shrugged. "Ha ha, I find it hard to believe too. Never would I have imagined myself holding my own against you like this. There's no way I could have gotten here by myself."

"It's her, isn't it?"

"It sure is."

"...Yeah." Sion closed his eyes. "I envy you, Abel."

The words flowed from his lips, and Sion realized they'd been waiting to be said for a long, long time.

So that's why. I'm envious of Abel. Have been for a long time...

The fact that he hadn't realized—hadn't *acknowledged* it—was almost laughable.

I knew I was dense, but this takes the cake... I'm a lot more inept than I thought.

He watched as Abel raised his sword high above his head. It held there in the same position it always did, uncaring of its circumstances. Having discarded everything else, it remained true to its one and singular goal. Just like its holder.

Sion envied its purity. *His* purity.

If only I could have been as single-minded. Maybe then, she'd...

He severed his thoughts with a swing of his blade.

"Let's do this, Abel!"

As he stepped forward, his body plunging toward his opponent, in his mind flashed the faces of his father the king, his mother the queen, his brother Echard, his loyal vassal Keithwood, Count Lampron, the chancellor, and countless nobles, along with countless more of the masses depending on the royal family for their peace and prosperity...

Of course. Sion smiled wryly. *Of course they'd be there...*

The next instant, his sword left his hand.

In the decisive moment, Abel's eyes stared straight at Sion. But Sion couldn't help but feel that they were directed not at him, but *through* him. They were eyes that saw only one thing.

One girl.

He fought for her only, whereas *he* fought for…

That was the difference that decided it all.

The sword, free of its holder, spun through the air before landing on the ground with a stiff clang. Like a bell, it signaled the end of the match, sending a wave of astonished commotion through the hall.

"Sion…lost?" Echard murmured in disbelief.

Sion spared Echard a brief sidelong glance before falling to his knees. He gazed at the floor until a hand appeared in his view. He looked up to find a grimacing Abel.

"Sion, you—"

"If," Sion interjected, holding his gaze, "you say anything to the effect of 'You'd have won if you fought properly, so this doesn't count,' I will *spit* on you."

Before Abel could utter anything in response, Sion continued.

"You and I, we both put something important to us on the line. We fought for it, and I lost. You took victory from me, Abel. I will not let you take my loss as well."

For a long second, they stared at each other. Then Sion's gaze suddenly softened.

"…And that's what we're going with, okay? Work with me here," he whispered.

A panicked Echard rushed up to him soon after.

"Sion…"

"As you can see, I have been defeated." Sion shrugged. "I'm not nearly as perfect as you think I am, Echard. I will fail. I will lose. Even when something important is on the line."

"No, but… Sion…"

Sion shook his head, urging his brother to be still.

"Besides, you were watching, weren't you? You must have seen the moment when Abel's sword trumped mine. He was unquestionably weaker than me. When we first went to Saint-Noel, I couldn't imagine myself losing to him. But he got better. With tireless effort and untold amounts of sweat and toil, he *got better*. And now, he's better than me. That…" Sion looked his brother in the eye. "Is my parting gift to you, Echard. With enough hard work, you can do the same. You can climb to whatever heights you wish, so long as you reach for it. Forget about me, Echard. There are higher, better peaks for you to strive toward. Remember that, and seize your own future."

"Sion…" Echard ducked his gaze.

Sion smiled and switched to a jocular tone. Whether to cheer up his brother or lighten the atmosphere, only he knew.

"With that said, I don't intend to keep losing. Neither to you, nor *you*, Abel."

Abel scratched his head and smiled.

"Sure, we'll fight again. And next time, I'll still win."

The two princes shook hands, and the ballroom exploded with applause. The audience heaped praise upon the two spectacular combatants. Amidst their thunderous cheers, Sion walked toward Mia.

Chapter 24: Someone Perfect for You Is Surely...

"Sion…"

Mia could but stare as Sion, his heart-stopper of a duel concluded, approached her. She was at a loss for words. What could she say? What *was* there to say? Should she comfort him? Angrily question his sanity? Or perhaps…

Flustered and confused, her thoughts spun in futile circles. Eventually, Sion stopped before her and quietly lowered his head. "I apologize, Mia, for using you for my own purposes," he said in a voice barely above a whisper.

"Using me…for your own purposes?"

"Yes. Echard seems to think—mistakenly, of course—that I harbor some form of affection for you. It was, therefore, necessary for my parting gift to him to end in my loss. And a meaningful loss at that. After all, I could hardly impress a life lesson upon him unless I made it look like I was putting something irreplaceably dear to me on the line." He covertly flashed her a grin. "Not too bad a performance, was it? I think I might have the makings of an actor."

"An actor? You were…acting?"

Mia gave a questioning tilt, to which Sion shrugged.

"Indeed, and I've clearly done a brilliant job of it, seeing as I've deceived even you. Unwilling though it might have been, your participation was nevertheless instrumental in making this work, and for that, I owe you my gratitude. Thank you for playing along."

With that, he turned on his heels and began to walk away. The speed with which he did so was, to Mia, telling. She felt the strain behind his nonchalance. A grunt escaped her as clarity dawned at last; she finally knew what it was that she had to do.

What I need to do...is give Sion a good lecturing!

Mia took stock of the situation. Sion's affection for her was very likely real. What did that suggest?

In that case, he must have been sending subtle signals all this time. Probably in a "Hey, I'm free to go on dates for a while, just in case you were wondering" sort of way...

She reasoned that he'd probably been playing the waiting game, hoping for her to make the first move. Unfortunately, that was a method destined to fail. She knew from firsthand experience. In the previous timeline, she'd played the exact same waiting game—with *him* as the target to boot—only to have every single one of her signals ignored.

Subtlety and waiting definitely won't work. After all, Anne said so, and she's my romance tactician. You need to be more direct with your signals. Modesty is still necessary, yes, but you can't let it get in the way of making your feelings understood!

Instead, Sion was trying to put an end to his feelings for her. That in itself was fine; the problem was his framing. To him, he was giving up on his love for the sake of his brother. That *wasn't* fine, because it muddled the cause of his romantic disappointment. His love remaining unrequited was in no way because of his brother. It was because he himself had made no serious attempt to approach her!

Granted, I already have Abel, so it wouldn't have worked out for him even if he did approach me properly. But if he keeps going about his romantic pursuits like this, he'll never get anywhere with anyone.

She knew well the words he needed to hear, for they were the same ones she'd heard when confronting her own past failures. In her case, it was Anne who'd pointed out her mistakes, allowing her to recognize that Sion's former frosty attitude toward her was the result of her own actions. Now, it was her turn. She had to tell him that his method was wrong. That no amount of wordless waiting would earn him the attention of his love. It was imperative that she hear his confession clearly and earnestly before turning him down. Otherwise, he would doubtlessly repeat his mistake in the future. Again and again, faced with the inevitable indifference of those he secretly adored, he would quietly nip the sprouting buds of his own loves, mistakenly judging his imperceptible advances rebuffed. Over time, that would surely leave his heart broken and, thus, vulnerable to manipulation by the Serpents.

That was an outcome she had to prevent at all costs!

As someone who has walked the brambled path of romance before...it is my duty to educate him!

Mia was, after all, a grown woman. Technically. As an experienced adult, she had an obligation to aid this young boy lost in love and show him the way.

Well, that's what she thought, anyway.

"Sion Sol Sunkland," she said, the tone of her voice stopping him in his tracks, "if you wish to thank me, then do not try to humor me with excuses."

Sion spun back toward her in surprise.

"If you have something to say," she continued, "then say it. Speak with your heart, so that I may answer with mine as well!"

"I..."

For a long second, silent astonishment filled his eyes. Then, he regained his usual composure.

"Hah... Fair enough. So be it." He quietly dropped to one knee before looking up at her. "In that case, Princess Mia, may I have your hand?" he asked, his voice ever so graceful.

She complied, holding out her hand to him. He took it in his and, ever so gently, placed his other on top, as if cradling a sacred artifact. Then...

"Forgive my heart, Your Highness..."

He touched his lips to the back of her hand and planted the tenderest of kisses.

"For it is hopelessly drawn to you. You are the object of my earnest affection. Would you be willing to requite my love?"

"Sion..."

Faced with the prince's confession, its ornate phrasing not entirely masking the awkward innocence underneath, Mia reached for her adult composure. She reached and reached, digging deep within, only to find it...completely gone!

"I-I h— Hem, ahem..."

She choked on her own spit. The adorably clumsy confession of an adorably handsome boy hit her heart with the force of a catapult.

C-Calm down! I need to calm down! she thought, rushing to pick up the pieces of her shattered composure. *Wh-What I need to do now is... Turn him down! Yes, that's it. I need to turn him down. A quick no. That's all it takes.*

Her mind refocused, she looked him in the eyes and...saw the intensity of his gaze. Suddenly, the duel she'd just witnessed replayed itself in her mind. There'd been no acting there. No deception. They'd fought each other with every ounce of their strength. All for *her.* In that moment, she realized that a quick no would not suffice. There was *weight* to Sion's confession, and it deserved a response of equal sobriety. Anything less would...be wrong. Or it'd make her feel very guilty, at least, and her chicken heart definitely didn't have the constitution to live with that kind of burden.

She drew a small breath and reorganized her thoughts. Then, she prepared to speak. Slowly. Carefully. But...

"Sion... Your duel with Abel was breathtaking. It really was..."

The words that left her lips came naturally, without conscious selection. She found herself commending his duel.

"Losing wasn't part of the plan, though," he said with a wry smile.

Mia shook her head. "It was still a wonderful duel, Sion. Just like yourself... You are a wonderful person."

Those were her true, unfiltered thoughts. For the first time in her life, she recognized, truly and honestly, that Sion was a wonderful individual. In this moment, after the conclusion of their duel, she finally found herself cognizant of his charm...and willing to admit it. She thought of how he'd dueled, relinquishing his characteristic swordplay to match Abel's guileless technique. She recalled how he'd leaped into a river to save her from drowning, how he'd stood against the wolfmaster to protect her, and how he'd erred, recognized his error and, despite the pain and guilt, still tried to keep moving forward...

In the previous timeline, Mia had known only his outward elegance. Now, she saw the true charisma it masked. And she couldn't help but think...what if?

What if something had been just a little different? Might she have fallen for him? Had she mustered the courage in her former life to take that crucial first step...and approach him not as the haughty princess of a mighty empire, but her honest, unaffected self... Could the two of them have shared a future?

No point contemplating that now... What I need to do is answer him. Properly.

She drew one last breath, allowed her nerves to calm, and regarded him anew.

"You are a wonderful person, Sion. That's why...I'm sure you'll find a more suitable partner," she said, hearkening back to the words she'd once spoken at a dance party. "A partner...more befitting you than myself."

Only this time, she *meant* it. Somewhere out there was a person perfect for Sion, and he would surely find that person. It was her honest wish, made with all the best of intentions. It was also a parting gift. From her, to him.

"...I see." Sion's lips tightened into a smile. "Very well. They're your words, after all. I'll...try my best to believe them."

With that, he walked off.

"Prince Sion..."

A pair of eyes watched him go, their brows furrowed with worry. They belonged to...

Chapter 25: As King and as Father

Let us turn back the clock a little.

Left alone with the king in his chamber, Tiona regarded him with no small amount of apprehension. "Um… Your Majesty?"

"My apologies for keeping you, Miss Rudolvon, but I wished to formally express my gratitude," said Abram as he respectfully lowered his head. "Thank you for stopping me earlier. You have saved not only my life, but Echard's as well."

"That's not— I, um…was just at the right place at the right time." Tiona backed away a step as she shook her hands furiously.

"I see… Still, just as bad deeds must be punished, good deeds must be rewarded. Such is the foundation upon which justice rests. If there is anything I can offer you as recompense…"

"N-No, that's not necessary at all."

"You needn't be modest. Simply speak your desires. Should no object interest you, then maybe some knowledge would? Is there something you wish to know, perhaps?"

This caused Tiona's shoulders to twitch.

Seeing her response, Abram smiled. "During the discussion, I noticed that you seemed a tad restless, as if there was something you wished to say. Or ask. Do you have any questions for me?"

Tiona made no reply.

"There are no ears here except ours, Miss Rudolvon. What is said in this room shall stay in this room. Even if you divulge it to someone by accident, so long as I do not admit it, it will not spread far. So go ahead. You are free to speak your mind."

Few would believe the words of a mere outcount's daughter if pitted against the denial of a king. In a he-said-she-said situation, Abram's advantage was absolute. In that sense, it opened the floor to questions of a less comfortable nature. She could inquire more pointedly, and he could answer with relative candor.

Tiona understood his intent.

"In that case," she said, looking back toward him, "I *do* have a question. Your Majesty, am I correct in assuming that you noticed when Prince Echard slipped something into the drink?"

It'd all happened in a split second, but Tiona hadn't missed it. She'd seen the grim look on Abram's face when he shot the briefest of glances at Echard.

Her question elicited a grimace from the king.

"You have sharp eyes, Miss Rudolvon... You are correct. I did indeed notice that the boy had put something into Sion's drink. I certainly did not expect it to be a lethal poison though... I assumed it was some sort of prank, and I intended to lecture him about why he shouldn't do such things."

"I thought so... Then, what about how you almost fell off the balcony? Was that on purpose?"

"Falling from the balcony would have obfuscated my cause of death, making it impossible to determine whether it was an accident or a poisoning. For most poisons, that is. Obviously, in this particular case, the facial symptoms of shadowbane would have become apparent sooner or later."

Abram had been trying to cover for his son. Tiona felt a wave of gladness at the realization. At the same time, it raised another question.

"I see. Then… Your Majesty, did you really intend on sentencing Echard to death?"

The king's actions were not lining up. It was as if there were two Abrams: one who could put his son to death without batting an eye, and another who was willing to kill himself to keep his son alive.

"It is true that Echard never *wished* to lethally poison me, but the fact of the matter is that he *did*, and the penalty for poisoning the king is surely death. Such an act risks throwing the entire kingdom into chaos. Therefore, it deserves the most severe of punishments. Such logic is not only just and fair, but should go without saying. Am I right?"

He certainly was. In any normal circumstance, his decision would be irrefutably sound.

"Arbitrary judgment of guilt undermines the king's justness, and the undermining of a king's justness results in the suffering of his people," said Abram with solemn conviction. Then, he added, "Of course, that logic only holds when it is the *king* that we are talking about."

"When it's the king? You mean…" At that, the dots connected, and Tiona realized the true nature of Abram's actions. "You…were going to abdicate? And have Prince Sion take the throne?"

"More accurately, I was going to *have already abdicated*. The official stance would have been that Sion had become king before the ball started. That way, Echard's transgression would be less severe. Furthermore, amnesty is often granted during the crowning of a new king, which could save Echard from the death penalty."

"But…what about the coronation ceremony? How can Prince Sion succeed the throne if that hasn't happened yet?"

The coronation ceremony was what informed local nobles and nearby kingdoms of the crowning of a new king. Normally, it was during the ceremony that the title officially passed from the previous king to the next. Given this dynamic, a secret succession behind closed doors seemed impossible.

Abram, however, shook his head at Tiona's inquiry. "A careful look through history will reveal that the coronation ceremony is not as ancient a tradition as many assume. The only rite that is absolutely necessary for a new king to take the throne is anointment by a priest of the Central Orthodox Church."

The legitimacy of all sovereignties in the continent were rooted in the Central Orthodox Church's Holy Book. According to its teachings, the Lord entrusted to kings the task of governing their lands. Therefore, the one observance those who inherit a throne must follow was to complete their anointment, through which they were granted their authority by the Lord. The process involved having oil, representing the blessing of God, applied to their head, thereby infusing them with the holy mandate to govern.

In terms of scale, anointment was actually a fairly small affair, and there had been plenty of instances throughout history when it had been conducted in secret.

"Fortunately for us, there just so happens to be someone here who is the equivalent of a priest of the Central Orthodox Church. More than equivalent, in fact."

"Miss Rafina…"

The Holy Lady was currently present. Therefore, so long as they coordinated their statements, it was perfectly possible for her to have anointed Sion before the ball. That gave them a chance to save Echard.

"You almost *abdicated*…to save Prince Echard…"

"Attempting to rescind Echard's death sentence without eroding the legitimacy of the throne is an inherently unreasonable endeavor.

I could hardly afford to be reserved in my means. If anything, I think abdication is almost too small a price to pay for the privilege I intended to exercise," the king said, his voice gradually gaining the soft breathiness of introspection. "Especially considering…I bear no small amount of blame for pushing Echard to the brink. As a father."

"Your Majesty…"

"To uphold justice as a king and to love my sons as a father… At times, the two are mutually exclusive. At that moment, with the kingdom and Echard in the balance, I reached for my son. It was the right thing to do as a father, but it damaged my legitimacy as king. Surely, that is reason enough to surrender the crown, don't you think?"

At that, Abram laughed.

"I must admit, though," he continued, "the Great Sage of the Empire's acumen far surpassed my own. Had this fiasco not occurred, I would have remained blind to Echard's struggles, likely leading him to make another such attempt at some point in the future. Left to his own devices, it might very well have been a matter of time before he ended up committing the grave sin of fratricide. What she accomplished…wove past the countless ways in which this could have ended in tragedy and led us to the best conclusion one could possibly fathom."

The quiet profundity of his tone suggested he was deeply moved.

Tiona nodded. "Yes. That's what Her Highness does. That's… the kind of person she is." She couldn't help but feel a tinge of pride at the fact that her dear friend had garnered King Abram's approval.

"Again, I apologize for keeping you. I had only intended to answer any questions you might have, but I seem to have subjected you to my idle ramblings instead."

"No, I appreciate it. Thank you…for giving me the chance to ask."

Abram gently smiled and lowered his head once more. "Thank you too, Miss Rudolvon. Princess Mia has done me a great favor, but so have you. Your denouncement of my failure to protect my family… It is something I needed to hear. And I am glad I heard it. You have my gratitude."

Tiona stepped out of the king's chamber. As she walked down the hallway, her pace quickened. A single thought filled her mind. She pondered—could do nothing *but* ponder—the solitude of the throne.

Kings, she realized, were so utterly, excruciatingly lonely. The more King Abram tried to be just and righteous, the more he was forced to relinquish his humanity. In her eyes, the crown seemed not a glory but a burden, isolating its wearer from those around him. And that wearer, for now, was Abram, but would one day be…

Sion leaped into her eyes as she entered the ballroom. His duel with Abel was just reaching its climax.

Chapter 26: The Night When Love Was Lost

Sion walked off. A pair of eyes watched him go. They belonged to…

Tiona Rudolvon, who soon hurried after him.

Having walked in on the climax of the princes' duel, she'd witnessed its heart-stopping conclusion. Her gaze trailed Sion as he, following his defeat, departed the ballroom. The next thing she knew, she was outside the ballroom as well, her steps tracing the same path he'd taken earlier.

No one had dared speak to Sion, much less keep him. Not Mia nor Abel. Not Echard either. Such was the seclusive aura Sion exuded, so strong it kept even his most loyal of subjects, Keithwood, from uttering so much as a word.

It didn't stop Tiona. Not even for a second.

A sense of urgency pushed her forward. She had to approach him. Speak to him. Before she knew it, she'd broken into a run. In any other circumstance, sprinting through the castle would have immediately earned her a scolding by the nearest guard. In fact, she caught the attention of plenty of patrols during her dash. Fortunately, they'd seen her helping Abram into his chamber, so her behavior, rather than rousing suspicion, earned her gestures of gratitude as she rushed by. Some even pointed her toward the direction Sion had gone.

Guided by their advice, she rounded corner after corner and turned from path to path. Eventually, she found herself at the entrance to a watchtower. Shadow and gloom welcomed her as she walked in. Carefully, she made her way up its helical stone stairs. Then, all of a sudden, the stony walls fell away, and moonlight fell on her face.

She'd reached the top. Stepping out into the open air, she looked around and discovered Sion at the edge of the platform. His arms and chest rested against the rocky parapet, and his eyes were distant as he gazed at—or perhaps past—the sprawling townscape.

"Prince Sion…"

"Who's there?!"

He spun with a sharp cry of alarm, his whole form tensing before the sight of the speaker prompted him to relax. "Ah… Miss Tiona. What brings you to a place like this? Did you get lost?"

He gave his head a curious tilt, his lips curling into his usual friendly smile. Tiona did not follow suit. She looked him straight in the eye.

"Why did you fight like that?"

"Ah, so you saw my duel. Ha ha, not my proudest of moments, I must say. I'm sorry you had to witness—"

"Were you *trying* to lose?"

For the briefest of moments, Sion froze. Then, his expression sobered, and he shook his head.

"That would do Abel a great disservice. I fought with everything I had, and I lost. That's all there is to it."

"But you could have fought differently. If you were only trying to win, you could have fought around Prince Abel's strength instead of directly against it. But you didn't… Why?"

"You know, your behavior today has made me realize that you're surprisingly…" Sion paused, then let out a soft sigh. "Were it a simple contest of swordplay, you would be right. There would certainly be a way for me to win. But…such a win would have been pointless. Call me self-absorbed if you want, but that wasn't a simple contest. Not for me. That…was a trial. A test of my spirit and soul. My love for Mia against everything I will shoulder as king," he said with a pained chuckle. "And guess which way the scales tipped? I couldn't let go of everything."

A flicker of light from the townscape danced across his brow. He turned toward it, gazing at the myriad streets and dwellings below.

"My father and my mother. Echard. Keithwood. Count Lampron. The royal attendants. The castle guards. And all the people—*my* people—who live down there… I couldn't let them go."

Tiona followed his gaze. Moonlight streamed down on the town. Within its silver silhouette, she saw countless figures moving to and fro. For a brief moment, she thought she could see each and every one of their faces. She felt their joys and sorrows, and the sheer presence of life—*lives*—gathered there.

"That's why I lost to Abel," said Sion. "He was pure. He fought for Mia and Mia only. I couldn't. There was…too much on my shoulders."

What might have happened had he won against Abel? There would have been no salvation for Echard. Furthermore, following through on his pursuit of Mia would likely have required Sion to forsake his kingdom.

He hadn't done so. Sion had chosen the opposite—to remain true to his duty as the next King of Sunkland. He had a responsibility to his people. To rule them justly and fairly, and to safeguard the peace and security of this land. It was a responsibility he bore earnestly, and one he had no intention or wish of abandoning.

There was a loftiness to him that reminded Tiona of his father, King Abram. She saw in Sion the same high-minded nobility, as virtuous as it was tragic, and she couldn't help but speak. But before she could find her voice...

"That's how it was supposed to play out, anyway..." Sion let out a deep sigh, and the ambience of their conversation noticeably changed. "But Mia didn't let it. She saw right through me."

"...Huh?" Tiona frowned at him, baffled by his statement.

"She refused to let me blame my actions on anything else," he said, shoulders slumping in defeat. "Not on king and country, nor on duty and responsibility. She made me confess my love to her properly...and turned me down. Knowing her, she was probably worried that an ambiguous end to my feelings for her would sow within me the seeds of bitterness, eventually causing me to resent my own kingdom. In that sense, I understand why she forced my hand. It must have been hard for her... But by the sun high above, I swear it's even harder for me..."

The sight of a dejected Sion visibly feeling sorry for himself tickled something in Tiona, and she heard herself say, "You know, Prince Sion, I never knew you could be..."

"Hm? Could be what?"

"So adorably kiddish."

"I—"

Sion choked on his words, causing Tiona to burst into a laugh. The rare crack in his armor of perfection afforded her a glimpse of the person underneath, and she found his vulnerability... delightfully endearing.

"Wow, you didn't have to laugh… In case it wasn't clear, I *did* just have my heart broken, you know?"

"Yes, yes, I'm sorry," said Tiona between giggles. "But it's just…"

Suddenly, she realized, inspired by her own laughter, the significance of what Mia had done. She'd taken Sion and pulled him from a king back into a man. The person standing before Tiona right now was no sovereign icon of justice—he was but a boy. An entirely human boy who'd had his heart broken by the girl he loved.

Her Highness…is so incredible. Tiona silently mouthed a heartfelt statement of admiration for her princess.

Mia, seeing that Sion was struggling with the strangulating obligations of his station, ripped from him all his masks and appearances, leaving him a mere boy. Having stumbled in love, he would hurt as a boy and then pick himself back up. Not as an aspiring king but as a boy. That, Tiona thought, had to be a good thing. But…

"Now then, Miss Tiona… Assuming my romantic travails have sufficiently amused you, could you leave me be? I would appreciate some time alone to compose myself," said Sion.

As he spoke those words, it was as if he'd aged in the blink of an eye, his face gaining a sudden air of maturity. His boyishness, so endearing mere moments before, was nowhere to be found, now replaced by a cold calmness that forbade approach. It was, she realized, the face of a king. Of someone who divulged no worries and showed no weakness. Someone whose heart and all its afflictions were his and his alone to suffer.

There stood once again the proud, lonely king.

But…she just pulled him back…

The thought urged her forward. She stepped toward him. His aloofly regal aura, his position as the crown prince of Sunkland, not to mention his direct appeal for solitude... There were a million reasons for her to leave. She heeded *none*. With unwavering stubbornness, she pushed her hands straight through them.

Sion was right there in front of her. Within reach. So she reached. He was hurting, and she'd managed to be here for him. What more reason did she need? Her mind set, she closed the last bit of distance and...

"Tiona? What—?"

His bewildered voice faded into her chest. She embraced him like a mother would a child. Or, perhaps, a sister would a heartbroken brother.

"What...is the meaning of this?"

Within his voice, she heard the flustered innocence of youth. It drew from her a breath of relief.

A long moment later, she answered.

"My little brother… He's fallen for Her Highness as well."

"Hm? I…see?" said Sion, baffled by her response.

"But," she continued, "his is also a hopeless love. Someday, it'll surely break his heart. So for a long time, I've been thinking…about how to comfort him when the time comes."

She'd thought and thought, wondering how she could cheer Cyril up when his crush inevitably hurt him. But no answer came. How could it? Tiona herself had never been in love. In the end, her conclusion had been…to hug him. And if he cried, cry with him. Ultimately, all she could do was to simply *be there for him*.

"But I'd like to get some practice beforehand. So if you don't mind…"

"Uh, I *do* mind, actually. Specifically, I don't appreciate being treated like a child, so—"

"When was your birthday, Prince Sion?"

"…About ten days ago?"

His answer elicited another giggle from her. "Well, mine was in spring, so I'm older. That makes me the big sister here, and when little brothers are feeling down, I think it's their job to let their big sisters comfort them."

"That's…nonsense," said Sion, his voice exasperated.

Tiona agreed. Even she thought what she said was nonsense. Nevertheless, she couldn't just leave Sion on his own like this, or she'd regret it for the rest of her life. How she knew that, she had no idea, but she did.

"Besides, there's nothing to worry about. I'm just an outcount's daughter. Even if someone tries to spread some weird rumors, no one will take them seriously."

"That's…nonsense…" Sion said again, his voice growing pensive before dropping to the softest whisper, "You…are surprisingly pushy, Tiona. So much so that it's very hard not to take you seriously…"

A third figure let out a deep sigh.

Praise the sun… Looks like my job has been done for me…

Keithwood smiled privately as he watched the two from afar.

It's nice that he's found a friend he can be vulnerable around… And I'd like to keep it that way. Despite what Miss Rudolvon said, this is definitely a scene that needs to be kept private. I guess I'll head back down the tower and play door guard for a bit…

Ever the loyal workhorse, the night of Keithwood was long, and it had only just started.

As for Mia, what was she up to during this time?

"Hmm… All this relief is making me hungry. I wonder if there's anything to eat around here… Where did that cookie go…?"

With the spectacle concluded, guests had begun to leave. She scratched her head and scanned the emptying ballroom.

"That's a good point. We weren't able to have much of a dinner, were we?" said Rafina. "How about we head to my room for a light meal? With plenty of desserts, of course."

"My, is that really okay, Miss Rafina?" Mia's expression brightened immediately. "In fact, I was just thinking I should thank the people at the inn. I do believe the juice that Anne brought was from them, after all."

"Perfect. Also, we should ask around and see if anyone wants to come along. Miss Esmeralda…might be occupied, but Miss Citrina and Miss Bel are certainly welcome to join us. Miss Anne as well, of course. We should probably meet up with Miss Tiona too."

Thus, it was decided that the after-party would be held in Rafina's room at the inn. The night of Mia and the girls was also long, and you can bet it wasn't going to end any time soon.

Chapter 27: The Brothers Embark

A few days after the incident at the heart of Sunkland, a public statement was put out, announcing that Prince Echard would head abroad to study at Saint Mia Academy. The official reason was to aid in the initial preparation for the Mianet, an extensive project spanning multiple kingdoms whose purpose was to rid the continent of famine. As the story went, King Abram expressed great interest in the project after learning about its noble ideal and declared that as a matter of policy, Sunkland would proactively participate in its organization. To that end, he arranged for the Second Prince, Echard, to study abroad in the Tearmoon Empire with the eventual goal of taking part in the Mianet's operations.

The announcement was initially met with some resistance by the conservative nobles who had been trying to prop Echard up, but the king's resolve was firm, and their protests ultimately proved powerless. This arrangement necessitated the postponement of Echard's marriage with the daughter of Duke Greenmoon, Esmeralda, which ruffled some feathers as well, but Count Lampron and the chancellor managed to smooth them out. In the end, Echard, with all the haste of an escapee, left for Tearmoon in Greenmoon's carriage. As it trundled off, he turned to give his fading home one last, longing look. Seeing his wistful expression, Esmeralda gently spoke to him.

"Don't worry. You'll be back. I know it might feel lonely for a while, but there's no need to brood. As soon as I can, I'll bring you here to Sunkland again," she said, figuring young boys of his age would surely be missing their parents.

Echard, however, shook his head. "No... Thank you for your concern, Miss Esmeralda, but I won't be returning. Not to Sunkland. There is something I must do," he replied, expression stiff, "and it is penance." After a pause, he looked up at her with eyes far too mature for his age. "That, with your gracious leave, is what I will seek in this arrangement."

Esmeralda regarded him, regarded his tight-lipped restraint, and felt...sorry for the boy. It made her heart ache. Which was why...

"No, Your Highness. You're wrong."

...She explicitly rebutted his claim with a solemn shake of her head and explained, "You have no need to do penance...because you have already been forgiven."

"...Huh?" The young prince frowned, puzzled.

She smiled at him. "It's all right. You can relax. There's no further punishment for you in store. After all, who can possibly carry out your death sentence? They would have to come all the way to find you, capture you, and bring you back to Sunkland. Do you think I would allow that? And not only me, but my dear friend Miss Mia? No, Your Highness. We won't ever permit such a thing to happen."

As she spoke, she could feel the logic falling into place piece by piece. Indeed, Echard's sentence was as good as null. For all intents and purposes, he'd been pardoned. Even if he wasn't capable of distinguishing himself by the time his reprieve expired, he would face no penalty. Whatever wrongs he'd committed, they'd be nothing more than artifacts of a bygone era. To resurrect his old sins would be beyond cruel, and Mia would hardly allow it. In fact, the suspension of his sentence that day in the royal chamber was very much an unspoken declaration of his amnesty.

"But... But then, what am I...?" Uncertainty entered Echard's eyes. He began to look around as if he were lost.

With her words, Esmeralda proceeded to point him forward. "Your Highness, you shan't face any further punishment. There is no need to feel pressured to make amends. You've been forgiven, so you should live like you're forgiven."

"Live...like I'm forgiven?"

"That's right. Miss Mia has forgiven you. So has His Majesty, and so has your brother. Think about how Prince Sion sent you off. He risked life and limb for that performance. Did that seem like the kind of parting gift he'd give to a sinner awaiting punishment? Absolutely not. That was a gesture of expectation. He has forgiven you, and on top of that, he's eagerly waiting to see you grow into a fine young man. The most you can do in return...is to show him exactly that, isn't it?"

The more she said, the more it made sense. If anything, it was ridiculous that she was only realizing now. This was Mia they were talking about. Would someone like her ever condemn someone to eternal penance? A life lived only to make up for past wrongs? Certainly not. Such cruelty was beyond her. How, then, would she hope to have Echard live? And what role did she expect of Esmeralda, having entrusted her with the young prince's future guidance?

She pondered, and slowly, she spoke. "How you should live, Your Highness...is to take the fact that you were saved by Miss Mia, and wear it proudly."

"Proudly..."

"That's right. To live with your eyes down and your back hunched, in constant fear of a sword over your head... Such a craven approach to life hardly befits someone blessed by Miss Mia's benevolence. You should follow her example and live with your head held high. It is my belief that only people who have pride in themselves can accomplish things that they're proud of."

For Esmeralda, that was also how a spouse befitting her should live. She had extremely high standards for husbands.

"That is how *I* hope you will choose to live, and I have no doubt Miss Mia feels the same. Should you do so, know that we will support you with all our heart and soul," she concluded, taking Echard's hands in hers and giving them a firm squeeze.

"U-Um… Thank you very much…"

There was a bashfulness to his voice that, at last, reflected his callow age.

After seeing off the departing carriage, Sion went to see Abram.

"Excuse me, father. There is something I wish to discuss with you."

"Is there? Go ahead, then."

Despite recovering from the poison, Abram had complied with the physician's advice to rest for ten days and temporarily withdraw from his official duties.

Sion eyed his father, who was seated comfortably in his chair with a book in his hand, and spoke. "The incident with Echard gave me a lot to reflect on…and I have some thoughts I'd like you to hear."

Abram quietly met his gaze and, ever so slowly, closed his book. "Very well. Let's hear them."

It was as if the room's air doubled in weight. In the span of a breath, Abram's aura changed from that of a father to a king. Sion drew in a breath, willing his nerves to calm, and slowly pushed it back out before continuing.

"Your Majesty, I..." he said, explaining in a voice steady but soft, "I wish to be—to remain—a man."

What was required to pass judgment that was fair and just? The expulsion of all personal feelings and interest. In that moment ten days ago, the onus that had befallen Sion was to judge Echard not as his brother, but as someone who had done wrong. A person—a *criminal*—the same as any other.

There had once been a Sion who would have done so without a second thought. To that Sion, it would have been natural and proper. As one who bore the weight and authority of the crown, such was simply his duty.

That Sion was no more, because he'd learned. He now *knew* that he was far from perfect. The current Sion was lacking too much to realize the ideals of justice and fairness. What was he to do then? Expunge every last piece of humanity from himself to become the ultimate embodiment of justice?

He'd deliberated long and hard, grappling with conflicting thoughts. In the end, the conclusion he arrived at was...

"I wish to become a king...who rules as a man. One who knows that man will err."

That was his answer.

"You wish to rule as a fallible king...who admits his fallibility?" asked Abram.

Sion nodded. "Is that not what it means for man to rule man?"

"I see... So that is the Sunkland you envision..." Abram exhaled through pursed lips, then closed his eyes. When he opened them again, they were fixed on Sion.

"If so...then what you need, Sion, is to create a system that rights the king's wrongs," Abram said, his voice imbued with a regal gravity.

"A system…that rights the king's wrongs?"

"Indeed. If you admit the fallibility of kings…and wish to become such a king, then a system must be in place to right your wrongs and uphold justice."

"What kind of system might that be?"

Sion's question was met with a narrowing of Abram's eyes and a stern reply.

"How should I know? That is for *you* to figure out. Struggle. Search. Plead. Impose on and indebt yourself to those close to you. That is your way of man, is it not?"

A gasp escaped Sion. Silently, he lowered his head.

"Good friends are a blessing," said Abram. "And yours, doubly so, aren't they?"

Slowly, but surely, Sion nodded. "Yes… Irreplaceably so."

The smile that spread across his lips was endlessly tender.

That night, Abram tapped his glass against his wife's. Though brief, they both made time to enjoy a bottle of fine wine in each other's company. Within their shared sip was an unspoken celebration of Sion's growth, as well as a wish for Echard to have a safe journey.

Side Chapter: Mialogy
–Ludwig's Unpalatably Delicious Wine–

Saint Mia Academy successfully wrapped up its third day of lectures.

Mialogy turned out to be a difficult class for Ludwig to teach. The difficulty was perhaps inevitable, considering how the object of the field of study, Mia Luna Tearmoon, was an extremely multifaceted person. Sometimes, she could exude kindness rivaling a saint, while other times, she could exhibit flashes of solemn but profound insight. Then, just as one thought they got a handle on her, she would surprise them with her unique humor before morphing into a sweet, guileless girl to perform an absolutely angelic dance. Those who assumed cold, unflappable calculation was the core of her person would find themselves dumbfounded by her displays of extreme courage that bordered on reckless as they watched her charge boldly into unspeakable dangers.

The only thing certain about her was her deeply human charisma. However, the way her facets often contradicted each other made it hard to present a complete picture of that charisma. Should Ludwig overly focus on any single facet, he would risk misleading his students.

For example, if he emphasized her serious side, the children who came from orphanages would likely become scared of her. Conversely, highlighting her abundant kindness risked trivializing her in the eyes of young nobles. Finding the right balance was exceedingly difficult. However...

"That was a pretty good lecture I gave today."

The episode he unveiled was one where Mia's quick wits and sense of humor shined. It was one of his favorites, and the students quickly took to it, leading him to speak with ever increasing enthusiasm.

Now, with his duties for the day concluded, he was enjoying a late lunch in the academy's cafeteria while savoring the lingering exhilaration of his lecture.

"Ah, Mr. Ludwig. There you are."

Hearing his name, Ludwig turned toward the voice to find a familiar face.

"Oh? What a pleasant surprise it is to meet you here, Mr. Cyril," he said, lowering his head in a deep bow toward the young researcher, Cyril Rudolvon. Not only was he the younger brother of Mia's friend, Tiona, and one of the leading botanists in the empire, he was arguably the savior of the whole continent. "I just happened to mention your sister in today's lecture."

"You mentioned Tiona? Oh, I know... It's that story, isn't it? You sure do love telling it," Cyril said with a resigned chuckle. "We Rudolvons sure have gained a good deal of fame thanks to that particular episode. It's even led to us becoming one of Her Imperial Majesty's closest associates. Who would have thought such a thing was possible? Certainly not me, and not my father either."

"Indeed. After meeting Her Imperial Majesty, all our lives have taken a good many unexpected turns."

A period of friendly catching-up ensued, after which Ludwig noticed the bottle in Cyril's hand.

"By the way, if you don't mind me asking, what might that be?"

"Oh, this?" Cyril held up the bottle, the motion causing the clear liquid inside to swish audibly. "This...is a new type of alcoholic beverage that I'm developing."

"An alcoholic beverage, you say?" Ludwig frowned.

In the empire, the term "drinking" was typically associated with wine. In fact, Ludwig had just received a report about the new infusion of technological know-how from Perujin Agricultural Country leading to an increasing number of nobles starting up private vineyards. It was a welcome development, for it signaled that more and more people were being liberated from anti-agriculturalism. In that sense, he could see how Saint Mia Academy might want to dip its metaphorical toes into wine research as well...but was it so important as to require the attention of a researcher of Cyril's caliber?

His evident confusion prompted Cyril to grin. "Have I piqued your interest? If so, would you like to come with me to take a look? I'm making it right here in the academy. At a certain facility."

"Very well. Do educate me." His spectacles glinting with curiosity, Ludwig rose from his seat.

Ludwig was led to Cyril's research lab, which stood on the periphery of the academy's grounds.

"So...this is where you do your work?" he asked, looking around.

For the laboratory of the botanical prodigy, Cyril Rudolvon, whose discovery of cold-resistant wheat rid the continent of famine, the room was...a tad odd.

No offense to Cyril, but this looks more like the inside of a witch's hut from some fairy tale than a research lab...

A massive metallic cauldron sat in the middle of the room. A tube extended from the gaping mouth, snaking its way into a bottle some distance away.

"I assume this is...some sort of research equipment?"

Ludwig was widely known to be an erudite individual. Thanks to his lengthy studies under the wiseman of the forest, Galv, he was well-versed in most scholarly pursuits of his era. However, the contraption before him was apparently of *too* specialized a nature for even him, as he couldn't make heads or tails of it.

And the surprises didn't end there.

"What the—? Is that a mountain of potatoes?!"

A glance at a corner of the room revealed a large wooden basket filled with dozens, maybe hundreds of potatoes. He walked over, picked one up, and examined it with a frown.

"These are…half-moon potatoes?"

"You know what they are?" Cyril's eyes lit up. "Your knowledge is truly encyclopedic, Mr. Ludwig. I didn't expect you to recognize these."

"I certainly know what they are…"

Ludwig's frown deepened as he tried to imagine to what end Cyril had accumulated this heap of tubers. Half-moon potatoes grew ubiquitously throughout the empire. On top of being astringent and bitter, they contained a mild poison that disturbed the bowels if consumed raw. The prevailing opinion was that they were unsuitable to eat. As far as he knew, they had no appreciable utility that was worth the effort of harvest.

"But *why* are they here? And in such numbers?" he asked.

"As a matter of fact, I'm trying to make alcohol using these very potatoes."

"Using half-moon potatoes?" Ludwig's eyes widened. "Why in the world would you want to do that? They're easy to obtain, I suppose, but…"

Admittedly, given that they were an agricultural nuisance, it would be great to find some use for them.

"That's *exactly* why. Half-moon potatoes are incredibly resilient. You can always find them, even during years of poor harvest. The prospect of making alcohol from this widely available crop was too intriguing to pass up. And while they contain some poison, it is neutralized by the process of distillation, so the resulting alcohol is harmless to consume."

"I see. One will at least be able to drink when there is little to eat, then... I can't say I find the idea of using alcohol to fend off hunger very appealing, but— Actually, hold on..." His grimace soon grew thoughtful as his well-trained mind reminded him to broaden his thinking. The utility of alcohol was not to be underestimated.

Strong drink buoyed the spirit and allowed for a temporary escape from distress. The despair of famine was all-encompassing. When there was nowhere to run, the ability to forget—even for a brief span of time—was certainly not without its merits.

"On second thought, I suppose the idea *does* have some merit." Ludwig nodded to himself.

Cyril, however, shook his head and chuckled. "There's value in providing solace for the people during tough times, yes, but that's not all. In fact, the primary purpose of this alcohol is not consumption, but medical treatment."

Ludwig narrowed his eyes. "Do explain."

"I heard from Miss Tatiana that apparently, alcohol can kill off the agents of disease..."

Cyril's explanation roused a long-forgotten memory of Ludwig's.

"Ah... Right. I do remember hearing something like that from my master as well. I believe he mentioned that when treating wounds suffered by soldiers on the battlefield, it's good to first wash the wounds with alcohol..."

"Yes, that sounds about right. Wounds are openings into the body, and the alcohol likely prevents the agents of disease from entering. Moreover, open wounds are not the only way into the body. The mouth is an equally accessible orifice for disease, and one can only imagine how much more vulnerable it becomes when the person is weak from starvation…"

"For the famished, even a minor disease can be fatal… I see. The depth and scale of your considerations humble me. The empire is lucky to have you," said Ludwig.

From the perspective of a chancellor, nothing was more terrifying than plagues. Widespread disease killed societies and toppled kingdoms. Furthermore, disease had a friend—famine. Those suffering sustained hunger were far more susceptible to illnesses.

"It never occurred to me to go after the root of the problem. To fight not the disease but its *agent*. Your mind, Mr. Cyril, truly works on another level. Clearly, your title of savior of the continent is well-deserved."

"You give me far too much credit. No one deserves such a lofty title," said Cyril with a shrug before reconsidering. "Except, perhaps, Her Imperial Majesty. If it wasn't for the Mianet, I'd never have met Miss Tatiana. Worse, the continent might be plagued by famine and disease by now. The only reason I'm able to focus on researching ways to prepare for future crises is because she laid the groundwork for me."

The Great Famine never came to be, and the Mianet started operating in Perujin. Thanks to a host of new policies and the educational enlightenment provided by Saint Mia Academy, the empire was palpably changing for the better, creating an environment in which people like Cyril and Ludwig could concentrate on getting things done without worrying about friction and resistance.

"Then, as her loyal subjects..." said Ludwig, understanding. "We can but redouble our efforts."

"Yes. Day by day, piece by piece, we'll work toward realizing her vision," agreed Cyril.

The two exchanged a meaningful look of shared duty before a thought occurred to Ludwig.

"By the way, this half-moon potato wine... Is it drinkable?"

Its primary purpose might be medical treatment, but if it was suitable for consumption, that would surely broaden its utility. After all, half-moon potatoes were destined to become little more than garbage, so discovering even the slightest of uses was an improvement. If they could somehow push it into the market, maybe producing half-moon potato wine could even become a viable business.

Cyril made no reply. Instead, he poured some out into a cup before saying, "Here, try some. I wouldn't drink too much if I were you, but..."

Ludwig pursed his lips and took the cup. He regarded the hesitant expression on Cyril's face, shrugged, and took a sip. A *tiny* sip.

And almost choked.

"Eegh—"

Coughing to clear his throat, he squeezed a few tears out of his eyes and grimaced.

"The taste...certainly needs some work."

"Yes, but I was thinking it might be a better use of time to focus on its medical purposes and forget about the taste. There are more and more people starting to make fine wine now, after all." Cyril poured some into his own cup, clinked it against Ludwig's, and said, "To the Great Sage of the Tearmoon Empire."

"To the glory of Her Imperial Majesty Mia," answered Ludwig.

The pair downed their drinks in unison.

And choked in unison as well.

The wine was, in a word, unpalatably delicious. Its taste was certainly bad enough to make grown men cry, but there was something else to the process of drinking it. Some sort of richness. A richness unrivaled by the finest of wines…that resembled the deep joy of a bright future.

Side Chapter: Empress Mia's Trick or Treat

The empress of the Tearmoon Empire, Mia Luna Tearmoon, was known to be a woman of great humor and playfulness. What follows is a tale that illustrates her mischievous side involving a prank that she planned and executed.

After finishing her work for the day, the young empress of Tearmoon, Mia, sat in the Whitemoon Palace, gracefully enjoying some afternoon tea. That is, you could call it graceful if you ignored the ravenous look in her eyes as she held her fork over the head chef's custom-made vegetable cake. Just as she prepared to thrust the prongs into a slice, a number of men from the central nobility walked in. They all belonged to the Bluemoon faction and had come to voice their dissent regarding something Mia had said some days ago. After a brief round of greetings, they promptly got down to business.

"Your Imperial Majesty, we implore you to reconsider."

"Oh? Reconsider what?"

"You know perfectly well what we've come for. The issue with Outcount Rudolvon and Viscount Berman, of course."

"My... Well, promoting Berman from viscount to count is perfectly reasonable, is it not?"

"It certainly is. Viscount Berman is one of the central nobility, and Princess Town is situated within his domain. His current title is unsuitably low for a man of his caliber. His extensive efforts in establishing Saint Mia Academy alone should qualify him for the title of count. Your Imperial Majesty's arrangement in this matter is entirely appropriate."

First, they presented themselves as supportive of her proposal. Then, figuring they'd ingratiated themselves with her, they went on the offensive. With a scoffing smile, one of them said, "But as for Outcount Rudolvon... Making *him* a count is far more questionable, is it not?"

The nerve of these people!

Realizing this was no time to be savoring vegetable cake, Mia sighed and lowered her fork. Then, she reconsidered and quickly thrust it into a slice, pulled off a big chunk, and stuffed it all into her mouth before actually putting her fork down.

"Mmmfmm, mmfm mm mm..." She swallowed. "Well, Outcount Rudolvon distributed the wheat from his own domain and saved many people from famine. Had it not been for his wheat, we would surely have lost many more lives. And then there's his son. You all recognize the significance of Cyril Rudolvon's accomplishments, right?"

The nobles looked at each other with reluctant grimaces.

"Of course, we are well aware of these facts. But we do not see how they entail making him a count."

"The guarantee of due reward and punishment is indispensable for proper governance of a kingdom, is it not?" The reply came not from Mia but Ludwig, who'd been standing beside her.

The noble shot him a look of disgust before shaking his head. "With all due respect, Ludwig, are you *sure* you understand the nuances of the situation?" the noble retorted. "These are, after all, the affairs of nobles, and you are of common birth." He gave Ludwig a condescending look before letting out a scornful laugh.

The fact that they were willing to acknowledge Ludwig's presence was notable, but it didn't come from a sense of respect for Ludwig's ability. They knew he was in Mia's good graces and figured that with her watching, dismissing him outright might give her a negative impression. Not that her impression of them could get any worse, mind you, considering they were not only wasting her time with their inane protest, they were wasting her *cake-eating* time. The latter was, if anything, the far more egregious offense, but sadly, they were entirely oblivious to its ramifications.

"I see," said Mia. "So what you're submitting is that it's unacceptable for an outland noble to be given the same rank as central nobility."

"Your Imperial Majesty is most perceptive. That is precisely what we mean."

The nobles lowered their heads in feigned respect—feigned, because the arrogance they exuded could hardly be masked by a mere gesture.

Well, the Bluemoon faction obviously wanted Sapphias to become emperor, so I guess it makes sense for them to hate me.

The thought was accompanied by a growing urge to turn all their protests into sweets and eat them. Her fanciful wish was interrupted by Ludwig.

"Your Imperial Majesty... How do you wish to proceed?" he asked.

"Hmm... Oh, I know! I just had a great idea." Mia grinned deviously. "In that case, why don't we change the spelling of the title, just a little...and turn it into a new one?" She spun a finger in the air as she pretended to deliberate. After a while, she held up the same finger as if inspiration struck. "How about...marcount? Just change the 'out' to 'mar.' It sounds better this way, and it'll feel like a bit of a promotion, right?"

Her suggestion was met with pursed lips from the nobles. Ludwig, however, froze for a second, his eyes widened with shock. A second later, he caught himself and adjusted his glasses to hide his surprise.

"'Marcount'...." mumbled a noble. "Fascinating. 'Mar' is the old word for fringes, I believe? It certainly does retain the term's rural feel... But will that really work?"

"What do you mean? Of course it will. It's all about the technicalities with these things. If we keep him an outcount, it'll go against the principle of due reward, but we can't make him a count either, so this is the only thing we can do, right?" She flashed another devious grin.

"I see... Very well. Your Imperial Majesty's brilliance never fails to impress."

With that, the nobles left the room, presumably satisfied by her answer.

Mia watched them go with a smile. Once they were gone, Ludwig leaned in.

"Your Imperial Majesty, if I'm not mistaken, marcount is already..."

"Oho ho, I see that you're aware." She steepled her fingers and reclined. "Exactly. The rank of marcount already exists. People stopped using it a long time ago, though. And since it's a foreign title, I can't really blame people for not knowing about it."

In other words, what had just transpired...was a trick. Or, perhaps, a bit of revenge. It was Mia's way of giving those annoying nobles a taste of their own medicine.

The rank of marcount was not something she made up on the spot; it very much existed. Or had existed, at least. It was a curious title—a count yet not. The "mar" in the term, however, was by no means derogatory. "Mar" was short for "march" which, unlike the nobles' interpretation, meant "borderland." The domains of marcounts had, therefore, been situated along the borders of their kingdom. Tasked with defending against invasion, they were the aegis of their nation. Often granted to those of royal blood or the most trusted vassals of a ruler, there had been times when the title of marcount rivaled marquesses in prestige.

And the nation where the rank had once existed…was the mighty Kingdom of Sunkland. There, the title of marcount—though long discontinued—still bore its former glory, frequently spoken of among the Sunkland populace with the kind of reverence usually reserved for kings.

Having learned about this piece of history in her classes at Saint-Noel, Mia smiled with satisfaction.

"Hah." Ludwig chuckled. "So their protest certainly changed things, but ultimately to their detriment. I wouldn't want to be in their position when they find out the truth."

"Mmm hm hm, that's what they get for interrupting my cake-eating time. If anything, they got off easy with a prank like this," said Mia before gleefully stuffing a whole slice of cake into her mouth.

A trick well played, and a treat well had.

Some time later, news of Outcount Rudolvon being promoted to the rank of marcount made waves among the central nobility. Those ignorant of the title's history were astonished to hear that it had once existed in Sunkland. As they asked around, their astonishment would turn to panic upon learning that its standing rivaled that of a marquess.

Meanwhile, those of the Four Houses who were close to Mia—Sapphias, Esmeralda, Ruby, and Citrina—could but shake their heads with wry amusement. Presumably, they figured, some members of the central nobility with more pride than sense had incurred Mia's wrath. Needless to say, Sapphias's amusement was the most short-lived, for he'd soon find out that the incurring members belonged to the Bluemoon faction. Rumors were that he'd visibly paled at the discovery.

Over time, however, the central nobility's consternation faded.

"Th-Then again, at the end of the day, it's only for show... The fact of the matter is that the rank of marcount never existed in the empire, and it's not like he gained any more territory or power. It's no problem."

Thus would they comfort themselves.

Unfortunately for them, their consolation would prove fleeting, for a subsequent development would make double the waves through their ranks. Their jaws littering the floor, they would soon receive news of...

The engagement of the daughter of Marcount Rudolvon, Tiona Rudolvon, to the young king of Sunkland, Sion Sol Sunkland.

Side Chapter: The Seed That Did Not Sprout

Sion Sol Sunkland became king shortly after he graduated from Saint-Noel Academy. Curiously, the timing of his crowning coincided almost perfectly with Mia Luna Tearmoon taking the throne as empress. The twin successions, together with the growth of the transnational organization, the Mianet, and the spread of the new strain of wheat, seemed to signal to the people the coming of a new era.

Amidst a confluence of sentiments—excitement, trepidation, ambition, hope—a piece of news rocked the Kingdom of Sunkland.

Their young king, Sion Sol Sunkland, announced his betrothal.

On the day of the announcement, the royal capital's taverns exploded with chatter. Needless to say, only a single topic was in discussion.

"But, uh, what's with the bride's family? I don't think I've ever heard of a Marcount Rudolvon before. I mean, a *marcount*, of all things? Who'd have expected to hear *that* word again? Is the fellow from some old-fashioned country somewhere?" asked a tavern-goer.

"No, I'm pretty sure the girl's a Tearmoon noble..." answered a second man, who then lowered his voice to a whisper. "Keep this between us, but I heard he's a marcount in name only, and it's actually an empty title."

"Really?"

"Yeah. I mean, it has to be, right? After all, marcounts don't exist in Tearmoon. They only have outcounts, and apparently, that's a term they use to mock the nobles who live in the countryside."

The more the men discussed, the more they felt offended, for the arrangement seemed like an affront to their king. However, just as their communal anger neared a tipping point...

"Gotta say, though, I don't know about marcounts, but the name Rudolvon sounds sort of familiar..."

A pensive remark from one of the gossipers gave them pause.

"You know, now that you mention it..."

It was then that another man joined the group.

"Oh, come on. You've got to be kidding me," said the new entrant, who was a traveling merchant. He rolled his eyes at the others. "Have you folks been living under a rock? Does Cyril Rudolvon ring a bell? You know, the one who discovered the new strain of wheat?"

"Ah—"

Realization dawned immediately. The mass production of cold-resistant wheat was a watershed event in the history of the continent. Nowadays, even the most average of joes knew the names of Cyril Rudolvon and Arshia Tafrif Perujin, for they were hailed as heroes.

"I see. So basically, thanks to Cyril's breakthrough achievement with wheat, his old man got a freebie promotion to marcount," reasoned one of the men.

The merchant, however, shook his head. "No, not necessarily. According to what I've heard, Marcount Rudolvon is one of the empress faction's earliest members, and he worked real hard to build up the faction and rally people around it."

The empress faction referred to a new political coalition that Empress Mia had sought to assemble as a counterbalance against the factions of the Four Dukes. Originally, it had consisted of a number of political newcomers who'd gathered under Mia's banner when she'd still been the princess, but now, they'd grown to the point of rivaling the other factions, effectively adding a fifth player to Tearmoon's traditionally Four-Dukes-dominated political landscape.

Among merchants, whose livelihoods depended on access to information, these developments in Tearmoon were widely known, but they had yet to trickle down to the ordinary Sunkland populace. As a result, the merchant's explanation was met with sounds of awe and approval, which tickled his ego enough for him to dole out some more information.

"On that note, have you folks heard of Count Berman? His domain borders the marcount's, and it's where the empress's private borough, Princess Town, resides. And that's where it gets interesting…"

"Hm? Doesn't that mean Saint Mia Academy, the place where they developed the new wheat, is also…"

"Exactly. It's also in Count Berman's domain," said the merchant in a conspiratorial tone.

Marcount Rudolvon and Count Berman were both known to have been a part of the empress faction at its outset, which lent credence to his implied intrigue.

"Both were early members of the empress faction who contributed greatly to Empress Mia's succession… I get it now. Making him a marcount wasn't an insult. It's the opposite. She was rewarding him for his services."

That painted Rudolvon in a very different light, for it suggested that his recently bestowed rank of marcount was a prestigious title specially created to rival the Four Dukes. This made sense to the Sunkland gossipers, who were used to thinking of marcounts as esteemed figures. How, they figured, could such a respected title possibly be given to some country bumpkin of a noble? The idea immediately seemed preposterous.

And it would have been, had the originator been a normal emperor.

"So Rudolvon is clearly a distinguished noble who had the honor of becoming the empire's very first marcount, meaning he's now part of the empress's inner circle...and his daughter is the one who's..."

On top of that, her younger brother was the hero, Cyril Rudolvon, who discovered the new strain of wheat. More and more, the engagement was seeming...not as bad as it had first appeared.

"But what about the girl herself? How is she as a person?"

"About that... Just between us, I'm a gardener for a noble family, and the husband told me something a while back..." said a nearby man who joined the conversation. "Marcount Rudolvon's daughter... She apparently saved the former king, His Majesty Abram's life."

"What? I've never heard of that."

"Of course you haven't. It concerns the royal family. They're not gonna just come out and tell commoners like us," the gardener said with a smug shrug.

His increasingly intoxicated audience could but nod in agreement, their mental faculties no longer up to the task of skepticism.

"Which means...His Majesty Sion's bride is..."

Through a fog of inebriation, the listeners forced their minds to work through the logic. The prospective queen consort, Tiona Rudolvon, had literally saved the life of their former king, Abram. She was the sister of Cyril Rudolvon, the savior of the continent. Moreover, her father was an eminent member of the empress faction whom Empress Mia trusted enough to bestow on him an entirely new rank, making him the first and only marcount in Tearmoon.

The more they thought about it, the more they realized that *this was actually a pretty good deal.*

Later, a message from the Holy Lady in which she personally blessed the upcoming union would further solidify their admiration of Tiona.

"Who would have thought that young woman would be an old friend of Lady Rafina's…?"

Every piece of additional information would add another facet to her ever-evolving image in Sunkland. It was amidst this atmosphere of speculation that Tiona, her reputation far preceding her, entered Sunkland. The people welcomed her with a mix of excitement and apprehension, unsure how much they knew about her was true, and how much was hyperbole.

The speculation did not last long. Very quickly, the Sunkland populace found themselves charmed by her down-to-earth personality. There was an endearing approachability to her that was absent in most prominent nobles. In her, Sunkland saw a fairy tale playing out in real life. The daughter of a commoner-turned-impoverished-noble overcame the towering barrier of the class divide to marry the prince of a great kingdom. It was the stuff of dreams and fables, forever popular among the masses, yet forever unattainable.

But she'd reached for it. And her timeless tale of romance became a vicarious vehicle for the people, who invested their hopes and wishes in her. Thus, despite some resistance, Tiona would find herself welcomed by her new home.

Sunkland was not, however, the only kingdom to be affected by this development. Within Tearmoon, it changed the power balance of the noble class.

Those who had thought of Marcount Rudolvon's new rank as an empty title with no real substance found their jaws on the floor.

Before they knew it, the marcount's family had expanded to include the *King of Sunkland*. At first, few among the nobility believed the news. They figured that, sure, the two were schoolmates, but there was no way the daughter of an outcount could ever marry the young Sunkland king.

To their dismay, reality hadn't seemed to have gotten the note. Not only did their wedding proceed, Tiona Rudolvon was warmly received by the people of Sunkland.

Now, it was the Tearmoon nobles' turn to panic.

"At this rate, the marcount title will end up having *actual* power!"

What was supposed to be an empty title had, through a matrimonial union with Sunkland's royal family, gained a significant amount of clout. One couldn't really fault the nobles for panicking. Actually, the sentiment wasn't so much panic as a sense of urgency—the kind of feeling that would one day be referred to as "massive FOMO." Hearing about a fellow Tearmoon noble marrying into Sunkland royalty made all of them think, "I need to get in on this."

As it turns out, nothing unites people quite like the bruising of a communal ego. Not to be outdone by a mere outland noble, the long-squabbling factions of the central nobility immediately dropped their grievances against each other and joined forces, seeking to marry one of their own into Sunkland's royal family as well. It didn't matter who, as long as the Tearmoon candidate hailed from a distinguished lineage representing the central nobility. The question, however, was who the Sunkland candidate would be.

That was when the nobles remembered something—during Abram's reign, Sunkland didn't have one, but *two* princes. There seemed to be some issues surrounding the other one, if gossip were to be believed, but that wasn't particularly relevant for the time being.

All they needed was Sunkland royalty, and the second prince fit the bill perfectly. On top of that, the boy had already been placed in the care of the Greenmoons as a future fiancé to the Duke's daughter.

It was simply too tantalizing an opportunity to pass up, and the Greenmoons suddenly became the center of attention. Numerous powerful nobles began to pay them visits, discreetly— and sometimes not so discreetly—probing about the arrangement with the Sunkland prince. If the Greenmoons planned to call off the engagement, they had every intention of recommending their own daughters as potential replacements.

Not too long after, Esmeralda was summoned by her father. Having been told that he intended to discuss her promised marriage, she showed up with a scowl.

"Ugh, *again*?" She shook her head. "Father, how many times must we go through this?"

Five years had passed since she'd brought Prince Echard back with her. Esmeralda was now twenty-three, putting her well within marrying age. If anything, she was already a little on the late side. Countless marriage proposals had already been sent her way, and she'd turned down all of them. The reason was simple: she had Echard. From the day she brought him home with her, she'd sworn to herself. Whatever mistakes he'd committed in the past didn't matter. He was the one for her, because she'd decided so.

Echard, for his part, steadily grew into a promising young man, almost as if he knew of her silent pledge and was trying to live up to it. Studying under Headmaster Galv at Saint Mia Academy, his academic performance was nothing if not exceptional.

Esmeralda believed in him. Believed that he would go on to do great things. The last thing she wanted to do was to betray his trust.

Whatever this new proposal is, I need to be very clear in turning it down. That's the least I can do for him.

With an aggressive huff and arms akimbo, she prepared to deliver the most resounding no her father had ever heard.

"Actually... I've had a lot of talks with people lately, and they're really starting to clamor for you to hurry up and finalize your marriage to Prince Echard..."

"I'm— Wait... Huh?" Esmeralda stared speechlessly, struggling to process what she just heard.

Her father grimaced. "I don't blame them, considering the recent developments. But I can't exactly tell them the truth about Prince Echard's situation..."

He rubbed his forehead in frustration, regretfully figuring he should have sent Echard back to Sunkland earlier. Esmeralda, however, did not share his remorse. With a puzzled tilt to her head, she slowly worked through the words.

"Finalize...my marriage...to Prince Echard?"

Thus, the pair's wedding proceeded at breakneck pace. Before long, they were married, with Esmeralda at the age twenty-three and Echard at fifteen.

More time passed.

Twenty years of time.

One day, Sunkland welcomed the homecoming of Echard and his family. After a blur of greetings and functions, he retired to a room in the royal castle with Sion. It had been a while since the brothers had seen each other in person. They clinked their wine glasses together, celebrating their reunion.

"When was the last time we shared a drink like this? A year ago?"

"Yes. That was during mother's birthday last year. It's good to see you again, Sion."

Echard smiled. It was a good smile, free of the stiffness and reservation that had, until only a few years ago, plagued his demeanor around Sion. Finally, they could speak to each other in a state of mutual comfort.

"I have to say though, the Mianet really is something," Sion said after a sip of wine. "I heard it's expanding beyond the continent and coordinating with kingdoms overseas now?"

The topic was a familiar one for them, as Echard was involved in the Mianet's operations.

"Yes. Greenmoon's connections really paved the way for us. The more kingdoms we can convince to join the network, the more people we can save. By sharing food and communicating with each other, it also improves diplomatic relations between nations. The work this organization does is profoundly valuable."

Though veiled by modesty, Sion nevertheless heard the pride in Echard's voice as he spoke. It was a good pride too—the kind exuded by adults who did work that they felt was meaningful. There was a mature radiance to his younger brother's expression that Sion found heartening. Almost a little dazzling. He nodded.

"That's very good to hear. Especially coming from you…" said Sion. "I'm glad to know that you're doing your duty as a member of Sunkland's royal family. And doing it well."

As the Mianet's negotiation officer, Echard was in charge of managing contractual obligations with numerous kingdoms. He excelled at his job, displaying a diplomatic prowess that was second to none. Sion had long heard that even among the experienced merchants who worked with the Mianet, there was unanimous agreement of Echard's superiority when it came to closing deals.

Sion's praise elicited a calm smile from Echard. "Thank you for your compliments, Sion. Knowing that you recognize the value of my work... It means a lot. More than anything else."

"The thing is... Sorry to change the topic, Echard, but recently, I heard a curious rumor..."

"A rumor? What kind?" Echard lifted an eyebrow.

"I heard from Miss Chloe that she discussed stepping down and having you succeed her as the Mianet's president, but you firmly refused," said Sion.

Seeing Echard in good spirits was reassuring, but there was one thing that still bothered Sion. For some reason, Echard kept turning down every job offer that came his way. Many of these were for high office or executive positions, but he'd never shown any interest.

Echard's time at Saint Mia Academy had been more than fruitful. Even by Sion's standards, he was impressed by the sheer talent and competence his younger brother now displayed. The vast majority of jobs should be manageable, if not trivial, for someone of Echard's ability. Nevertheless, he'd adamantly refused to assume any sort of prestigious or important position. Sion couldn't help but suspect that his brother was still haunted by a lingering sense of guilt from that incident long ago.

"I think it's a fine job for a Sunkland royal, and I'm sure Miss Chloe offered you the position because she had every confidence you'd be up to the task... So why? Why did you say no?"

"Uh... Well, that's..."

Echard shifted uneasily in his seat and mumbled something under his breath before scratching his cheek and offering a hushed confession.

"It's because... If I'm too busy, Esmeralda gets lonely..."

And what a confession it was!

For a long moment, Sion stared in silence at his brother's reddening face. Then, he burst into laughter. "Bah hah hah hah! Does she, now? Well, that's certainly a very valid reason to turn down a job. I'm not sure I can even think of a more valid one. Ha ha ha."

It was then that Sion finally laid his worry to rest. At long last, he could say with absolute certainty that the seed Echard had sown so long ago had withered for good, never to sprout ever again...

There was something else he could now say with absolute certainty as well—as a married couple, Echard and Esmeralda were doing *just fine*.

Thus, the insidious rift between Sunkland's royal brothers was finally mended, bringing a long and potentially tragic chapter to a mirthful close. And it was all thanks to...

Mmm hm hm. Outcount and marcount... All I changed were the first three letters, and on the surface, they both mean the same thing. I bet those stupid nobles won't realize what I actually did. Serves them right for pestering me when I was trying to enjoy my cake!

The initial sentiment behind the long chain of cause and effect leading to this conclusion would forever be lost to history...

Chapter 28: A Delightful Gathering of Girls –Princess Mia Is Filled with a Sense of Duty–

After the conclusion of the ball at the royal castle, Mia and her friends relocated to Rafina's room at the inn, where they intended to enjoy a girls-only after-party.

The first thing they did upon arriving was seat themselves at a dinner table, which was soon garnished by a tantalizing pot of steaming cream stew. Floating inside the rich liquid were large cuts of bread. Well-boiled pieces of sunny sweet potatoes lent the stew a golden-yellow color which, together with the faintly sweet fragrance, left Mia all but spellbound. She spooned some into her mouth. A piece of sweet potato touched her tongue and all but unraveled into pure deliciousness, leaving behind a rich sugary flavor and a fruity aroma that melded with the creamy texture of the stew. Blowing out quick, steamy breaths, she probed the rest of the stew, searching for her prize until… There!

She found it, its body mostly concealed by the stew except for a small portion that poked out the surface. It resembled some sort of seaweed, but it was no marine vegetable…

"Is this…the legendary mushroom, sambapilz?"

"Yes," answered the server. "It is said that those who eat this mushroom find their tongues dancing with delight from its exquisite flavor. They are easier to find around here in Sunkland."

"My, how wonderful!"

Without further ado, she spooned a piece into her mouth. Its thin, flexible texture caused it to jiggle, resulting in a unique mouthfeel—almost like it was dancing on her tongue. She couldn't help but giggle. As she bit down on it, rich mushroomy goodness spilled out into her mouth. The flavor was magical, as if all the delicious essences of Mother Nature had been distilled into this single bite. Combined with the stew, it made for an indescribably wonderful experience.

"Mmmmmmmmmm… It's *so* good…"

From the stew-soaked bread to the soft-boiled sunshine carrots, everything about the stew was deeply satisfying.

Hm, if Esmeralda marries Prince Echard, then our ties to Sunkland will naturally get stronger, which means they might gift us these mushrooms from time to time… But it's not just the mushrooms— this whole stew is an exquisite work of art!

After her rather filling late-night snack of stew, Mia started to feel sleepy. It was, after all, human nature to seek a good sleep after a good meal, and Mia, ostensibly a paragon of humanity, was all about being human.

"Hnnngh… I'm not really feeling up to making the trip back to Count Lampron's…" she mumbled as she stifled a yawn.

For some reason, this caused Rafina to perk up. The Holy Lady then took a deep breath before regarding the room with the most serious of expressions.

"I completely agree. It's hardly a good idea for young ladies to head out when it's already so late. How about you all stay here for the night?"

"Huh? Is that…okay?" asked Mia, trying and failing to keep the sleep out of her voice.

"Of course. This is an inn, and they have plenty of rooms. Besides, there are *Serpents* out there, so it's definitely safest to stay here," said Rafina, fists balled persuasively.

"Fwaaaah… That's…a good point. I guess I'll take you up on your offer… Rina? Bel? You're okay with that, I assume?"

So, it was decided that Mia and friends would spend the night with Rafina in the inn. Figuring they'd all fit in one room, Mia's four-girl group consisting of her, Bel, Citrina, and Anne proceeded to rent…absolutely nothing! They stayed exactly where they were! Because…

It was time for a five-girl pajama party!

Soon, the girls were in full sleepover mode. Having changed into pajamas—all provided by Rafina—they were huddled on the two beds in her room and ready to talk the night away.

The all-jammies look had, in fact, been Rafina's idea.

"Once we're in pajamas, there's no telling who's a noble and who's a commoner, right?"

With that one statement, she'd effectively offered Anne an invitation to join them, allowing each and every one of them to huddle together on the beds of sisterhood.

Mia, for her part, had been ready to crash out at a moment's notice, but with so many young maidens gathered after witnessing such a heart-stopping duel, sleep was all but an impossibility. There would be no rest until they'd exhausted every topic of romantic interest they could think of!

"Prince Sion was so cool back there!" Bel took the first shot, opening with a short but effective declaration of her idol's performance.

"Tee hee, you sure are crazy about Prince Sion, aren't you, Bel?" said a giggling Citrina, her tone facetiously dismissive.

Bel nodded firmly, the joke having either soared straight over her or slid right off her. "Of course I am! I mean, he's just too cool! Don't you think so, Rina?"

Mia regarded the girls with droopy eyes as their conversation flourished. Despite the excitement in the air, sleep still hung heavily over her. That is, until…

"What about you Moth—? Miss Anne? Is there anyone that you're crazy about?"

…Bel went for the jugular. Mia perked up immediately. Her drowsiness had vanished in the blink of an eye.

She'd asked Anne for love advice countless times, but it just occurred to her that she'd never asked about *Anne's* love interests. With intense curiosity, she turned to look at her faithful maid, who…

"No. I won't marry, because I plan to stay at milady's side and serve her for as long as I live. Oh, assuming, um…you're okay with that, of course…"

Anne turned nervously toward Mia. Their gazes met.

"If I'm okay with that?" Mia frowned. "Why would I not be? You've been nothing but helpful all these years. In fact, I have every intention of retaining your services as my maid-in-waiting even after you get married. Oh, but once I have children, maybe it'd be better to employ you as my wet nurse… Anyway, the point is that even if you have a husband, there's no need to quit your job."

Frankly, Mia wasn't entirely comfortable with engaging in displays of affection while Anne was around. Something about the idea of her flirting with her boyfriend while her loyal maid remained single made her feel guilty. Just as food was best enjoyed together, love was best experienced concurrently as well.

240

"Milady…" Tears of gratitude welled up in Anne's eyes.

"But, you know," continued Mia, "if the problem is that you're too busy for romance, then it'll fall on me to find you a good partner. To that end, I'll need to know your preferences. So go ahead; tell me your taste in men."

Another bout of excited girl-chattering ensued, after which the topic shifted again.

"By the way, Miss Rafina, what kind of person are you into?"

Mia wasn't entirely sure who asked the question, but its content demanded her attention. Her *undivided* attention. She even sat up a little straighter. After all, who didn't want to find out what the Holy Lady was looking for in a man? Mia just hadn't had the courage to pose the question herself.

I don't know who was the one with the guts to ask Miss Rafina, but thank you.

She mentally saluted the nameless daredevil's courage and turned her attention to Rafina.

"What kind of person I'm into? Hm…" Rafina touched a finger to her cheek and tilted her head. "I…don't think I'm into any type in particular."

"Huh? But what about Prince Sion?" asked Bel, astonished that there could exist someone immune to Sion's charms. "He's so dreamy! And Keithwood's really cool too!"

Dauntless, unwavering, and with no concern for propriety or etiquette, Bel kept pressing. Her memories of the nightmare that was the Empress Prelate had all but faded. Probably.

"Hmm… They're both marvelous individuals, that's for certain, but…" Rafina smiled. "Not exactly the kind of person I find attractive."

Just like that, she let the blade of rejection drop on the pair of grade-A Sunkland bachelors. Mia shuddered a little, inadvertently recalling the times when she'd seen that expression in the previous timeline. Rafina really could kill with her smile.

"Seriously? Huuuuh. What kind of person do you find attractive then?" Bel puffed out her cheeks indignantly and kept asking, evidently dissatisfied with the lukewarm answer that her personal best candidates had received.

"Hmmm, good question…" Rafina paused for a while before conceding in a bashful mumble, "If I had to choose, I guess it'd be… someone who could carry me in their arms like a bride."

The Holy Lady had apparently lost her mind.

Mia stared at Rafina in disbelief. She quickly took a sip of the drink in her hand. As far as she could tell, it did not contain any alcohol. She then stared at Rafina again. Then took another sip, just to be sure. It was literally a double double take.

She's…not drunk, right?

Rafina seemed perfectly normal. Mia shot a sideward glance at Citrina, who promptly sneaked in a quick whiff of Rafina's drink before dipping her tongue into her own drink for comparison. Citrina nodded.

It really was just juice. Whatever this was, alcohol was not to blame.

But…a bridal carry? That's just…too out there. It's so surreal…

Not that bridal carries weren't done, of course. Plenty of people performed it. The issue was how nondescript it was with regard to a potential love interest. So vague was Rafina's response that it offered absolutely no concrete picture of the actual person.

Mia was suddenly struck by a sense of a looming crisis. She swiftly scanned the room before whispering to Bel, "By the way, Bel... did the Empress Prelate version of Rafina ever marry?"

Bel gave her a baffled look. "I can't imagine anyone having such a death wish."

Right, of course... Not that I'm surprised...

"Oh, but maybe General Dion! Someone like him can probably handle it!"

I...can't believe you just had that thought. Also, you're probably right!

After privately acknowledging the potential in her granddaughter's just-so-crazy-it-might-actually-work suggestion, Mia recomposed herself and took another look at Rafina.

You know, now that I think about it... Miss Rafina seems like the type who's going to have a lot of trouble finding a husband.

Now, being the daughter of Duke Belluga, it is highly likely that her father will bring her a suitable groom in due time. It is similarly likely that she wouldn't outright refuse such an arrangement. However...

Considering her father's the type to have a portrait of her drawn every year...

The duke was clearly overly fond of her. Which was fine. There was nothing wrong with a father doting on his beloved daughter. It was even understandable, to a degree, to order a new portrait of his daughter every year—just an overeager fatherly expression of affection. But *selling* the portraits to all the neighboring kingdoms was probably crossing the line. That was like climbing onto a roof and yelling, "My daughter is the cutest-schmoochest little girl in the world!" at the top of your lungs to the whole town. It was simply too much. And it was exactly what the duke did on a regular basis.

Duke Belluga would probably get along very well with Mia's own father.

Knowing how her father is, if Rafina has even the slightest grievance about the potential groom, there's no way he'd push her to go through with the arrangement.

While that was a nice gesture on the part of the duke, it'd make it terribly difficult to settle on a partner. Rafina would likely go through candidate after imperfect candidate to no avail, every failed attempt leaving another scar on her psyche until…the Empress Prelate was born!

Right now, I'm pretty sure Miss Rafina thinks of me as a friend… Which means the onus is on me to live up to our friendship.

Suddenly, Mia was filled with a sense of duty. A friend duty—but more importantly, a seasoned-expert-of-romance duty. She needed to use her experience to find and introduce the perfect man to Rafina, thereby ensuring she'd remain her friendly, non-prelate self. It was imperative to keep her desires fully satiated—her romantic ones, mainly, but her culinary ones wouldn't hurt either. Mia wouldn't mind having a comrade in the world of F.A.T.

"Miss Rafina, you and I are in a position that will eventually require us to produce heirs. It is something that we need to do if we want to keep our kingdom prosperous and our people happy. To that end, when it comes to the type of men you prefer, it might be wise to think in terms that are a little more specific."

"Hmm… I suppose you do have a point."

Mia's suggestion prompted Rafina to adopt a more serious expression.

"In that case…" said Rafina, a thoughtful hand on her cheek, "Someone I can respect, perhaps?"

"Respect…"

"Yes. Someone selfless, who won't hesitate to act for the good of others. Someone kind to children and the elderly alike, and who has compassion for the weak…but will firmly oppose oppression by powerful people. He doesn't have to be physically strong, so long as he stands up to tyranny. Someone who fights quietly, but tenaciously… I'm pretty accommodating, so as long as he's got those qualities, then I don't really care much about the rest."

"Mmhm, mmhm. Okay, I…see?"

As she pieced the laundry list of qualities together, the face of a certain individual flashed across her mind. Faced with the cold, uncaring cruelty of the world, the man had doubtlessly fought against it. Quietly and tenaciously. He worked himself to the bone trying to protect poor children. Despite the extreme deficiencies of his surroundings and environment, he always put the children first, tending to their needs before his own. He was selfless, he acted for the good of others, and he had endless compassion for the weak…

The priest! In the Newmoon District!

Granted, he was a bit older than her. Well, actually, he was *a lot* older, but he was also a member of the Central Orthodox Church. Surely, he was at least a viable candidate. To make sure, Mia decided to ask a few more questions.

"By the way, what do you think about muscles?" she asked.

"Huh? M-Muscles?"

Rafina frowned, puzzled by the abrupt question. Mia, recognizing the inherent faux pas in the question, quickly shook her hands.

Ugh, what was I thinking? Ruby's the only one who gets excited when she sees big, muscular men. For most girls, their romantic preferences don't include muscle mass!

She cleared her throat and started anew.

"Well, not just muscles, but more like…stature? You know, how tall they are and how big they look. The face is important too. Also, how good they are at swordsmanship or academics… And what their rank is…"

"Personally, I have no preferences regarding any of those qualities."

"What about age then?"

"In terms of public image, it would be problematic if he was too old, but for my part, I don't particularly care."

That made sense; being too old to produce heirs would defeat the purpose of the exercise. Mia recalled the priest's visage.

Hmm… I wouldn't call him too old. Maybe this might just work?

"So long as we share the same faith, and his love for me is true, then I'm happy to marry whoever asks for my hand."

Wonderful! The priest of that church loves Miss Rafina to death! I think I've found the perfect candi—

"Oh, actually, I have one more condition," said Rafina with a clap of her hands. "And this one is *very* important."

"Oh? One more condition?" asked Mia, prompting her to continue.

Rafina, with the most serious expression she'd worn yet, said, "Yes. They can't own a portrait of me."

"Ah. Well. That…makes sense."

So much for the priest. Mia promptly erased him from her mental list of potential candidates.

The conversation went on and on until a little past midnight, at which point Rafina, having ostensibly gotten her fill of girl talk for the time being, said, "Phew… Well, how about we call it a night?"

Seeing that she could finally enjoy some long-awaited slumber, Mia threw herself onto one of the three beds.

Yes, three.

Anne had insisted on sleeping on the floor, but Rafina adamantly refused to allow it.

"When wearing pajamas, we're all equals, so we should sleep as equals too, no?"

At Rafina's demand, they'd gotten a third bed and pushed it beside the previous two so everyone could sleep together.

This...gap between the beds... It seems like you can fall through... thought Mia as she yawned.

Before she had a chance to drift off, she heard Rafina's voice.

"By the way, Mia, has the whole engagement issue with Miss Esmeralda been straightened out yet?"

"Hmmwha? Uhh... Yes, pretty much..." Mia reflexively answered before her drowsy brain got around to comprehending the question.

The subsequent chill was definitely enough to wake her up. Had she told Rafina about the real reason for her trip to Sunkland? No... She never mentioned anything about the complicated circumstances she'd come to sort out.

Uh-oh. This might be a problem...

Too late now.

"I see..." Rafina's expression grew pensive. "There was something I wanted to discuss with you, but... You probably have plenty on your plate already, and I'd rather not burden you any further. Also, the situation has changed a little, and it doesn't seem like I'll be needing your help immediately, so just keep what I'm about to tell you in the back of your mind, okay?"

After that oddly long preamble, she began to quietly tell her story.

"You see, Malong came to me the other day and asked for some advice."

"Malong? What kind of advice?" asked Mia.

"You're probably aware already, but lately, there's been reports of a gang of horseback bandits causing mayhem in Sunkland…"

"Ah… Those people…" Mia wasn't just aware. She'd come face-to-face with the very same bandits.

Moons, I completely forgot about those people… They were the ones who were originally supposed to assassinate Sion.

"I certainly do know about them, but… What's the matter?"

"Within Sunkland, there is a growing contingent of voices claiming it's the Equestrian Kingdom's doing, and that war is inevitable. However, Malong doesn't think the bandits are from his kingdom."

"I see. So that's why you're here. I assume you came all the way to Sunkland to mediate that issue in person?"

"If hostilities break out, countless lives will be lost. No amount of effort is too much when it comes to preventing war," said Rafina, her voice calm but resolute. "The issue is, well… Even if it's not the Equestrian Kingdom's doing, to some degree, it still concerns them."

"What do you mean?"

Her curiosity thoroughly whetted, Mia couldn't help but turn toward Rafina…only to discover Rafina doing the same. Both girls ended up on their sides, regarding each other from across the thin chasm between their beds.

"Have you ever heard of…" began Rafina, holding Mia's gaze. "The lost clan of the Equestrian Kingdom?"

"Lost…clan?" Mia blinked with obvious confusion.

"It's said that long, long ago, the Equestrian Kingdom was made up of thirteen clans. Granted, this is something I've only ever heard about from other people, and the Equestris have no cultural custom of recording their history on parchment, so everything is preserved through word of mouth and ends up being oral tradition.

Even within the kingdom, no one has any direct knowledge of these events… But anyway, the point is that supposedly, there's a clan that no longer exists—the lost Fire Clan."

The surname of Equestris represented the clan they belonged to. The "Lin" in Lin Malong, for example, meant "forest." Malong, therefore, belonged to the Forest Clan. Some of the other clans included Wood, Tree, Wind, Mountain, and Hill. Mia was aware of all twelve existing clans, but she'd never heard of the Fire Clan— those with "Ka" as their clan name.

"And the bandits causing trouble in Sunkland might be from the lost Fire Clan…" said Rafina. "That's what the people in the Equestrian Kingdom suspect, anyway."

"I see. So they're not directly responsible, but it might be the doing of people who used to be part of their tribe…"

Mia mulled over the implications. Fortunately, the story proved interesting enough to slightly lift the fog of sleepiness. In addition, thanks to the mental stimulation of their extended discussion of romantic interests, her brain still had enough juice left to do some work. When in romance mode, Mia was neither an introvert nor an extrovert. She was an *amorvert*, who recharged by thinking and talking about love-related matters.

"In that case, I suppose we can't *entirely* blame Sunkland for misunderstanding the situation."

"Indeed… Though it's also possible that their misunderstanding is intentional…"

They could be using their suspicion of the Equestrian Kingdom as a pretext to justify an invasion for the purposes of annexing the Equestris' land. It was a line of thought that had no doubt crossed the minds of the more militant Sunkland nobles. Many of them were probably delighted by the situation.

"True. That's a definite possibility. I assume the purpose of your visit this time is to push back against those voices, then?" asked Mia.

"It's one of them. The other purpose is to look into the possibility that the assassin who attacked you might be a member of that lost clan. I've been asking around to see if there's anyone in the gang of bandits who resemble that assassin."

"You mean the wolfmaster…"

The whisper came from neither of them. Glancing toward the speaker, they found a grimacing Citrina. Her face seemed a tad bit pale.

"Don't worry, Rina," said Bel, who noticed her friend's discomfort. "It's okay."

The young girl rolled over and gave Bel a tight hug. "Thanks." Citrina nodded. The tension in her expression eased every so slightly.

"Bel's right. I wouldn't worry too much about him. After all, even I managed to shake him off… Oh, I know. How about we all go for some horse riding lessons together?" Mia suggested on a whim.

To be clear, she didn't "shake him off." She'd miraculously survived his pursuit, and it had been the closest of shaves.

It'd be good for Bel and Rina, in case they ever end up in a situation when they need to escape. If they have some experience on horseback, they'll be able to ride on their own, which frees me up to ride alone. And riding alone…means riding lighter. And my horse will run faster, making it easier for me to get away.

Make no mistake—first and foremost, Mia was always looking out for number one.

"Together? Um… Mia, would that happen to…include me as well?"

"Hm?" Mia arched a brow at the dumbstruck look on Rafina's face. "Well, sure. I don't see why not. You should definitely join us, Miss Rafina. We can even try going on some long rides. They're great for clearing your mind."

"Long rides..." Rafina whispered to herself. "Going on long rides...with friends... I was just invited... This is— I can't believe..." Her indistinct mumbling continued for some time before she replied. "Yes... Yes, I think I will, Mia. I'd love to go on long rides with you!"

Mia had expected Rafina to agree. What she hadn't expected, however, was the immense amount of accompanying enthusiasm.

The following morning, Mia was nowhere to be found. On the beds, that is.

Chapter 29: Miabel's Nearly Spine-Chilling Waking of Suspense and Horror

"Mmm… Hm?" Bel quietly woke to the gentle sensation of morning light upon her skin. "It's…morning?"

She sleepily smacked her lips a few times and yawned. Rather, she was about to when the sensation of wetness at the corner of her mouth gave her pause. This was quickly followed by the discovery… of a drool stain on her pillow!

"Her blood flows through you. Go, and hold that proud name close to your heart."

Familiar voices echoed in her mind, belonging to the women who'd raised her like their daughter.

"Mother Elise… Mother Anne…"

Their words reminded her of something important. The name she'd inherited was a proud one, and she had a duty to uphold that honor. With that noble thought in mind, Bel…quickly flipped over her pillow! No evidence, no embarrassment. Her grandmother's honor had been defended.

She let out a breath, then looked around. Citrina was curled into a ball, evidently feeling cold. The process of hiding evidence seemed to have displaced their shared blanket. Bel softly got off the bed and put the blanket over her friend again. Only then did she realize that the headcount was off.

"Huh? Miss Mia's gone…"

Mia was supposed to be at the center of the beds, but she was nowhere to be found.

"Maybe she's out for a morning walk."

Bel scratched her head.

"Walking through the streets of Sunkland in the morning… Yeah, that does sound fun."

But was it a fitting activity for a princess like her? Sure. Learning about the townscapes of other kingdoms seemed like a worthwhile usage of time. With the educational value of her walk justified, she promptly changed and headed out.

What she didn't notice…were the faint groans coming from that thin chasm between the beds.

"Hnnngh… Hnnnnngh…"

They would have been a spine-chilling thing to hear, making for a waking of suspense and horror, but alas, it was not meant to be. Whatever nightmares roiled down there would find no audience today.

Stepping out of the inn, Bel was greeted by a brisk morning breeze. Within the refreshing gusts, she caught the scent of a town that was just waking up.

"Mmmm… This is so nice."

She stretched and filled her chest with fresh air. It reminded her of when she'd been hiding in the Newmoon District. Back then, this time of the day had been her favorite. The Great Sage of the Empire had loved the Newmoon District, breathing new life into its people and businesses. Never was her accomplishment more apparent than this time in the morning, when the denizens woke up and the district came to life. It was endlessly exciting, and Bel could never get enough of it.

She'd sneakily peer out from her window and appreciate the townscape until Mother Anne called her for breakfast. She'd head to the dining room, where Mother Elise, having stayed up late writing, would drowsily walk in rubbing her eyes and greet her with a sleepy but tender "Good morning."

They were some of her most treasured memories of her most cherished times.

"Mother Elise... Mother Anne..."

She was so fond of them. So terribly, *painfully* fond... She rubbed her eyes.

"Hm? You're..."

Hearing someone's voice, she turned and squinted at the speaker through blurry eyes. Her sentimental moment immediately ended upon discovering who it was.

"Th-The Libr— I mean, Prince Sion? G-Good morning."

"Good morning to you too, Miss Bel. What are you doing out and about so early in the morning?"

Before her stood the crown prince of Sunkland, Sion Sol Sunkland, and his attendant, Keithwood. The prince's silver hair glowed gently in the sun, and as Bel stared at him, she found herself mesmerized by the deep compassion radiating from his eyes. She quickly caught herself and smiled.

"I'm going on an adven—tour through the town."

Sion chuckled. "An adven-tour through the town, huh. Fair enough. Towns are indeed the kind of things that invite adventourous souls to explore them," said Sion, returning her smile.

Keithwood, his expression as level as always, leaned in and said, "It's not every day you run into a familiar face out here. How about it, then? Would you like milord to give you a tour of the town?" He glanced at Bel before turning back to Sion and shrugging.

"As a veteran adventurer of towns, it seems appropriate for you to show your junior the ropes."

Sion pursed his lips for a second, then nodded. "Good point. I've been meaning to take a look around the town myself, so this is perfect timing."

Bel's eyes widened with excitement. *I-I get to go on a morning date with the Libra King?! Wow! Thank you so much, Keithwood! You're the best!*

She privately applauded Keithwood's thoughtfulness. Little did she know, he was acting out of not consideration but caution, for he'd already witnessed her fearless impetuousness last night when she'd gone on an adventure through the castle.

This little one is even more of a handful than Princess Mia. The princess already has a penchant to dive headfirst into trouble, but in her case, she's the type to walk into danger without even realizing it... If I let her roam around, I bet she'll end up strolling into risky areas like the open market without a second thought. Leaving her alone is out of the question!

To Keithwood, Bel was pretty much a walking, talking bundle of trouble. Fortunately, she was oblivious to his opinion of her. Had she known, her excitement would surely have—

Heh heh heh, I don't know what Keithwood's thinking, but I couldn't care less. As long as I get to go on a date with the Libra King and Keithwood the Loyal, I'm happy! Aaaah, I can't wait! Let's go already!

Or...maybe she'd be just as excited.

Meanwhile, Mia was...

"Mmm... Mm? My, where am I? How odd... I can't move my body... And it's so dark. Oh no, don't tell me... Was I kidnapped by bandits in my sleep?!"

…Waking up to a good deal of suspense and horror. The reality, of course, was that she'd rolled off into the gap and gotten herself stuck between the beds, but…

"I-Is anyone there? A-Anne? Anne…?"

She even supplied a bit of suspense and horror to everyone around her, as her ostensibly disembodied voice rose from the chasm and echoed through the room.

Luckily, Bel was out on a walk and would remain oblivious to this embarrassing mishap. The honor of her grandmother had been duly defended!

Chapter 30: Bel Asks the Hard Questions

"Um, Prince Sion, do you often go for walks around town like this?"

"I do. Whenever I'm in Sunkland, I make an effort to walk through the streets as often as I can. As someone in a position of power, it's my duty to have a firsthand understanding of the lives and circumstances of my people."

"Which is a sublime aspiration, milord, but I must once again remind you that you are *working me into the ground* here. Please start arranging for a proper escort of guards on your excursions before I fall over from exhaustion."

Keithwood gave a tired shrug, to which Sion grinned.

"Owing to the much-appreciated dedication of a highly capable attendant, I enjoy the ability to perambulate through my kingdom at will. I must say, I'm not particularly minded to forfeit such a convenience."

"Well I *am*. For the sake of my own well-being."

For a good long while, Bel enjoyed their banter until a thought occurred to her. She tilted her head curiously. "Prince Sion, is it just me or…are you more cheerful than usual today?"

"Huh?"

Caught off guard by the question, Sion blinked a few times.

"If I had to describe it, it feels sort of like…a weight has been taken off your shoulders," Bel added.

"Huh. How surprising. You're more perceptive than I thought."
Sion leaned in and studied her face. "That reminds me, you're related
to Mia, aren't you? Hm…"

He crossed his arms in thought. After a while, he asked, "I'm
not sure if I should be asking this, so I'll first apologize for any
possible offense, but… I heard that you share her blood. Is that true?
Are you imperial kin?"

Upon hearing the question, Bel immediately straightened, for
it was no simple query; it concerned the very essence of her person
and pride.

"Yes, Prince Sion. I am Miabel Luna Tearmoon. The blood that
flows through my veins, I share with the princess of the empire, Mia
Luna Tearmoon."

The dignified gravity with which she answered left Sion
momentarily dumbstruck. He widened his eyes, regarding anew the
girl before him. Gone was the carefree aura she so frequently gave off,
replaced by what could only be described as the air of regality.

"I see…" he said, recognizing the truth of her words. "In that
case, it's probably in your interest to tell you…" With a sigh, Sion
proceeded to explain. "About what transpired last night. I assume
you've already heard about it from Mia, but my brother, Echard,
committed a grave error, and the one who'd caused him to do so…is
me. For far too long, he has struggled with the fact that he couldn't
become a second Sion. From his swordsmanship, to his deportment,
and much more… In all those facets, he has been trying to catch up
to me, convinced that he must do so or else be deemed a failure."

"That's… That's just wrong. He can't become you. He *shouldn't*."
Bel recalled the teachings of her former teacher, Ludwig.

*"Miss Bel… For what will surely be the rest of your life, you will
find that time and again, you will be compared to the Great Sage of
the Empire. People will wish for you—expect you—to become her.*

Even your foster parents, Anne and Elise, might eventually push you to do so. In fact, even I myself might succumb to the inclination."

The future that Ludwig described was, in a way, a happy one. With the triumphant return of Princess Miabel to the throne, the empire would be rebuilt under her leadership. Of all the struggles one could face, that was probably the most auspicious one, lying far down a very narrow path of possibility.

"However, remember this well: There is no need for you to become her. You are you, Miss Bel. You cannot become Mia, not because of a lack of effort or will, but because you are Miabel."

She could still recall the introspective tone of his voice as he'd said that, almost as if the caution had been meant for himself.

"That's why... Well, I suppose that's why there's nothing I can do about your tendency to fall asleep during lectures..."

In that moment, the struggling camel that was Ludwig's pedagogic soul came within a single straw of breaking.

"Anyway, just...try your best within the limits of your capabilities, Miss Bel. That will surely be what's best for you."

Those words had long buried themselves deep within Bel and taken root. She must live in a manner that did not besmirch the good name of Mia, the Great Sage of the Empire. However, she did not need to *behave* like Mia. Based on this logic that Ludwig had engrained in her, Echard's approach to his life was undoubtedly incorrect.

"He's just...him. He's Prince Echard," said Bel.

"Yes... I agree. I was hoping he'd come to that realization on his own eventually, but, well... Look what happened. My inaction has led us all to the very worst result. But..." Sion paused for a second as his gaze grew distant. "Normally, what he did would absolutely warrant the death penalty. But Mia... She refused to settle for that—

for an irremediable end. So she fought, and by doing so, won Echard the chance to make amends. To pick himself up and stand again."

His statement led Bel to strike her palm in sudden comprehension.

"Oh, I get it now. So that's what happened yesterday... Oh! Then that's also what you were talking about with Miss Mia in the ballroom last night, right?"

"...Hm?"

Sion's arched eyebrow was lost on Bel, who was too busy nodding to herself.

"I knew it. That conversation felt odd to me the whole time. I mean, she *turned down* a declaration of love from you. I mean, who does that? You're Prince Sion! She'd have to be crazy. Right, Keithwood?"

Keithwood's lips tightened into a strained smile. "Ha ha ha, well, uh... I suppose so. It's a...complicated affair, after all. Anyway..." He spared a glance at Sion, who groaned while clutching his chest, before continuing. "The point is, milord was happy to see that his brother had been given a chance to redeem himself. Isn't that right?"

"R-Right... Yes, that's what I meant," Sion agreed in spite of his pained grimace. "The fact is that...I also committed a grave error in the past."

"Huh? You did? But you're *the* Prince Sion!" said Bel, her wide-eyed disbelief clearly implying *Prince Sion doesn't commit grave errors!*

His grimace deepened.

"I brandished my own justice like a sword, blind to its dangers and wrongs, and as a result, I almost took the life of a friend. And when I was about to succumb to the weight of my sins, Mia came to me and, just like with Echard, granted me a chance to redeem myself," said Sion, his gaze shifting upward with nostalgia.

"She did me a great favor then, and I remind myself every day never to forget the debt of gratitude I owe her. Faced with my error, I believed that my royal status required me to forfeit my life as recompense. It was her who showed me a different way to take responsibility for my wrongs. The second chance she afforded me that day is something that I now believe every person in the world deserves."

Sion balled his fists.

"If you are indeed a scion of the imperial family, then remember this: the one thing Mia is terrible at is giving up. That's just the kind of person she is."

"Not giving up easily... That's the way of Miss Mia..." Bel repeated in a whisper before looking back over her shoulder.

A vision of that death-defying dash across the winter plains resurfaced. It was the same back then. Mia had defiantly, *stubbornly* refused to give up on life. She was bad at giving up on others, yes, but she was also bad at giving up on herself.

That lines up with what Grandmother Mia said after coming back from Perujin. A lot of people have done a lot for me, and she told me that if I want to pay them back, I should pursue the best life possible and live up to their kindness by living for myself.

To Bel, it felt like Mia was telling her to endure and survive, no matter the circumstances. To cling to life with dogged determination, and in doing so, repay the services of compassion she'd received. Suddenly, she was reminded of where she'd come from.

That world of despair...

What if one day, the time came for her to return to that desperate, desolate life? How would she act then?

I don't know, but even if I have to go back to that place, there's one thing I should make sure I don't do...and that's giving up and letting myself go.

Life, its weight, its value, and how it should be used, as well as the stubborn resolve to never give up on living… These were the things she learned from her idol, the Libra King.

While Bel was learning important lessons about life, Mia was… being rescued from the inter-bed chasm.

"Huh… Bel's nowhere to be found, you say?" she asked after her liberation, which Anne had so graciously waited for before giving her the news.

Mia felt a sudden pang of worry. What if Bel had suffered the same fate as her? Just as she was about to conduct a panicked search of the remaining chasms…

"I heard from the innkeeper that she is apparently out on a walk with Prince Sion."

Rafina offered the answer she sought.

"Ah. With Sion. I see…"

That was all the information Mia needed to infer the sequence of events that led to Bel's absence.

I bet she walked out of the inn, ran into Sion, and just followed him around from there on…

"I can't believe she went off on her own," protested a pouting Citrina. "She could have asked Rina to go with her."

Mia gave her a mollifying smile. "I'm sure she'll be back by breakfast. I know that girl, and she's just like me in that she won't miss a meal for the world."

Hearing that Bel was with Sion, Mia relaxed. Tension flowed out from the muscles in her shoulders. And the ones around her gut. As a result, her stomach gurgled.

Hm, maybe I can start eating breakfast while I wait—

The thought was interrupted by a knock on the door.

"Excuse me, Miss Rafina. A guest has arrived."

"A guest? Who is it?"

A roomful of puzzled gazes focused on the door, which swung open to reveal…

"Hey, Mia. Good morning. And greetings to all you fine ladies too."

Abel Remno, who strode in with a charming smile.

Chapter 31: Onward! To the Equestrian Kingdom!

With Abel's arrival and Bel's timely return with Sion and Keithwood in tow, Mia and all her friends ended up having breakfast together in the inn's cafeteria. Interestingly, Bel's return was *so* timely that she'd shown up exactly when the bread came out of the oven. Even Mia, who'd predicted that the girl would be back by breakfast, couldn't help but be impressed by the ability of her granddaughter to follow her nose.

Not that Mia's own gluttonous tendencies paled in any way, mind you. Be it morning, noon, or night, she ate whenever and wherever she wanted. Like grandmother, like granddaughter.

Furthermore, Rafina was apparently aware of this fact, judging by the impressive portions that were brought to the table for breakfast. One plate held a veritable heap of freshly baked bread, and beside it was a large bottle of jam.

The sight caused Mia to nod in satisfaction. Just as she reached for the bottle...

"The jam is very good, of course, but the butter is no slouch either."

Rafina's comment forced her to reconsider. She was going to have some bread with her jam—note the sequence of wording—but perhaps...

"Oh? Is that so...?" she murmured.

After some thought, she spared a final longing glance at the jam before complying with Rafina's suggestion and spreading the butter over the bread instead. The butter immediately began to melt on the hot bread, giving off a tantalizing, sweet aroma.

"Oooh… This is…"

Her appetite fully whetted, she took a big bite. With a satisfying crunch, a mouthful gave way.

"Mmm!"

The rich fragrance of milk wafted through her nose as creamy goodness filled her mouth. Every successive bite produced another crunch of bread, each of which followed by a delicious burst of butter. She let out a sigh of pleasure.

"This…is a marvel of gastronomy." She wolfed down the rest of the bread and spun toward the innkeeper. "Please accept my compliments, master. The bread was baked to perfection, of course, but it's this butter that truly stands out. I've never had butter this good…"

"I am overjoyed to hear that it was to your taste. This butter was, in fact, made with sheep milk."

"My… Sheep, you say?"

"Yes, and it is procured from the Equestrian Kingdom. Their sheep produce extremely fine milk that tastes richer than milk from cows."

"Really? I had no idea…" Mia nodded with fascination as she reached for another slice of bread and spread a thick layer of butter over one side. Then, she turned to Abel. "So, Abel, what brings you here so early in the morning?"

"Right, about that. Since we're all here, I figured that we might as well head back together, though I won't be able to join you for the whole trip."

"Oh? What do you mean? Aren't you heading back to Saint-Noel?"

"No, I've got some business to attend to. I'm thinking of paying Malong a visit."

"My, Malong... So you're going to the Equestrian Kingdom?" Mia frowned. *Crunch. Crunch.* "Speaking of which, the Kingdom of Remno has some ties with the Equestrian Kingdom, right?"

"Yeah. My kingdom puts a lot of effort into our military drills, and we have an arrangement with the Equestrian Kingdom to dispatch instructors to us for our warhorse training. Of course, the purpose of this training is to use horses as instruments of war, so they've never been particularly enthusiastic to comply..."

"Ah, right. That's to be expected, I suppose."

Mia knew enough about the Equestrian Kingdom to see how they would take issue with the purpose of the arrangement.

Crunch. Crunch.

"So, I've actually known Malong for a long time, and a while back, I got a letter from him saying there was something he wanted to discuss..." said Abel.

"Hmm... I see." Mia frowned in thought, summoning a mental map of the local geography.

Crunch. Crunch.

The Equestrian Kingdom had no concept of borders. It was composed of twelve clans, and ten of those clans would take their sheep—their main assets—with them as they roamed around the vast grassy plains south of Sunkland between the Holy Principality of Belluga and the Kingdom of Remno. Due to their nomadic nature, while that general area in which they roved could be said to be the kingdom's territory, it lacked well-defined borders.

The remaining two clans were known as townwardens. One was permanently settled in the north capital near Sunkland, and the other in the south capital near Remno. As their title suggests, they were charged with defending the two settlements.

Once every few years, a clan council would be held in one of the capitals, during which the clans would assess the state of the grassland and discuss their respective movement plans for the future.

Remember the self-preservation scheme Mia had concocted in case Sunkland invaded Tearmoon? The one that involved befriending Remno so they could hit back at Sunkland with a pincer attack? The fact that the Equestrian Kingdom existed between the other two had not been lost on her. She'd given the thought of establishing some sort of friendship with the Equestris plenty of thought, as their high-skilled cavalry was something she absolutely wanted on her side.

Not that it matters a whole lot now, of course, since it doesn't look like Sunkland is going to be invading us any time soon.

In any case, she now understood Abel's situation. Since they were headed for Saint-Noel, it was certainly possible to drop by the Equestrian Kingdom along the way.

"Hmm… The Equestrian Kingdom…" she murmured as she glanced at the bread she was holding.

Well, the bread she'd been holding, because for some mysterious reason, it was nowhere to be found!

"Huh?" She raised an eyebrow at her breadless hand. *How odd. Where did it—*

"Excuse me, milady…" Her thought was interrupted by Anne, who discreetly leaned in and wiped the corner of Mia's mouth.

As she pulled away, Mia caught a glimpse…of a bread crumb on the handkerchief! "Hmmm…"

She then looked at the table, on which lay more of the fresh-baked bread. After a contemplative narrowing of her eyes, she reached for another slice and quickly applied a smooth layer of butter. Another round of crunchy crunching followed.

Hmm… It's just so good. Honestly, if we're going to pass by the Equestrian Kingdom, it might be a good idea to stop and talk to them about procuring some of this butter.

If she, with Ludwig's help, could get them to do business with the empire as well… She'd have access to this delicacy for breakfast every morning! With lips pursed in overeager calculation, Mia eyed Sion.

"I'll have to run the idea by Esmeralda and Tiona too… Actually, Esmeralda has Echard with her, so she probably can't make any detours. On that note, Sion, what's going on with Tiona? I was told by Keithwood yesterday that she spent the night at the castle."

"About that… There's something that happened for which I owe you an apology."

"Oh, do you? What for?"

"Miss Tiona, you see, wasn't feeling too well. She…was exposed to some chilly air, and I suspect she might have caught a cold."

"My, is that…? Hm? But wait… Then why do you owe *me* an apology?" Mia asked with unwitting pointedness. "I was going to ask her to join us for our girls party last night, so I went looking for her, but she was nowhere to be found. Are you telling me she was at *your* place?"

"Hm? Oh, uh, well… I suppose so. Father wished to thank her in person, so he asked her to stay," Sion answered with an odd sense of nervousness.

"Huuuuh." Mia's gaze lingered curiously on Sion for a second. "I see. So that's why."

"Anyway, the point is that she's a little sick, so we figured we'd have her stay a little longer. It'll give her time to recover, and we can treat her to some more of our amenities as both apology and thanks. I don't want to keep the rest of you though, so I'm planning to arrange for a ride back to Saint-Noel for everyone at Sunkland's expense."

"Hm…"

If Tiona wasn't feeling well, it would be unreasonable to force her to come along to the Equestrian Kingdom. At the same time, Abel had matters to discuss with Malong, so he couldn't afford to linger in Sunkland. As Mia weighed her options, her wandering gaze stopped on Bel, who was munching on bread like she didn't have a care in the world. Despite having left Ludwig in charge of Bel's education, she didn't seem to have done much studying since coming to Sunkland.

I can already see her struggling on her future exams. I'd better get her out of Sunkland as soon as possible.

Her mind made up, Mia nodded. "Very well. In that case, I'll leave my dear friends in your hands. Do make sure they are taken care of."

"Of course. They will be afforded every luxury," Sion answered with a nod.

Just when she thought they'd wrapped up this topic, Rafina waded in with a comment of her own. "If you're going to make a stop at the Equestrian Kingdom, then I'll come along with you."

"Miss Rafina, you will?"

"Now that I've discussed the Sunkland issue with His Majesty, I need to inform the Equestrian Kingdom of our conclusions. There's a lot of information I need to communicate, including the situation with the potential Serpent, so I'd prefer to speak to them in person."

"I see. It looks like we'll be showing up in a big group... Oh, in that case, why don't we get some horse riding practice on the way there?" Mia suggested in a flash of inspiration.

"Huh? B-But that's..." Rafina stammered, caught off guard by the sudden idea.

Mia couldn't resist a private grin at the sight.

Oh, Miss Rafina. I bet she's scared of getting on a horse. Oho ho, I never knew she could be such a child. How adorable.

Feeling a sense of duty as the veteran equestrian, she put a fist to her chest, determined to allay the fears of her new apprentice.

"Oho ho, don't worry. I'll show you the ropes. As long as you follow my instructions, you'll be riding in no time."

"Well, if you so strongly insist... I'm looking forward to learning from you then," said Rafina, who played with her fingers as a faint sheen of pink engulfed her cheeks.

Chapter 32: The High Priestess of the Serpents Dances

There was a place that had been lost to time. A place that had faded from history and memories alike. It lay at the foot of a steep and treacherous mountain that rose between the Kingdom of Remno and the Holy Principality of Belluga.

Tucked deep within a sea of trees, a small castle long abandoned stood, alone and desolate. Rather, it was not a castle. It lacked the dignity, the visual elegance and architectural sophistication that defined castles. No, this was a relic of past times—the stony remains of what had once been the ephemeral dream of an ancient people. They had built it, rock by rock, in this place to which they'd fled. Here, the defeated would rally. And rise again. This would be the site of their glorious revival.

That day never came. The dwellers lived there. *Died* there. Empty and lordless, the fortress saw not a single battle through its misguided existence before it was excised from the annals of history. Now, weathered by time into stony ruins, the old edifice had become a meeting place for the Serpents.

At the center of the small stronghold was its throne room, in which a lone woman danced. She looked to be in her midtwenties, and her glossy jet-black hair swung and swayed as she moved.

Wordless and expressionless, she danced with single-minded concentration. Her motions were erratic. Odd. *Disquieting.* But inarguably beautiful. Belonging to no particular form or style, their unique dissonance was equal parts enchanting and ominous.

It was difficult to imagine a dance more befitting the Chaos Serpents, who sought to destroy all order. However...

"What the hell are you doing?"

The man who walked into the room shot her a bemused look.

"Performing a dance," she said, placidly answering the wolfmaster's question, "as an offering to the Archdaemon. What do you think?"

Despite the sudden interruption, the woman stopped dancing without the slightest hint of reluctance. She dabbed away the sweat on her forehead with a look of boredom.

"I made it up, but I think it actually passes for a ritual dance. Personally, I feel like I really evoked the image of the high priestess of the Serpents being an apostle of the Archdaemon."

The high priestess favored the wolfmaster with a bewitching smile. The wolfmaster remained unmoved. "I don't remember us becoming apostles of the Archdaemon."

"We are...and we aren't. It's a fuzzy line. What we do is destroy order. Sometimes, as apostles of the Archdaemon. Other times, as atheists. So long as we can destroy this hellish invention of order that is the source of our endless persecution, we will become whatever, whenever. We are shapeless and formless, united only by our goal and suffering. That is our greatest strength, no?"

The wolfmaster was well aware that a portion of the Serpents' adherents were devout Archdaemonists. The high priestess, though... He knew beyond a shadow of a doubt that the woman before him did not believe for a second the existence of such a deity as the

Archdaemon. And it was *because* she didn't believe that she could conduct herself as the ideal priestess that her followers desired. Her irreverent objectivity made her an extremely effective leader who could unravel all forms of order with great efficiency and composure. She was, in short, a consummate actor whose ideology was rooted in destruction.

"So? What is it? Do you have some news?" she asked.

"I received a report from Ka Kunlou. He'll go into hiding instead of coming back here."

"Ah ha ha, okay then. I wouldn't worry about him. He's a shaman, after all. Wherever he goes, I'm sure he'll be a model Serpent and do a great job of destroying all sorts of order."

The high priestess smiled her bewitching smile again.

"But isn't it dangerous to fly solo right now?" asked the wolfmaster. "The Holy Lady Rafina… Given her recent actions, there seems to be a significant risk of being captured by agents of the Central Orthodox Church."

"Just as one cannot change the flow of a river by scooping out its water, there is a limit to the degree of impact the actions of a single agent can have. Should he fail, it will be a minor setback. Should he succeed, his feats will compensate for the failures of other agents. All is but a small drop in the greater current of things." Her smile grew even sweeter. "The fact that he left Sunkland, well… I assume that means he successfully planted the seeds, in which case, I think we should wait a while. Then, we'll spread a new rumor that says Prince Echard is hiding some poison. If they plan to hide the fact that he used the poison, then the rumor will damage trust in Sunkland's royal family. If he hasn't used the poison yet, then it should still stir up a lot of suspicions."

Her tone was so insouciant that it sounded like she was planning a simple prank rather than plotting to the downfall of people and kingdoms alike.

"Sounds dangerous to me. Are you sure we should be going so deep into Sunkland?"

"There's no need to worry. Even if our actions lead to our ruin, the Serpents won't die. There's Kunlou and the other shamans. A new high priestess befitting the times will rise and lead the Serpents anew. In fact, the existence of a high priestess itself is in no way critical. It all depends. Whatever is necessary, the Serpents will create, be it a priestess, a princess, or even a king. That is our way, is it not?"

"And you're okay with that? Even if you're not there to see it all happen?" asked the wolfmaster. "Wasn't the destruction of order your dearest wish?"

She regarded him for a moment, then shook her head and smiled. "Men are such glory-seekers. You seek simple outcomes. Ones that visibly distinguish your accomplishments. Not that I don't understand this desire of your kind, of course… But I personally couldn't care less about any of that. Ruin is inevitable, after all. Eventually, everything will be destroyed." She spoke with no passion or zeal. To her, it was merely a statement of fact. "What do you think is the strength of the Chaos Serpents?"

"Beats me. The ability to manipulate people with words?"

"That is neither true nor correct."

The priestess fixed the wolfmaster with a look. It was calm and unassertive, but there was a depth to it, as if she were peering into some cosmic truth.

"The strength of the Chaos Serpents," she explained, "is that they cannot be killed. They cannot be eradicated. They may not succeed today, or tomorrow, or the day after, but they are eternal. And with enough time, they will eat away at the world until nothing is left. So long as humans continue to exist, so will Serpents. That's how this world works. And how it will unravel. There is no future in which we fail." She folded her hands before her chest and closed her eyes. "And no one can change that. Not even the Great Sage of the Empire."

Then, a playful smirk spread across her lips.

"Unless, of course, she replaced all the humans in the world with those horses your people love so much. Then, the Serpents would indeed disappear. Because it is the ever-unchanging nature of humans that the Serpents are a curse upon."

She paused. Her pursed lips suggested the abrupt emergence of a thought.

"That reminds me. Your little sister... Is she out plundering again?"

"We need enough food to feed the clan, after all, or our people will starve. I believe she's operating near the Sunkland border..."

"Is she? Well, tell her to come pay me a visit some time. It's high time we had some tea together again."

She smiled, this time with all the grace and polish of a princess.

Short Story

Chancellor Ludwig
Loves His Wine

During the final years of the revolution in the Tearmoon Empire, when most had turned their backs on the ailing nation, there was one man who refused to forsake the land of his birth. He kept doing everything he could to sustain the empire and continued to support Princess Mia until the very last moment when the imperial capital Lunatear fell to the revolutionary army. He was a young and industrious official of Tearmoon, and his name was Ludwig Hewitt.

The historical footprints of this capable retainer continued up to the execution of the lady he served, Princess Mia, after which they abruptly disappeared from the official record. Thus did the annals of the empire document his final moments…

Following the execution of Mia Luna Tearmoon in the Grand Square of the imperial capital, Ludwig vanished. No individual has ever claimed to have seen him since.

That is, of course, according to the *official* record. Real people don't simply vanish. Though unlikely to ever make their way into the likes of history books, his subsequent actions nevertheless left a small but definite mark on the world. The story that follows is compiled from fragments of memories belonging to those with firsthand experience of an episode involving a bit of trouble that occurred in a certain tavern.

In a small town near the empire's border stood a small tavern. It was crammed full of people, and the limited space inside reverberated with bright laughter. The air was brimming with an unqualified mirth that had never existed before—not during the Great Famine, nor the revolutionary period that followed.

"Mmmm, this is some fine wine."

"It sure is. Made in Belluga, you know? And blessed by the Holy Lady herself."

"Heh heh heh. Gotta salute the Sunkland prince and Lady Tiona. It's thanks to them that we get to sit here and enjoy such great drinks."

With the old oppressive regime overthrown, the people were ready to welcome their liberation. At the end of a righteous war, an evil tyrant was deposed, paving the way for a new age of freedom and hope. So intoxicating was the cheery atmosphere that even the abstinent members of the populace found themselves drunk on mirth. Amidst this ambience of grins and laughter…

"Such blatant propaganda…"

A bitter utterance was spat into the air, reaching no ears before drowning in the surrounding glee. The speaker—a man—was seated in a nook of the tavern. Unaccompanied, he fumed alone as he peered out from behind his slightly cracked spectacles and scanned the room. Dark discontent exuded from his eyes as he reached for his glass.

"What awful wine…" he said with a snort. The man, Ludwig Hewitt, grimaced as he slammed the glass back onto the table. A few drops of wine splashed onto the ground.

"Hey, mister, watch what you say." The tavern owner, having heard Ludwig's grumble, shot him a furrow-browed glare. "I ordered that wine straight from Sunkland, you hear? It's not every day you get to drink something this good."

The tavern owner was clearly offended by the comment. Before his anger could build, a third person stepped in with a mediating comment.

"Hey, sorry. Don't take it personally, barman. This guy's just in a bad mood. More importantly, could you get me some wine too? I'll take a bottle of your finest."

The newcomer wore an affable smile. His magnificent blond hair and well-kept beard suggested he was not the type to pinch pennies. The tavern owner immediately matched his smile.

"Well, good sir, that would happen to be this high-quality wine I just procured from Sunkland a few days ago. It's going to cost a fair bit, though—"

"Will this be enough?"

The man tossed a small pouch at the tavern owner. As he caught it, some of its contents fell out onto the counter, revealing themselves to be shiny gold coins.

"This…is too much, good sir."

"Don't worry about it. Consider it reimbursement for the disturbance. It's pretty crazy out there these days. Doesn't hurt having some extra cash, so just hold onto it, okay?"

"Heh. I'll take your advice then. Thank you, sir," the tavern owner said with a servile smile before placing the bottle in front of the bearded man and retreating to the back of the tavern.

The man watched him go before turning to Ludwig.

"I've been looking high and low for you, Ludwig. What've you been doing all this time?"

"Balthazar."

The bearded man was Balthazar Brandt. Like Ludwig, he was also a former disciple of Wiseman Galv. The two had studied together under their master.

"You came back, huh? I sure didn't expect to see you here in the empire. I assume that means the chaos from the revolution has died down enough for some serious money to start flowing here."

"Right on. Your hypothesis is entirely correct. The business of rebuilding Tearmoon is something that Prince Sion is heavily involved in. From Sunkland's perspective, they absolutely cannot afford for this project to fail, or it'll damage their reputation as upholders of justice. Unsurprisingly, I heard that the scale of the assistance they're going to provide is pretty massive."

"Yeah, that makes sense. No surprises there."

Given the propaganda being spread, what Balthazar just described was easily inferable; he had just witnessed an example in the tavern himself, in fact. There was no way they'd allow anything to mar the reputation of Prince Sion, who was now the savior of the empire.

"And once all that Sunkland money starts pouring in, merchants from all over will flock here to get a piece of the golden pie," mused Ludwig.

"Apparently, Belluga is also prepared to fully cooperate with the effort. Chances are, the rebuilding is going to start in the south around Outcount Rudolvon's domain."

"Huh… Clever bastards, aren't they?"

This project should allow the empire, after struggling and suffering for so long, to finally put itself on the road to recovery. Food should become more abundant. Fewer people should starve. Those were undoubtedly good things. But for some reason…Ludwig couldn't wholeheartedly celebrate the development.

Balthazar poured some wine into Ludwig's glass before narrowing his eyes. "By the way, you haven't answered my question. What've you been up to?"

Ludwig took a quick glance at his glass, then downed it in a single gulp. "Nothing, really."

"Nothing, huh?"

Balthazar's lips tightened slightly as he regarded his longtime friend, more beaten and weatherworn now than he ever remembered. Then, with a shrug, he dismissed whatever somber thought had entered his head.

"All right, good. Good for you. You worked way too hard these past few years. You definitely needed the rest," he said, more to himself than Ludwig, as he took a sip of his wine as well.

Slowly, he swished it around his mouth, savoring the taste before closing his eyes and swallowing. "Mmm. The price is justified, I see. This is indeed very good wine." He filled Ludwig's glass again. "But…what's next? After you get enough rest?" With intentional bluntness, Balthazar pressed his friend further.

"What's next, huh…?"

"Yeah. This is *you* we're talking about, Ludwig. There's way too much talent in you to let rot. The empire needs you. This is no time to be appreciating the hermit life." His expression then softened. "If you won't work with Sunkland or the revolutionary government, then how about coming with me?"

Ludwig was reminded of a past rumor he'd heard. Balthazar Brandt had given up on the empire long before the revolution and gone abroad. After making his way into a certain merchant company, word was that he'd quickly distinguished himself as a talented asset. Considering the offer he'd just made, it became apparent that the rumor was true, and he'd gained a good deal of influence in his current role.

"Ah. First, you push me to work under the revolutionary government, knowing I don't want to. Then, you propose a more stomachable compromise. Start strong and ease off. Negotiation 101."

"Oh, quit being such a cynic. Miranada's a great place, you know? Being a kingdom of merchants, the only thing you're judged on is your commercial talent. Granted, you've always had a stubborn streak, so your business acumen could be a tad suspect, but… Wait, didn't you grow up in a merchant household? That's good. It'll be easier to make the case for bringing you in…"

Ludwig didn't respond. He silently appraised the man before him, whose friendship he'd enjoyed for so long. It was clear that Balthazar was being considerate and trying to do him a favor. Nevertheless…

"Sorry. I'm not interested in running a business."

"Come now. Don't be like that, Ludwig. You don't have to decide right away. Sit on it for a bit. To let a great mind go to waste does a disservice to not just yourself and your nation, but the whole world," Balthazar said before looking off into the distance. "Besides…I'm sure our master wouldn't want to see a dear disciple whom he taught and trained turn into a grumbling recluse."

"Master Galv, huh…"

Sighing, Ludwig closed his eyes. A vision of Galv flashed across his mind, reminding him of his master's many faces—at times gentle, and at times strict. Sometimes, the old wiseman would simply shake his head in resignation at the antics of his disciples. Ludwig had learned a lot from his master, and one of the most important lessons had been something he lived by to this day. Knowledge was key. With enough of it, one could do anything…and fulfill the many duties one had to their kingdom and world.

"Well, I suppose you have a point. There are a tad too many years left in me to be writing the final chapter of my life already."

Just as Ludwig opened his eyes again, some chatter entered his ears.

"But man, we sure are living in better times now. Much better than when the last emperor was still reigning."

"Hear, hear. It's been exactly a year since that good-for-nothing princess was executed. Cheers to this new era of the empire."

It was the drivel of drunks. Taverns never had any shortage of such talkative types, who ran their mouths with such impudence that it was hard to tell whether they themselves believed what they said. Casual contempt of this nature was everywhere. To bristle at every instance would be folly. Heck, he'd endured plenty of abuse like this back when he was running around the kingdom with the princess. Why get worked up now?

He could think of dozens of reasons to show restraint. After systematically appreciating the rationale for each and every one, he let out a long breath…and quietly tightened his grip around a nearby wine bottle!

"Whoa, whoa, whoa! What're you going to do with that bottle, Ludwig?" Balthazar exclaimed in alarm.

Ludwig shot him a rebuffing glare before flashing a toothy grin. "Nothing much. I just feel like smashing this over something round and headlike, that's all."

"Okay, slow down, buddy. We both know you're not the bar-fighting type. Just sit down, take a deep breath, and hand me the bottle…" Balthazar carefully pulled the makeshift weapon out of Ludwig's hand and placed it back on the table. "Look, there's still some wine left in it. You wouldn't want to waste such fine wine, would you?"

He poured some into his own glass, then filled Ludwig's as well. Even then, the bottle was still half-full.

"This bitter mood hardly befits our long-awaited reunion. What say we wash away the troubles with this delicious beverage? Just for today. Let us drink not in spite but in celebration." With that, Balthazar downed his wine in one gulp.

"Hm…" Ludwig regarded his friend. "I suppose it would indeed be a waste…" Nodding, he picked up the bottle and slowly began to fill Balthazar's glass again.

"Ah, thanks," said Balthazar, lifting his glass a little as a gesture of respect.

Ludwig continued to pour. And pour. And pour. The wine started spilling from the overburdened vessel.

"H-Hey! It's full already!"

Balthazar rushed to put his mouth to the glass. As he did, Ludwig withdrew the bottle, gave it a good shake, and examined its contents.

"You know what? You're absolutely right, Balthazar. It's not like me to waste things. This wine might be awful, but it deserves to be used."

Ludwig let out a booming laugh as he threw back his head and drained his glass. Then, he held the wine bottle high above his head. "Now, my good friend, let us drink to our dear princess, Her Highness Mia Luna Tearmoon, whose foolishness was surpassed only by her persistence, and who worked harder than anyone for the empire!" he declared in a voice that reached every corner of the tavern.

In the ensuing silence, he put his lips to the bottle, gulped down the remaining wine in a long swig, and flipped the empty container in his hand. Then, he charged at the men.

"You idiot! Augh, for the love of—"

Ludwig didn't care that he could hear Balthazar furiously protesting his behavior behind him. He didn't care that the men had every right to voice their long-simmering grievances about the former imperial family. Mia had been foolish, yes. She was arrogant, annoying, and utterly clueless. One could hardly find a more ineffectual princess. But Ludwig *didn't care*. Because she'd tried. She'd tried her heart out.

She deserved better.

And the fact that there was no one here to dissent on her behalf— to raise their voice in indignant protest—was utterly unacceptable. So, Ludwig solved the problem.

"Huh? What the hell do you think yo— Auuuugh?!"

The outcome of that outnumbered brawl...is not known to history. How many men did Ludwig strike down with that wine bottle? Did he strike fear into their hearts? Was he even any good at fighting? The answers to these fascinating questions would, unfortunately, forever evade us, because at the end of the day, it was nothing more than a minor, inconsequential scuffle—the kind that, during times of change, occurred with far more abundance than anyone cared to document.

But its inconsequentiality did not change the fact that it was a fight in which one man fought for his pride and all that he believed in.

So, on and on the wheel of time spun, in its ever wayward fashion...

"Hnngh? Ugh... What a dream..."

287

Ludwig shook his mildly aching head and looked around. The room's solid, stately furnishings were unfamiliar. It took him a while to remember that he was in the guest chamber of the Sunkland noble, Count Lampron.

"That's right… I came to Sunkland."

He'd apparently fallen asleep at his desk. Removing his glasses, he rubbed his eyes and let out a deep sigh. That dream he just had was the strangest thing. He couldn't make heads or tails of it. All he remembered was getting into a crazy melee with a bunch of drunks at a tavern.

"It must be because of that wine bottle I was holding during the ball… Ugh, what a pathetic reason. I guess the moral of this story is to stick with what you're good at instead of trying to be a hero."

At the time, he'd been singularly focused on the potential danger to Mia and acted mostly on instinct. The objectivity of hindsight, however, only put the perilous nature of the situation in the ballroom into clearer focus. They'd come exceedingly close to absolute disaster. Even now, the thought caused him to break out into a cold sweat.

"The sheer tension of that confrontation must have made its way into my dream. Good god, I'm more fainthearted than I thought. If only I could be as fearless as Her Highness, but ah, that is quite the tall order…"

In actuality, the heart of Her Highness was probably equal— if not greater—in faintness to his, but no one was present to point out the inaccuracy of his assessment. As he grimaced at his own ostensible timidity, there was a knock on the door.

"Who is it?"

"Hey, Ludwig. You up for a drink?"

The door opened to reveal the Empire's Finest, Dion Alaia. In one of his hands was a bottle of wine, which he brandished along with a pair of wine glasses in his other.

"Ah, Sir Dion. What of Her Highness's security?"

"My men are handling it. Not that they have much to do, considering Count Lampron's guarding her like his life depends on it. Which, you know, it probably does. I wouldn't worry much about the princess's safety," he said with a shrug.

"Fair point," Ludwig agreed. "If not his life, then at least his reputation. I have indeed noticed that Count Lampron has been rather *enthusiastic* with his security arrangements."

The ball was Count Lampron's responsibility. Given that the evening's ghastly proceedings had already left a stain on his good name, he could hardly afford another blunder.

"All right. A drink it is, then."

Ludwig rose and walked toward the wall to pull over a spare chair. In the meantime, Dion quickly placed the glasses down on a table and started filling them. To Ludwig's surprise, the liquid that poured from the bottle was not the familiar red of wine. Instead, it was a clear amber fluid.

"Is that…Sunkland wine?"

"Hm? Oh, I know what you're thinking, and the answer is no. I didn't appropriate it from the ballroom. I tried some there, and I gotta say, noble wine doesn't sit right with me. Too posh. This here, I had a couple of my most loyal men procure from the town," Dion said with a knowing grin.

Ludwig's concern, however, proved disparate. "Are you sure about this? I feel like Sunkland wine isn't known to be particularly good…"

He wasn't sure where or when, but he vaguely remembered trying some high-end Sunkland wine at some point and finding it highly distasteful. An attempt to recall the flavor dredged up an overwhelming sense of helpless anger.

"Oh yeah? News to me."

"Mm, well, on second thought, I can't seem to recall where I heard it. Which makes it likely to have come from some bigoted opinion unworthy of serious consideration."

Ludwig mentally admonished himself for blurting out such an unexamined thought. He looked at the label on the wine bottle and found…nothing on it that he recognized.

"Anyway, gotta say, our princess sure is something else. Not only did she sniff out an assassination attempt on royalty, she even resolved the issues and bad blood that caused the attempt in the first place. Pulled all of them out by the roots, just like that."

"And she did it without a single casualty," added Ludwig.

Dion silently chewed on the appended comment with pursed lips. Then, he uncorked the bottle with a knife. "You know, throughout this trip, I've been giving some thought to…your proposal. The idea of being the sword of our princess. Of the Great Sage of the Empire. It has occurred to me that what she requires is not the power to kill. Rather, it is the very opposite. To subdue her opponents *without* killing them."

"Correct, and there is no man more suited to the role than yourself, Sir Dion. I believe I am correct in my understanding that incapacitation is far more difficult than simple slaughter? After all, only through overwhelming superiority can one defeat opponents without killing them."

Dion shook his head as he filled his own glass. "It's not *that* simple. Even I have my limits. For example, if I'm up against people like the Adamantine Spear or the wolfmaster, I sure as hell can't be playing with my food. And if they were to come at me two-on-one, it'd take all I've got just to protect myself. My hand might very well slip at some point and kill one of them by accident," he quipped with a shrug. "But well, jokes aside… To be frank, I'm not generally fond of getting dragged around by the whims of nobles. The princess, though… She's different. The way she goes about it… Those aren't whims. She's got some sort of conviction—some unshakable core belief that underlies all her actions. You can tell she thinks things through."

Now, to be fair, Mia did indeed subscribe to an unshakable core belief. The philosophy that underpins everything she does is, of course, the now-familiar doctrine of Mia First. As for why she never killed people, well… She simply didn't want anyone to leap back through time like she did and take revenge on her. Not the most impressive of motivations.

Ludwig, of course, was entirely oblivious to Mia's actual guiding principles, so he responded with a heartfelt nod. "Indeed… What you described is the very essence of Her Highness. It is her number one gift. At times, it drives her to behave in roundabout ways that baffle us onlookers… But in the end, their inherent wisdom and compassion always become clear," Ludwig said with almost religious reverence.

In a way, his "number one gift" comment just about grazed the truth. It just wasn't the "gift" part that mattered. What concerned Mia was what came before it—in the end, it always became clear that Mia was looking out for number one. Sadly, never in a million years would he imagine how close his words had come to touching upon the *true* essence of Her Highness.

"That said," Dion replied, his grin growing more knowing, "wasn't there a little more that could have been done this time around?"

"A little more, you say?"

"Yeah, you know, a little more that could have been gained. Like, for example, *control over the whole of Sunkland*?"

Ludwig grimaced, realizing there was a fundamental assumption that Dion was making. "Correct me if I'm wrong, Sir Dion... But would you happen to believe that the ideal framework of this world is one in which Her Highness stands at the top of all nations?"

Dion didn't answer immediately. He scratched his chin in thought before reverting to his grin.

"Yeah, I guess I do. Well, I don't know if it's the *ideal* framework, but it's definitely a workable one. Not that I'm entirely on board with Sunkland's philosophy, mind you, but if everyone were ruled by a single wise monarch, it'd be impossible to start a war. That sounds like the kind of world the princess wants, doesn't it?"

"Indeed it does. If the untimely death of people is what Her Highness most wishes to abolish, then war is undoubtedly the worst of options. Having her directly rule all the nations in the world to ensure that no war ever breaks out is...an entirely sensible proposition. Logically speaking. However..." Ludwig put a finger to his glasses' bridge, then shook his head. "Her Highness is all too aware of the essence of nations and what it is that keeps them functioning."

"And...what exactly is that supposed to mean?"

"If we push your argument to its logical conclusion, Sir Dion, then having Her Highness directly rule over all humans would theoretically be a permanent solution to all problems of governance. And this might even be true. Being an exceedingly capable individual, Her Highness could very well manage such a feat. She can, as far as I know, handle anything on her own, from politics to

CHANCELLOR LUDWIG LOVES HIS WINE

education to business, and maybe even military affairs," said Ludwig, regarding Dion with a gaze that grew increasingly sharper. "But… a nation cannot function like that. Kingdoms are built on and sustained by the work of their people. Only when each and every citizen fulfills their duties to one another does a nation truly exist. That includes, of course, those in positions of power, be they nobles or royalty."

"So what you're saying is that…Sunkland should be ruled by Sunkland's nobles and royalty? That they should be the ones to solve their problems?"

"This continent is far too vast a land to be governed by a single person. Or perhaps it's not. Perhaps *she* can indeed govern it… But she does not. Presumably because doing so would defeat the point."

Again, Ludwig got close, but he only scratched the surface of Mia's wisdom, which had all the depth of a cake plate. Ruling over every nation in the continent? Never! That'd be such a pai— presumptuous thing to do! She *certainly* didn't want a job like that! Sunkland should absolutely be governed by Sunkland's royalty. Heck, they should just throw everything to Sion and call it a day. For Mia, she just wanted to avoid dealing with issues that could cause discord between subjects and rulers or give other nations fodder for attack.

"Well, well, well. Looks like I've got my work cut out for me, then," quipped Dion.

"That makes two of us. But life's more interesting that way, isn't it?"

"Hah. It sure is."

The two men shared a laugh, right after which there was a knock on the door.

"Ludwig, do you have a moment?"

The door opened to reveal the very person they'd been talking about.

"Ah, Your Highness. What can we do for you?" said Ludwig, inviting the princess in.

As Mia took a look around the room, her gaze stopped on the table, where two full glasses of wine stood.

"My, Ludwig, what's this? A wine party with Dion? I had no idea you drank. You never really seemed like the type."

Her surprise was met with a wry smile. "I certainly do drink, Your Highness, even if it is not an activity I partake in with any regularity. One can hardly engage in diplomatic talks without a few sips to start things off, after all."

Garbed in thick, symbolic livery made all the heavier by the duty they shouldered, envoys spoke not as humans but as conduits for their nations. Frankness was frequently in short supply, for their roles stiffened their lips and constrained their words. It was in these cases, when fellow envoys engaged in conversation, that an appropriate amount of alcohol could serve as a fine lubricant for the tongue. Overindulgence could certainly be disastrous, but like any tool, it was all a matter of proper use.

"Hm… Is that how it is?" Mia smiled at them. "Then I'm looking forward to the day when I share a drink with the two of you as well."

"As are we, Your Highness. I assume, however, you did not come to discuss matters of drink? Does something require my attention?" said Ludwig, his expression sobering.

"Ah, right. Actually, I came to tell you that I'd like to make a slight change to our itinerary for the return trip."

"A slight change?"

"Yes. I'd like to make a stop in the Equestrian Kingdom and spend some time there."

Ludwig immediately referenced a mental map of the local geography. Between Sunkland, Remno, and Belluga was a vast grassland. Somewhere there lay the Equestrian Kingdom.

"Oh, and Miss Rafina will be coming with us," she added.

"Ah. Will she, now? So we'll be guarding the Holy Lady of Belluga all the way to the Equestrian Kingdom. This job never gets easier, does it?" Dion sighed.

Mia smiled at him. "I believe in you, Dion. And not just you. All of the Princess Guard has my unconditional trust."

That caught him off guard. He blinked at her a few times before scrunching up his face and saying, "Could I trouble you to say that to the men in person? It'll help with morale."

"Certainly. I'll do so tomorrow," Mia said with a contented nod.

"By the way, Your Highness," said Ludwig, "is escorting Lady Rafina the sole purpose of our journey to the Equestrian Kingdom?"

"No. I have of course my own reasons for going as well. It is my opinion that there will be much we stand to gain from the Equestrian Kingdom."

She said nothing more, favoring them with only a knowing smile.

"Heh, well, looks like we'll have to put our wine party on hold. You sure are one busy man, Ludwig. Must be tough being you," said a grimacing Dion after Mia left the room.

"Indeed. Since I can no longer afford any significant inebriation for the rest of the night, I suppose I'll just finish this one glass," said Ludwig as he reached for his wine. "With that said…I wouldn't exactly describe my circumstances as 'tough.' It's certainly exhausting work, and there's never any lack of stress, but…I find it immensely fulfilling to work for Her Highness. And I mean every word of that."

Though he spoke from the heart, his sudden sincerity left him mildly embarrassed, so he quickly changed the topic.

"Besides, good labor—good, worthwhile labor—will elevate even the cheapest of wines into fine vintage."

"Oh? Now that's new. Since when did you become a wine philosopher, hm?" asked Dion with an arched brow.

Ludwig shook his head. "Hardly. I'm just parroting my master's words. His insight into the nature of drink far surpasses what I am capable of."

With that, he raised his glass high above his head. Dion did the same.

"To the Great Sage of the Empire."

With a mutual clink, the pair toasted in unison.

The moment Ludwig brought his glass close, a peculiar aroma tickled his nose. Rich and full-bodied, it smelled of a unique mix of herbs and grasses. He tipped the glass. As the amber liquid flowed across his tongue, he felt its heat. The fiery alcohol all but assaulted his throat. He came close to choking, but he held on and swallowed. It burned all the way down. His stomach roiled in the sudden warmth. What was left in his mouth, however…was a refreshing— no, *exhilarating*—aftertaste.

"Aaaaah… Delicious. Now *this*…is some good wine." He let out a satisfied breath.

Dion, having downed his glass as well, studied him for a second before nodding. "Heh, it sure is." He placed his glass down on the table with a firm thud. "It sure as hell is. I guess this means we did some good, worthwhile labor." He then took Ludwig's glass along with the bottle and moved them away. "Now then. Let's do some more. So that our wine tomorrow will be just as good."

Thus, the two men—both pillars of Mia's projects—turned their attention from table to desk. For the rest of the night, they would drink not sherry or vermouth, but the burgundy marks on the many maps now spread before their eyes.

Though they'd sipped but a modicum of wine, that lone glass of amber goodness was enough, for it filled their souls with a profound sense of satisfaction.

Ludwig Hewitt, Chancellor of the Tearmoon Empire.

In addition to being the right hand of Empress Mia, he was known for his love of wine. Interestingly, he was by no means an avid drinker. Though no alcoholic, he succumbed quickly to its effects and was rarely seen partaking in the activity of drinking. Those who *did* have the chance to share a drink with him, however, would all claim the same.

"That man finds flavor in even the cheapest of wines. His love for alcohol must run as deep as it does wide."

Mia's Diary of Deeper Dining
—Three Exquisite Sunkland Dishes for Those Who Wish to Deepen Their Appreciation of Food—

Sun Crownberry Pie

This pie is made with crownberry, a local specialty of the Kingdom of Sunkland. A crispy, flaky crust surrounds a creamy, rich filling that turns into delicious sweetness in the mouth, all of which is complemented by the perfect touch of sourness from the crownberries.

Once it comes out of the oven, the crust goes mushy after about a hour, making it a very short-lived pastry, but its fleeting nature only makes it that much more delicious when you bite into it fresh.

An indisputable masterpiece!

Highly recommended ☆x5

Ray Beef Stew

You can't talk about Sunkland without mentioning its beef, and fillet of their famous ray beef is undoubtedly the best of the best. Served with a rich demi-glace sauce, the meat melts on the tongue, leaving behind a thick, beefy flavor to savor.

When you're hungry and looking for something substantial, you simply cannot go wrong with this marvelous dish. Just be careful with ordering it at restaurants with generous portions, because you might end up with more meat than you can reasonably stuff into yourself.

Not that it'll stop you from trying, though, which I suppose could be considered a downside, especially for those who want to slim down.

Highly recommended ☆x4

Freshly Baked Bread with Equestrian Kingdom Butter

Freshly baked bread is so wonderfully fragrant. When it's made with flour from high-quality wheat, the crust is nice and crisp while the inside is soft and doughy. The flavor is excellent too. On top of that, we add the marvel of cuisine that is butter from the Equestrian Kingdom. You'd think a chunk of such rich butter would feel really oily in your mouth, but it doesn't at all! In fact, it has a wonderfully gentle and elegant flavor. Never leave home without some. Or stay home, for that matter.

Highly recommended ☆x5

How terribly baffling. This diary...has finally turned completely into a food notebook. It even lost the dates. The food-report-ization curse is still alive and kicking!

It's so strange. I can clearly remember writing daily entries in my elegant, flowing prose. In fact, I wrote one yesterday, and it was particularly poetic. But when I flipped the diary open today, they were all gone! It honestly makes no sense.

Maybe it's sort of like how that bloody diary works, and the stuff written in this diary will change from time to time? I guess it's not impossible. Maybe I should do some experiments later to confirm.

Anyway, the disappearing diary entries aside, it's good that everything worked out in the end.

We managed to prevent Sion's assassination, and King Abram is safe too. I'm so glad Rina was there. She really saved the day. Tiona too. Thanks to the two of them, we got everything wrapped up without any serious problems.

Of course, none of this would have been possible without my brilliant decision to bring them along. I have such an eye for people. Good job, me!

I must say, though, the Chaos Serpents are a serious pain in my rear. I can't believe they actually tried to snake their way into Sunkland's royal family. How would things have played out had I not been here this time? Moons, I don't even want to imagine...

Pretty soon, we're going to see poor wheat harvests, which will cause enough trouble on their own. The last thing we need right now is for King Abram or Sion to be incapacitated. Sunkland is a big kingdom, and anything that happens to them will surely affect the empire. If Sunkland fell into chaos... That's the kind of thing that would keep me up at night.

And it's not just about Sunkland either. I need to warn all the other king— Oh wait, that's not my job, is it? I'll probably ask Miss Rafina to do that.

In any case, that's one problem solved, at least.

Judging by how things ended, I think Sion and Prince Echard won't have too much trouble making up. I swear, those two... What a handful they are.

Sion, though... *The* Sion...came to me and...

Did I just throw away the opportunity of a lifetime? I mean, he *is* very handsome...

No, what I did was correct. I'd be acting on bad faith otherwise. Sion was honest with me. I owe him the same.

Actually, now that I think about it, hasn't he been nothing but infuriating all this time? How could I possibly be in a relationship with someone like that? Forget bad faith—there's no bad faith when dealing with bad people. If anything, I should have taken the chance to have some fun at his expense. Use my adult charms to really get into his head…

But then again, he *has* saved me a couple times. I'd feel bad about toying with his feelings, and it'd be awkward if my irresistible charisma was too much for him and he ended up taking me seriously.

Which means the answer I gave at the time was indeed the correct one. Mm-hmm, yes. It definitely was.

That mushroom, though… It's too bad I missed the chance to bring some back with me. It was extraordinary. Maybe I'll order some from Sunkland when I get back. One can never have too many exotic mushrooms to try, after all.

The Equestrian Kingdom's butter was something else too. That was so good. Who knew their sheep produced such high-quality milk?

I definitely need to get my hands on some during this trip.

Afterword

Happy New Year!

I am Mochitsuki, and I hope we'll all have a great 2022.

This time, a drama CD was simultaneously released with the volume, which is not something I ever expected myself to say. It's honestly quite overwhelming, so much so that both Mia and I are still coming to terms with this incredible development. Having a voice actor narrate the audio book was already an electrifying experience, and now, a drama CD...meaning there will now be many voice actors each playing the role of a different character. It's crazy, honestly, when you stop and really think about it.

Also, the name "Ludwig"—and this is something that actually occurred to me back when the stage play was ongoing—is seriously a mouthful, isn't it? Not the easiest name to say. His lines are minor tongue twisters too. Every time I heard them spoken, I felt like apologizing to the actor.

Mia: "They sure are. I apologize on behalf of that stupid four-eyes. Oh, you know what? Why don't we just call him that? From now on, his name can officially be stupid four-eyes."

Mochitsuki: "Uh, we can maybe discuss that again later. For now, let's talk about the drama CD. I mean, it's a *drama CD*! Can you believe it?"

Mia: "What's a CD?"

Mochitsuki: "Ah, right. So, a CD is a round disk that sound comes out of. I was really into radio dramas and drama CDs during my high school years. There was this time when I bought a twenty-disk set of drama CDs for this certain game..."

Mia: "A twenty-disk set, huh? That sounds like a pretty good idea. We should release a twenty-volume set of these drama CDs for Tearmoon Empire too and sell them for ten full golds a piece. That'll surely put the empire's finances on better footing, right? Mmmm, I really like where this is going!"

Emperor: "Ooooh! Great idea! All right, in that case, we should give a golden Mia sculpture as a special gift to every loyal subject who purchases one. Chancellor, have our people start preparing the gold immediately!"

Mia: "Hm, on second thought, I think the slow-and-steady method is better. We should put these out one volume at a time instead of coming out with twenty all of a sudden. It's too much, too fast. As for your special gift idea, father, we'll think about it some other time. (If we started giving out golden sculptures, we'd just end up running the empire's finances even further into the ground. It's too bad. Instead of shooting for the stars, we'll have to keep our feet on the ground and do this one step at a time.)"

And now for some words of appreciation.

Thank you to Gilse for the adorable illustrations. The drama CD Mia is so beautiful it made me say "Whoooa!" out loud. Ha ha ha.

Thank you to my editor, F. From the recording for the drama CDs to many other things, you've been nothing but helpful.

To my family, thank you for your enduring support. I'll keep pressing forward.

AFTERWORD

Finally, to all the readers who picked up this book, thank you very much. The story will be moving from Sunkland to the Equestrian Kingdom, where Mia's adventures will continue, so I hope you'll stay with us on this journey.

SERVING BIAS

MY, PRINCE ECHARD.

YOU DON'T SEEM TO BE ENJOYING YOUR MEAL.

HNGH...

WHAT? MUSH-ROOMS?!

STARE!

THIS STEW HAS MUSH-ROOMS IN IT...

MY, YOU DON'T LIKE MUSH-ROOMS?

NO, IT'S OKAY, MISS ESMERALDA.

JUST LEAVE THEM. YOU DON'T HAVE TO FORCE YOURSELF.

THE CHEF PUT HIS HEART AND SOUL INTO MAKING THIS.

IT WOULD BE SELFISH OF ME TO WASTE THE FOOD THEY PREPARED.

HOW COME THERE ARE NO MUSHROOMS IN MINE?!

SHAKE SHAKE

MY... HE'S QUITE MATURE.

HEART THROB

...A ...OR

Tearmoon Empire Vol.9

THANK YOU FOR PURCHASING THE BOOK!

Mizu Morino

NOVEL
VOLUME 10
ON SALE
WINTER 2024!

2

MANGA
VOLUME 2
ON SALE
OCTOBER 2023!

Tearmoon Empire

MANGA: **Mizu Morino** ✦ ORIGINAL WORK: **Nozomu Mochitsuki** ✦ CHARACTER DESIGNS: **Gilse**

Live!

Endo and Kobayashi
THE LATEST ON TSUNDERE VILLAINESS
LIESELOTTE

Light Novel
& Manga
Available
Digitally!

Author
~uzu Enoshima
~strator

NOVEL
VOLUME 10
ON SALE
WINTER 2024!

2

MANGA
VOLUME 2
ON SALE
OCTOBER 2023!

Tearmoon Empire

MANGA: **Mizu Morino** ✦ ORIGINAL WORK: **Nozomu Mochitsuki** ✦ CHARACTER DESIGNS: **Gilse**

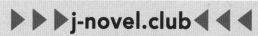

J-Novel Club Lineup

Latest Ebook Releases Series List